Four Shades of Gray

Platform Studies

Nick Montfort and Ian Bogost, editors

Racing the Beam: The Atari Video Computer System, Nick Montfort and Ian Bogost, 2009

Codename Revolution: The Nintendo Wii Platform, Steven E. Jones and George K. Thiruvathukal, 2012

The Future Was Here: The Commodore Amiga, Jimmy Maher, 2012

Flash: Building the Interactive Web, Anastasia Salter and John Murray, 2014

I AM ERROR: The Nintendo Family Computer / Entertainment System Platform, Nathan Altice, 2015

Peripheral Vision: Bell Labs, the S-C 4020, and the Origins of Computer Art, Zabet Patterson, 2015

Now the Chips Are Down: The BBC Micro, Alison Gazzard, 2016

Minitel: Welcome to the Internet, Julien Mailland and Kevin Driscoll, 2017

Super Power, Spoony Bards, and Silverware: The Super Nintendo Entertainment System, Dominic Arsenault, 2017

The Media Snatcher: PC/CORE/TURBO/ENGINE/GRAFX/16/CDROM2/SUPER/DUO/ ARCADE/RX, Carl Therrien, 2019

Who Are You? Nintendo's Game Boy Advance Platform, Alex Custodio, 2020

Four Shades of Gray: The Amazon Kindle Platform, Simon Peter Rowberry, 2022

Four Shades of Gray

The Amazon Kindle Platform

Simon Peter Rowberry

The MIT Press   Cambridge, Massachusetts   London, England

The MIT Press would like to thank the anonymous peer reviewers who provided comments on drafts of this book. The generous work of academic experts is essential for establishing the authority and quality of our publications. We acknowledge with gratitude the contributions of these otherwise uncredited readers.

This book was set in Filosofia OT by Jen Jackowitz. Printed and bound in the United States of America.

Library of Congress Cataloging-in-Publication Data

Names: Rowberry, Simon Peter, author.
Title: Four shades of gray : the Amazon kindle platform / Simon Peter Rowberry.
Description: Cambridge, Massachusetts : The MIT Press, [2022] | Series:
    Platform studies | Includes bibliographical references and index.
Identifiers: LCCN 2021013279 | ISBN 9780262543507 (paperback)
Subjects: LCSH: Kindle (Electronic book reader) | Electronic book readers.
    | Electronic books.
Classification: LCC Z286.E43 R689 2022 | DDC 004.1675—dc23
LC record available at https://lccn.loc.gov/2021013279

10 9 8 7 6 5 4 3 2 1

Contents

Series Foreword

How can someone create a breakthrough game for a mobile phone or a compelling work of art for an immersive 3D environment without understanding that the mobile phone and the 3D environment are different sorts of computing platforms? The best artists, writers, programmers, and designers are well aware of how certain platforms facilitate certain types of computational expression and innovation. Likewise, computer science and engineering have long considered how underlying computing systems can be analyzed and improved. As important as scientific and engineering approaches are, and as significant as work by creative artists has been, we also have much to learn from the sustained, intensive, humanistic study of digital media. We believe it is time for humanists to seriously consider the lowest level of computing systems and their relationship to culture and creativity.

The Platform Studies series has been established to promote the investigation of underlying computing systems and of how they enable, constrain, shape, and support the creative work that is done on them. The series investigates the foundations of digital media—the computing systems, both hardware and software, that developers and users depend on for artistic, literary, and gaming development. Books in the series will certainly vary in their approaches, but they will all share certain features:

- A focus on a single platform or a closely related family of platforms
- Technical rigor and in-depth investigation of how computing technologies work

- An awareness and discussion of how computing platforms exist in a context of culture and society, being developed on the basis of cultural concepts and then contributing to culture in a variety of ways—for instance, by affecting how people perceive computing

Acknowledgments

Four Shades of Gray was greatly strengthened by thoughtful suggestions from colleagues including Daniel Allington, Greg Barnhisel, Giles Bergel, Kathi Inman Berens, Chiara Bernardi, Karen Boyle, Inga Bryden, Dorothy Butchard, Eddy Borges-Rey, Daniel Boswell, Nick Canty, Laura Dietz, Beth Driscoll, Toke Riis Ebbesen, Carolin Esser-Miles, Andrew Ferguson, Molly Flatt, Simon Frost, Danielle Fuller, Alan Galey, Matt Hayler, Richard Haynes, Leslie Howsam, Matthew Kirschenbaum, Anouk Lang, Marcus Leaning, Fran Mason, John Maxwell, Tom Mole, Jim Mussell, Sarah Mygind, Simone Murray, Naomi Nelson, Corinna Norrick-Rühl, Stephen Pihlaja, Melanie Ramdarshan-Bold, Padmini Ray Murray, Staci Rowlison, Jonathan Rose, Matt Rubery, Mark Sample, Matt Schneider, Greg Singh, Claire Squires, Bronwen Thomas, Whitney Trettien, and Maria Velez Serna. Julian McAuley generously shared his Amazon data set with me.

The research was supported by a semester of research leave at the University of Stirling in autumn 2018 and a SHARP-RBS grant to attend the Born Digital Materials: Theory and Practice course at Rare Book School. Archival research at Stanford and the Computer History Museum was supported by generous funding from the Bibliographical Society of America and a Carnegie Trust Research Incentive Grant. My argument also benefited from feedback during invited talks at the Media History Seminar, the University of Edinburgh's Centre for the History of the Book, and UCL's Department of Information Studies, as well as conference papers at SHARP, By the Book, NUI Galway, Digital Humanities 2014, The Reader in

Stylistics, Digital Reading Network, Society for Textual Scholarship, The Book in the Digital Age, and Resurrecting the Book.

This research would not have been possible without the help of librarians and archivists. The interlibrary loan departments at the Universities of Southampton, Stirling, and Winchester were supportive in locating material. Aurora Tucker and Sydney Olson were instrumental in providing me access to the Computer History Museum's archive materials, both written and machine. The whole team at Stanford University's Special Collections was exceptionally helpful, including Tim Noakes and Leif Anderson.

I am also grateful for the support from MIT Press, from Nick Montfort and Ian Bogost's helpful early suggestions on improving my proposal through to Liz Agresta, Susan Clark, Bill Henry, Doug Sery and Noah Springer's support in turning the manuscript into a book. The three anonymous reviewers' helpful suggestions have ensured the final book is much stronger.

Parts of chapter 1 previously appeared in "Ebookness," *Convergence* 23, no. 3 (2015): 289–305; and sections of chapter 7 appeared in "Commonplacing the Public Domain: Reading the Classics Socially on the Kindle," *Language and Literature* 25, no. 3 (2016): 211–225, which both appear with kind permission from SAGE. Sections of chapter 7 were previously published as "The Limits of Big Data for Analyzing Reading," *Participations* 16, no. 1 (2019): 237–257, an open-access journal.

This book would not exist without the support and kindness of Marina, Michaela, Chris, Karen, Hannah, Will, Ellie, Pam, and Geoff.

A Note on Spelling

Ebook: The term "ebook" has three primary spellings: ebook, e-book, eBook. Just as email lost its hyphen, I use "ebook" to reflect the naturalization process that has occurred over the last decade. The only exception will be when referencing brands that have used variant spellings (e.g., Franklin eBookMan, Open eBook).

Amazon: While the full company name is Amazon.com Inc., for the sake of readability, I use "Amazon" to refer to Amazon.com Inc. and denote regional variants (e.g., Amazon.co.uk) where appropriate. "Amazon" will also incorporate subsidiaries such as Amazon Technology.

Reading system: When talking about the combination of hardware and software and its influence on the appearance of ebook texts, I use "reading system," a term coined for the EPUB specification that is roughly equivalent to the web browser terminology "user agent."

Introduction

When Jeff Bezos founded Amazon in 1994, he chose to sell books as a pragmatic business decision rather than from a sentimental attachment to print. Books can survive the rigors of the postal system and are easy to store in warehouses. Over the past two decades, Amazon has grown from a book-selling start-up to a technology giant valued at over $1 trillion in February 2020, with Bezos named the richest man in the world since 2017 even after a divorce settlement in the region of $40 billion.[1] Although Amazon has developed services far beyond the scope of publishing, books remain a core part of the company's brand in the popular imagination. Amazon solidified this connection with the launch of the Kindle in 2007, demonstrating the company's commitment to books even though up to 35 percent of sales came from "non-media" products in 2006.[2] After a half decade of stagnation for ebooks following the promise of the early 2000s, the Kindle was a necessary intervention and boosted the medium from a niche market to a stable revenue stream for publishers.

In the decade since the Kindle's launch, ebooks have come under sustained attack by traditional publishers.[3] Arnaud Nourry, the CEO of Hachette Book Group, rallied against ebooks during an interview in 2018, arguing that "the ebook is a stupid product. It is exactly the same as print, except it's electronic. There is no creativity, no enhancement, no real digital experience."[4] Nourry's statement reflects the commonly perceived rivalry between ebooks and print rather than how the two formats influence each other. Despite the Kindle's many limitations, and resistance from print-oriented publishing, Amazon's entry into ebook hardware irrevocably changed publishing. The device had a dramatic impact on digital workflows by encouraging publishers to adopt new processes that enhanced the quality of all publications, both physical and digital, since readers would now expect an ebook edition.

Beyond pushing publishers to embrace digital forms, the Kindle empowered some previously marginalized readerships. The emergence of Kindle exclusives demonstrates the demand for genres not traditionally supported by publishers. Readers not catered to by print-oriented publishing's drive toward best sellers can now find an abundance of reading material. Ebooks also offer new physical accommodations: parents can hold a Kindle in one hand while attending to their child, but a print book may be preferable to read in bed. E-readers require less space than physical books for people who cannot build a large library. Readers with visual or motor impairments may benefit from the ability to change font size or use text-to-speech features, and the introduction of the OpenDyslexic font in 2015 catered to the needs of readers with learning differences. Despite these improvements, critics and publishers assume that digital publishing should integrate multimedia, virtual reality, and video game elements.

Nourry's comments reflect the antagonistic relationship between Amazon and the book trade stemming from ongoing concerns about Amazon's sales strategies. Discussions of ebooks are often polemics around "disruption" or the superior materiality and smell of print.[5] Publishers have developed a niche market for luxury hardcover editions in response to readers who remain committed to print. Digital evangelism is pitted against print Ludditism, emphasizing extreme positions rather than considering the two media as complementary. In this book, I move beyond this antagonism to assess the impact of publishers, and the book industry at large, ceding the development of ebooks to a company that exemplifies the excesses of late capitalism and surveillance culture. Through this lens, I analyze how the Kindle has been a boon for publishing while simultaneously limiting the opportunities for developing an inclusive and forward-thinking digital platform.

The name "Kindle" reflects the tensions that have plagued the platform. The name was met with negative reactions owing to potential links to Ray Bradbury's novel *Fahrenheit 451* and book burning. Bezos pleaded innocence, arguing the name was an attempt "to talk about the future of reading, but in a small, not braggadocio way," to spark the imagination through reading.[6] He hoped the Kindle would become synonymous with ebooks as a verb akin to googling: "When I'm stuck in the airport or on line, I can *Kindle* my newspaper, favorite blogs or half a dozen books I'm reading."[7] According to Brad Stone, a technology reporter for *Businessweek*, the platform's development was driven by a desire "to thrive as a bookseller in a new digital age, [through owning] the e-book business in the same way that Apple controlled the music business."[8] After the iMac's success on Steve Jobs's return to Apple, the company noticed a growing market for digital music. To capitalize on this trend, Apple released iTunes in January 2001, with the iPod following nine months later. The combination legitimatized digital music consumption at a time when Napster and other peer-to-peer networks dominated the public imagination. The iPod also removed barriers to entry through vertical integration of hardware, software, and services from purchasing music to listening on the go. This required substantial investment from Apple. Ebooks were in a similar position by 2007, with a loyal community of dedicated hobbyists but no single catalyst for broader uptake.

The Kindle as Platform

To subvert the antagonistic comparison of digital reading with print, *Four Shades of Gray* tackles ebooks as *digital objects*, focusing on the Kindle as the largest platform. While other ebook platforms exist, none have been as transformative as Amazon's, owing to its unparalleled technical and social infrastructure. Nick Montfort and Ian Bogost proposed platform studies as a tool for the "serious and in-depth consideration of circuits, chips, peripherals, and how they are integrated and used" for creative computing.[9] For example, my title *Four Shades of Gray* refers to the limited color palette of the first-generation Kindle that Amazon used to guide the aesthetic of the device's screen savers, discussed in further detail in chapter 1. Platforms range from a video game console to an operating system or smartphone. Excavations of the Atari VCS 2600 or Adobe Flash are not mere technical excavations but considerations of the technology in its broader cultural and historical context. The Kindle was far from the first e-reader to market, but Amazon integrated a range of services and offered a large catalog of titles to create a more print-like experience than its rivals. As Montfort and Bogost argue, "A platform in its purest form is an *abstraction*, a particular standard or specification before any particular implementation of it."[10] A mature ebook standard could not just replicate the form of print but needed to capture the book's functionality and replicate the networks of its creation, distribution, and reception.

The Kindle must negotiate the inherent tensions between print and digital reading through existing simultaneously as a born-digital platform and a surrogate for print. Platform studies document the connections between computational architecture and creativity, but how does this work when a platform is constrained by the norms and expectations of another medium? Audiences consume differently in print and digital form. For example, romance has enjoyed a resurgence digitally, while the full size of the market was never explored in print. Otherwise, the ebook acts conceptually a lot like its physical equivalent. Experimental forms of "electronic literature," including Amaranth Borsuk and Brad Bouse's *Between Page and Screen*, develop the expressive vocabulary of digital media. Borsuk and Bouse's book is unreadable without the use of a webcam-enabled computer, as the pages feature hieroglyphics that display poems rendered in three dimensions in front of the reader once presented to a camera.[11] These playful experiments have a shorter shelf life than print: *Between Page and Screen* relied on Adobe's Flash Player, which was rendered obsolete by Apple's decision not to support the web browser plug-in for the iPhone. Further tensions persist between the long-established traditions of publishing, where many of the largest companies were founded before the 1930s (Penguin is a latecomer in 1935), and the meteoric rise of Silicon Valley as a hub for digital innovation in the latter half of the twentieth century. Throughout the book, I assess the consequences of the book trade's ambivalence toward digital media and how Amazon filled this demand with a technology-first approach. While this decision was mutually convenient for both parties initially, the longer-term impacts are still unraveling over a decade after the Kindle's launch.

The relationship between digital and print publishing challenges traditional notions of platforms as discrete entities. Tom Boellstorff and Braxton Soderman propose the term "transplatform" to describe the generative creativity encouraged by rivalries such as Intellivision and Atari or Sega versus Nintendo.[12] When placed in direct competition, technology companies innovate to outsell their rivals. The perceived antagonism between print and ebooks is a further example of a transplatform rivalry, but this is complicated by the internal cross-platform nature of the Kindle as a dedicated hardware range available for web browsers, personal computers, and mobile devices. The Kindle exists "in the weird liminal spaces that bridge one computational architecture to another."[13] Thomas Apperley and Jussi Parikka argue that "the platform requires a degree of *stability and consistency* as a technical object."[14] This is less clear here: What do we count as the Kindle platform? The dedicated e-readers? The content? The services?

The Kindle further complicates the notion of platforms through its position at the intersection of two often-conflicting definitions of digital platforms. This book is part of the Platform Studies series, which pioneered what Esther Weltevrede and Erik Borra term approaching "platforms as architecture," or analyses of the sociotechnical infrastructure of specific platforms and its influence on the production of creative content.[15] Since the publication of *Racing the Beam*, this technical approach to hardware's materiality has been overtaken by Tarleton Gillespie's more popular notion of "the politics of 'platforms.'"[16] This definition of platform serves as the prefix for several neologisms, including "platform politics" and "platform capitalism," which stem from the distinction between platforms, supposedly neutral sites for users to consume and share content, and publishers, the curators with direct responsibility for material they disseminate. The Kindle is a platform from the perspective of computational architecture, but within the broader Amazon ecosystem, it also functions as a political platform. By emphasizing the synergies between these two definitions in relation to the Kindle, I address the blind spots around how users engage with platforms in the architectural approaches and the technical limits of political economy analyses.

In an interview with the journalist Steven Levy to promote the Kindle, Bezos stated, "Books are the last bastion of analog. . . . Music and video have been digital for a long time, and short-form reading has been digitized, beginning with the early Web. But long-form reading really hasn't."[17] Resistance to extended reading on-screen dates back to at least the 1990s with publications such as Sven Birkerts's *The Gutenberg Elegies*, which challenged electronic media's ability to replicate the immersive experience of print.[18] The line of criticism has continued into the ebook era, with several studies documenting a gap in comprehension between students reading a text in print and digitally.[19] These projects often focus on reading to learn rather than as a leisurely pursuit, where accurate recall is less important. While the web revolutionized journalism, reference, and academic publishing, the strengths of trade publishers remained staples of print. The book trade predates other media industries, and practices from analog culture are deeply ingrained within the conventions of the industry. Since the advent of the personal computer, a *cultural* shift had occurred in publishing toward using digital tools to create and market print books. For example, the introduction of Standardized General Markup Language (SGML) in the 1980s allowed publishers to typeset digitally, a practice that became widespread by the early 2000s. Less attention was paid to the *media* shift of digitization, or converting books into digital publications. Print presented unique hurdles for digital consumption: five centuries' worth of history to convert, the lack of an established format for reading, strong associations between the materiality of print and content. The problem was exacerbated by distracting speculative visions of digital publishing: Spotify for Books, blockchain for managing rights, data-driven acquisitions. A large gap exists between publishers' desire to step into an entirely new paradigm (without the investment required) and focusing on a more organic evolution of the current strengths of digital publishing.

Ebook platforms are part of broader transformations of publishing in the early twenty-first century, especially in digital publishing.[20] For example, Matthew Kirschenbaum's "Book.Files" project reveals the challenges of publishers' reliance on digital asset management (DAM) for the preservation of contemporary book publishing.[21] *Four Shades of Gray* builds on this work to demonstrate the impact of the publishing industry ceding control of digital distribution to a technology company at the expense of the industry's own autonomy and the interests of readers. As a result, the market for ebooks has largely diverged from print, enabling new genres to thrive rather than supplementing existing revenue streams. Publishers' stronger embrace of audiobooks shows that the industry has the will to adapt to digital distribution, so why did they not prioritize ebooks?

Publishers and technology companies can be an uneasy mix. Obsolescence timescales differ substantially between the two. Publishers proudly market any Nobel Prize winners or *New York Times* Best Sellers on their lists decades after their initial publication date, while smartphones are called obsolete within a matter of years. Lisa Nakamura extends this logic, arguing that "older reading platforms like the first-generation Kindle may be worth studying because they were quickly obsolescent"[22] Her comments were published six years after the Kindle 1's launch but failed to account for the longevity of the hardware, which received its last update in March 2016 to ensure it remained compatible with changes in Amazon's wireless network.[23] The long-term support for hardware does not extend to services, however, as many functions available originally on the Kindle 1, and many later generations, are no longer available. The platform is constantly in flux, prioritizing short-term policy and experimentation rather than ensuring permanence and archival consistency.

The Kindle has stagnated, allowing for a moment of reflection on the state of the platform after its first decade. This book tackles the Kindle's impact from the perspective of *technology*, *texts*, and *uses*. By analyzing the interconnection between these three areas, I argue that Amazon's influence on publishing extends beyond "disruptive technology" to embedding itself in all aspects of the contemporary trade. This analysis can only be conducted through separating the publisher and technology company discourse from actual uses. The Kindle is a vast and complex platform with over five million ebooks, fifteen hardware launches, and forty million users.

A single book could never cover all facets of the platform, and my perspective is constrained to an Anglophone context, but I hope my work here will encourage further accounts of the Kindle's influence in other contexts. While individual chapters will primarily appeal to readers interested in computational culture, bibliography, or reception studies, the three themes clearly overlap. Amazon is first and foremost a technology company, and this context is vital to understanding the company's impact on a creative industry that prioritizes cultural influence and tradition over digital experimentation. Frederick Kilgour saw the "electronic book" as the "seventh punctuation" in the history of the book, an event on equal footing with clay tablets, the printing press, and offset printing.[24] It is still too early to judge the long-term impact of ebooks compared to these older technologies, but the shock waves of the Kindle continue to shape publishing.

When Jeff Bezos revealed the Kindle on November 19, 2007, critics lauded the device's combination of previous ebook successes while learning from other companies' mistakes.[1] Amazon's strategy was encapsulated in Bezos's comment that the Kindle "isn't a device, it's a service."[2] The Kindle is synonymous with ebooks as both hardware and consumable media because Amazon strived to emulate the book trade rather than focusing on translating print directly onto the screen. Criticisms of the Kindle often focus on visible design flaws or comparisons with the benefits of print, ignoring the platform's complex back end. Ebooks are best defined according to their own media specificity and materiality rather than just their relationship to print.

Resistance to ebook hardware stems from its disruption of the "natural" practices of reading print. Matt Hayler argues that the perception of print's naturalness is the result of its normalization through centuries of use. The ebook's artificiality can further be ascribed to "the sense that the text is somehow placed *behind* the object, that there is an additional layer of visceral insulation that must be fought through before it can be accessed."[3] Ebook users must charge batteries and purchase content separate from the hardware.[4] Amazon's marketing of the Kindle 1 emphasized the benefits of ebookness, including a screen that "looks and reads like real paper," and a device "lighter and thinner than a typical paperback."[5] The advertising also offered rebuttals to common worries about computers, including promises that the device was "simple to use: no computers, no cable, no syncing," and "the screen never gets hot."[6]

The name "ebook" attempts to resolve the tension between print and digital consumption. As with "email" and "electronic signature," the "electronic" book denotes only a conservative departure from its source material. Ebook hardware might extend features from print culture, but unlike an app or web page, an ebook will never challenge the fundamental concept of a "book." Ebook standards including the Kindle and EPUB are primarily designed for trade publishers such as Penguin or Hachette, which publish material for the broadest possible audience. Trade publishers were skeptical of digital publishing's benefits, so the ebook's success relied on conservative changes (synchronizing progress across devices, changing font sizes) rather than experimenting with form. Amazon's marketing and hardware design instilled ebookness in the public imagination.

From Book to Ebook

In an interview promoting the first Kindle, Bezos acknowledged the book's technological advantage over ebooks: "You know, the physical book is so highly evolved and so elegantly suited to its purpose that it's hard to improve on. It isn't like some other artifact, some other object. It's something very, very emotional and personal for people. But the book has a feature which I think is hard to notice, but it's the book's most important feature. And that is that it disappears."[7]

As Bezos notes, it is impossible to understand the Kindle's success outside of the wider context of book history. Ample scholarship exists in the field, but four core aspects influenced the ebook's development: *discrete characters and words, mass reproduction, paratext*, and *sociality*.[8] The invention of the alphabet as a set of discrete characters kick-started the book's development. The shift from *scriptio continua* (continuous writing) to spaces between words accelerated the process of abstraction in language, forming the discrete units of words, paragraphs, pages, and books.[9] This rigid codification of text as distinct from oral culture enhanced the prestige and authority of textual transmission. Gutenberg's introduction of movable type to Europe in the mid-fifteenth century solidified the book's importance by emphasizing mass reproduction. Print's perceived fidelity through perfect replication elevated the medium as the gold standard for knowledge exchange. The publishing industry therefore resisted the challenges faced by the perception of fluidity in digital publishing.

In the centuries after Gutenberg's breakthrough, the growing market for books developed conventions for tackling the overwhelming volume of text. Publishers created what Gérard Genette terms "paratext," including indexes, page numbers, and tables of contents to aid navigation.[10]

Print-based paratext took advantage of random-access features of the codex, a collection of bound pages, to allow readers to quickly navigate through the text. The ebook could not replicate this essential affordance, leading to experimentation with alternative navigation systems. *Sociality*, the final characteristic of the book, was part of a shift that the librarian and bibliographer David McKitterick describes as a transition from the "public word, mediated on stone, metal or paint on buildings," to "the privately mediated word."[11] Although readers engaged with words in a private space, the book remained a social object through marginalia, sharing, and substantial alterations of texts.[12] A sustainable ebook platform needed to engage with the long history of print to establish how digital reading was compatible with conventional models of consumption.

Because of this long evolution, the physical book endured as the "last bastion" of mass analog consumption despite several prophecies of the ebook's imminent arrival.[13] Television shows such as *Star Trek* primed consumers for the ebook's arrival. After the original series replicated the computational architecture of its time (large mainframes with whirring tape machines), *The Next Generation* envisioned speculative technology including the Holodeck and voice interfaces.[14] A place for linear reading still exists in the *Star Trek* universe, since crewmembers read on single-use hardware, called Personal Access Display Devices (PADDs), which resemble modern tablet computers.[15] PADDs are signifiers of busyness, with Captain Jean-Luc Picard's desk frequently seen scattered with the devices. A scene from a 1996 episode of *Deep Space Nine*, "Homefront," reveals the differences between *Star Trek*'s model of ebookness and the realities of ebooks in the mid-2000s. In the episode, Captain Ben Sisko carries an attaché case containing several PADDs to hand out for a meeting.[16] PADDs were depicted as single-use devices with no apparent mechanism for sharing content between them, a clear oversight when compared to the real-life e-readers that would come to market just two years later.

Beyond *Star Trek*, Michael Hart's Project Gutenberg was the most pervasive example of ebook culture before the Kindle. Hart aimed to create a digital "Library of Alexandria" from public domain texts. Project Gutenberg removed the text from its container. Slow internet connections made high-quality facsimile photographs impractical for transmission, so the project instead extracted the text rather than replicating the original book's format and layout. Progress was slow, however, as a small team digitized just ten titles between 1971 and 1989. Productivity increased with the uptake of the web in the early 1990s and the 2000 launch of Distributed Proofreaders, a tool designed to allow multiple users to proofread a text simultaneously. The project has digitized more than sixty thousand titles since 1994. Project Gutenberg is widely regarded as the original ebook project, but this title cannot relate to the project's launch in 1971, as its first nine publications, including Lincoln's inaugural speeches and the US Constitution, are documents. Hart himself referred to the project as the "National Clearinghouse for Machine Readable Texts" in early correspondence, and the resulting digitizations are called "e-texts" rather than "ebooks."[17] Project Gutenberg released its first recognizable ebook with the monumental digitization of the King James Bible in 1989.[18]

Project Gutenberg's shift to ebooks corresponds with wider conversations about the digital future of the book at the beginning of the 1990s. The *Oxford English Dictionary* notes Robert Olsen's use of "ebook" in his speculative future of publishing in 1988, which included nonstarters such as coin-operated CD-ROM jukeboxes and optical-media warehousing. Olsen describes the ebook as "a small, hand-held, flat recording device able to replay text as a portable cassette player replays sound. Libraries who argue that mass storage devices could never replace the book may be wrong—you *can* cuddle up with the E-book."[19] Olsen also made some incorrect predictions, including the ability to record and replay text directly on an e-reader. The concept of the ebook remained fluid and experimental until the arrival of commercial devices in the late 1990s.

The prehistory of ebooks before Project Gutenberg's publication of the King James Bible in 1989 resists strict linear treatment, and we can identify no clear candidate for the "first" ebook. Advances in optical-media storage and playback during the early twentieth century led to conceptual *mechanical* books as precursors to the ebook. Bob Brown's Readies from 1929 and Vannevar Bush's Memex from 1945 predicted the emergence of digital reading platforms but offered substantial changes to the reading process.[20] Brown was inspired by the New York Stock Exchange's Trans-Lux movie ticker, a back-projected ticker tape launched in 1923 that "could project a block of eight lines of text."[21] He envisioned a portable device that used microfilm to replicate the ticker tape's motion to allow users to speed-read a text in linear order. Bush was more ambitious in viewing the potential for nonlinear traversal of a microfilm workspace using a modified desk. These visions of the future of reading emphasized the manipulability of print in a digital environment at the expense of simulating the book.

Alan Kay's vision of the Dynabook in 1968 more directly connects to the contemporary ebook reader.[22] Similar proposals appear in patent filings from the 1970s onward, although none of these projects resulted in a commercial product.[23] The US Army's collaboration with academics at the University of Colorado on the "Personal Electronic Aid for Maintenance"

(PEAM) between 1982 and 1989 represents the earliest evidence of a physical ebook reader. PEAM was an attempt to create a portable device that used the nonlinear functions of the computer to improve the retention and speed of officers conducting maintenance work in the field. Hyperlinks allowed engineers to cross-reference unfamiliar processes at greater speed than traversing bulky print documentation. Contrary to research that digital readers retain less knowledge than with print, this early study concluded that nonlinear instructions were best followed using the prototype hardware.[24]

The first commercial "electronic book player," the Sony Data Discman, launched in 1990 and "sold 100,000 units in its first nine months at a list price of 58,000 yen (about $430)."[25] Other Japanese technology companies developed similar devices to capitalize on this trend, including the Fujitsu ViewArt and NEC Digital Book Player. The NEC device met with reasonable commercial success on its Japanese launch in 1994, but the ViewArt was never released.[26] These devices focused on the nonfiction reference market with encyclopedias, dictionaries, and travel guides, reflecting a common skepticism about the market for fiction ebooks.

The 1990s and early 2000s marked a sustained period of experimentation with ebook hardware in North America, coalescing in the launch of two devices that attempted to enter the fiction market. Softbook released its first hardware in 1998, and Franklin's eBookMan followed a year later. Franklin had a pedigree in digital publishing after pivoting from bootleg Apple computers to portable digital dictionaries in the late 1980s. Both companies struck deals with major publishers including Simon & Schuster and HarperCollins to distribute popular titles. This substantial investment ensured initial interest, but the technology was not sufficiently advanced. The devices were hampered by low-quality LCD screens and limited storage space. While conceptually mature, the technology required to make the ebook a success was not yet commercially viable.

Nonetheless, the early 2000s were a veritable gold rush for ebooks. In 2001 a joint report by the American Association of Publishers and Andersen Consulting valued ebooks at $2.3 billion by 2005.[27] Publishers conducted several high-profile business model experiments, including Stephen King's foray into ebooks in 2000 when Simon & Schuster sold his new novella *Riding the Bullet* exclusively as an ebook for $2.50. When the novella sold over 100,000 copies, King decided to reissue an earlier novel, *The Plant*, as a serialized ebook on an "honor fee" system. Users could download each chapter for free, but if 75 percent of users paid a voluntary charge of $1 for chapter 1, or $2 for subsequent chapters, King would continue to publish the material. King grossed over $600,000 from 150,000 users with the first chapter, but he stopped at chapter 6 after payment dipped below the threshold with chapter 4. King only posted the final two chapters because the material was already prepared.[28] The failed experiment with alternative economic models for ebook publishing served as a warning about the conservatism of ebook uptake. Amazon and other ebook platforms would reinforce the perceived ideals of print culture rather than attempt to challenge the conventions established over the preceding five hundred years.

The initial excitement of King's experiment encouraged Amazon to sell ebooks in the early 2000s. The "Ebooks and E-Doc" store featured ebooks available as Mobipocket and Microsoft Reader files. The store remained open until 2006, when the company was gearing up for the launch of the Kindle. Bezos argued that Amazon's previous attempt to sell ebooks was a failure: "We'd been selling e-books for a long time. Nobody has been buying e-books. So, very very small."[29] Amazon was happy to erase this footnote to emphasize the Kindle as a clean break from the previous stagnation.

The Kindle succeeded where previous attempts by Amazon and others had failed because the company understood the importance of developing infrastructure alongside hardware. As the book still evokes a stronger material nostalgia than other media—preference for analog film or audio is often framed as hipsterism, while it is normal to seek comfort from the materiality of print—ebook designers needed to "out-book the book," a task Bezos himself considered foolhardy, to encourage early adopters.[30] Gregg Zehr, the project manager for the Kindle 1's development, noted the challenges of creating a better ebook: "those business relationships, those technical connectivity issues, the wireless, the hardware, battery life issues, the software issue of on-store commerce or on-device commerce, straight from the device without any intermediary."[31] Anyone brave enough to develop an ebook platform was in an unenviable position of building a platform that improved on both books and digital media to create a distinctive sense of "ebookness."

Developing the Kindle

The Kindle was not Amazon's first encounter with ebook hardware, as the company had rejected an early offer to invest in NuvoMedia's Rocket eBook in 1997.[32] The company was instead acquired by Gemstar, an interactive television guide company, in 2000. Gemstar merged NuvoMedia with Softbook to create the RCA REB 1210, which sold 100,000 devices by March 2001.[33] Gemstar closed its ebook division in 2003, marking the end of the first major wave of ebook hardware after Franklin stopped producing eBookMans in 2002.[34] By mid-2003, the initial hype in ebooks had dissipated as major retailers such as Barnes & Noble closed their ebook shops, believing the concept was not marketable.[35] The following three years marked a fallow period in ebook history while Amazon and Sony were secretively developing the next generation. Amazon analyzed the fallout of the early 2000s ebook bubble and worked to ensure that its platform had an appropriate catalog of ebooks and the hardware would correct the limitations of earlier devices.

While others were struggling to develop viable ebook platforms, Amazon quietly built infrastructure. The introduction of the "Look Inside the Book" feature in October 2001 represented the company's first step toward the Kindle.[36] Readers could use this feature to preview books they considered purchasing. "Look Inside" predates the launch of Google Books by three years and was publicly open a year before Google's "Project Ocean" began in earnest with a partnership between Google and the University of Michigan.[37] Although Amazon launched its service earlier, Google Books has historically been considered the landmark moment in book digitization owing to its vast and overreaching early ambition.[38] Amazon had a smarter strategy for digitization: Google Books aimed to enhance the company's search index instead of creating a broader public good, while Amazon marketed the benefits of "Look Inside" to publishers as the equivalent of flicking through a book in a brick-and-mortar shop. Google's relationship building with large academic libraries was less fruitful than Amazon's direct engagement with publishers, as it ensured the rights holders felt in control of their intellectual property. The approach worked and allowed Amazon to build the foundations for the Kindle, while Google Books remains caught up in litigation for over a decade.

The launch of "Search Inside the Book" in October 2003 marked a transition from using scanned material for marketing to extracting the text from the page. Gary Wolf proclaimed this shift toward accessible text as the "Great Library of Amazonia."[39] Before the launch of the Kindle, Amazon and publishers mutually benefited from the "Search Inside" as a marketing technique, replicating the ability to flick through a book in a physical bookstore. Pearson led the charge of publishers agreeing to "Search Inside" deals in 2006 just before the Kindle's launch.[40] The retailer incentivized participation by offering to digitize books, defraying costs for publishers who would need to convert the material for other purposes.[41]

As with many Amazon initiatives, the benefits of digitization extended beyond ensuring the Kindle had sufficient content. The company announced "Amazon Pages" in November 2005 as "a program that would let consumers view parts of a book online on a pay-per-view basis." The project launched in May 2006 as the rebranded "Amazon Upgrade," a service that allowed readers to access full facsimiles of previously purchased print texts online for a small fee.[42] "Amazon Upgrade" covered over 100,000 titles, largely content from professional publishers who required high-fidelity facsimiles rather than reflowable text. Amazon discontinued the service in August 2016, when it was consolidated with Kindle Match-Book, the equivalent business model for purchasing discounted Kindle copies of print books bought through Amazon, launched in 2013.[43]

"Look Inside" and its derivatives including "Amazon Upgrade" provided the raw materials for the Kindle, but the company had to develop a wrapper for the text. The company revealed its intent with the acquisition of Mobipocket, an ebook platform, in 2005. Mobipocket had built a viable ebook format for the burgeoning Palm OS ecosystem, which had hit sales of ten million units by early 2001.[44] The Mobipocket bookstore listed 50,000 titles in early 2007, allowing Amazon to capitalize on previously digitized titles when boasting of its 88,000 ebook catalog.[45] Palm OS and other personal digital assistants (PDAs) filled the void left by the exit of e-reader hardware manufacturers in the early 2000s, and Mobipocket had developed the de facto reading system for Palm OS, while Microsoft invested significant resources into Microsoft Reader for Windows CE. Mobipocket had developed significant infrastructure and had a record of sales directly via Amazon. Bill Rosenblatt noted that Amazon's acquisition of Mobipocket "completes the realignment of the ebook industry," where the company replaced Adobe as an industry leader.[46] The acquisition of Mobipocket marked a transition between generations of the ebook after Gemstar's hardware failure and Barnes & Noble's high-profile exit from the market in 2003, after the end of the first ebook gold rush.[47]

Project Fiona

While "Look Inside" ensured Amazon had sufficient content for launch, hardware was more complicated. The Kindle would be Amazon's first hardware launch, so the company created a separate hardware division, Lab126 (code for Lab A–Z), in 2004, based in Palo Alto, at a distance from Amazon headquarters in Seattle. Lab126 was tasked with "Project Fiona," the ambitious project that coalesced into the Kindle. Fiona was named after the protagonist of Neal Stephenson's *The Diamond Age*. Bezos had long admired the author, and the code name references Stephenson's prescient vision of ebookness in the novel, describing "smart paper [as] a network of infinitesimal computers sandwiched between mediatrons. A mediatron was a thing that could change its color from place to place."[48] The reference therefore signaled the grander aspirations of Lab126 to recreate Stephenson's vision of "smart paper." Traces of this early code name remain in Amazon's URLs in the help pages for the Kindle to pay homage to the novel's significance to the platform.[49]

Bezos solicited the headhunting of Gregg Zehr, then hardware developer for palmOne, to work on Fiona. Zehr was approached to "create a new electronic book reader for Amazon" that would "change the world."[50] Bezos believed that Amazon needed to design the Kindle "to look for things that ordinary books can't do."[51] At the same time, "it must project an aura of *bookishness*, it should be less of a whizzy gizmo than an austere vessel of culture."[52] Amazon was keen to market this ethos through its secretive undertakings at Lab126. A 2005 version of the subsidiary's website quotes the jazz musician Charles Mingus: "Making the simple complicated is commonplace; making the complicated simple, that's creativity."[53]

The Kindle 1's firmware (the core software shipped with the device) referred to the "Fiona computer platform" as the code name shifted from a hardware prototype to the temporary name for the underlying architecture.[54] Unlike the remnants of "Fiona" in Kindle-related URLs, references to the "Fiona computer platform" in the source code were phased out as Amazon transitioned from its experimental to mature hardware. The second-generation devices stored these files in a "Fiona Legacy" folder while the Kindle hardware engineers continued to mine *The Diamond Age* for code names. The Kindle 2 was named Turing, after a character in the novel named after the early computer scientist Alan Turing, and the DX was named after the novel's protagonist, Nell. The scope of code names expanded beyond Stephenson's novel with "Tequila" (Touch), "Bourbon" (Basic), and "Pinot" (Oasis).[55] Where the hardware received alcoholic names, the software referenced games culture: Lab126's version of Linux 2.6.22 was dubbed "Mario" for the Kindle 2. This was followed by the Kindle 3's "Luigi" platform.[56] These code names situate the Kindle as a device clearly tied to speculative visions of the future of reading while remaining connected to entertaining pursuits such as video games and alcohol.

The development of Kindle hardware remained a well-kept secret until September 2006, when *Engadget* published a leaked Federal Communications Commission document containing the hardware specifications.[57] The FCC approve any hardware emitting radio frequency, and Lab126 was required to disclose the Kindle's specifications to the FCC before launching the device.[58] The leak was accidental, since Amazon had filed nondisclosure agreements. The specification was quickly deleted once news sources began reporting on Amazon's entrance into the reinvigorated ebook hardware market after Sony's announcement of the Librie in 2006. In the subsequent final FCC filing for the Kindle in March 2007, all mentions of "Kindle" and "Amazon" are redacted in the user manual.[59] Nonetheless, the leaks built a yearlong period of anticipation among ebook enthusiasts.

The external design of the first-generation Kindle was settled as early as 2005. Zehr's physical prototype of Fiona, which now resides in the Computer History Museum's *Raiders of the Lost Ark*–esque Milpitas warehouse, mirrors the final design's form.[60] Without the final external plastic casing, the asymmetry of the keyboard, navigation buttons, and overall form is emphasized. The final product showed only minor changes, except for the removal of a built-in reading light peripheral that was designed and mentioned in the FCC filings.[61] The wedge shape and asymmetric navigation design were both already present, although some of the final aesthetic flourishes were still being debated. Lab126 wanted to acknowledge the long influence and evolution of print culture on the ebook with engraved letters on the device's rear. Two prototypes from 2006 show the two final designs: one features exclusively cuneiform, the Sumerian writing system, arranged into a neat grid; the other features a waterfall-like arrangement starting with runes that slowly transform into the Latin alphabet.[62] The latter version was implemented in the final product and was used on

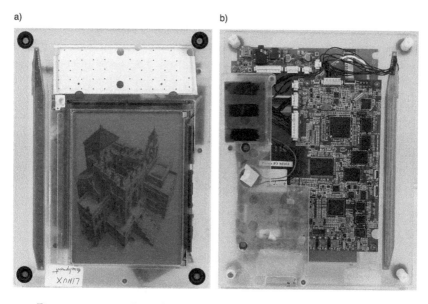

1.1 Fiona prototype unit housed at the Computer History Museum's Milpitas warehouse. © Computer History Museum.

the rubber rear cover and featured prominently in the Kindle 1's book-like box packaging.

While the hardware presented substantial design challenges, the rise of open-source software such as Linux afforded the Lab126 engineers the opportunity to adapt a preexisting operating system.[63] Linus Torvalds conceived of Linux in the early 1990s as a freely available and reusable version of the popular Unix operating system. Linux gained popularity, as it was designed to work with a variety of processors rather than remaining restricted to a single type of computer. As with other companies, Lab126 customized its version of Linux, derived from release 2.6.10, to remove superfluous hardware driver files and reduce the operating system's overall size by 45 percent to 110 megabytes decompressed, an important consideration when the device's overall storage space was limited to 256 megabytes.

Hardware choices were made on similarly pragmatic grounds. Lab126 chose ARM processors, which had a track record with Palm OS devices, iPods, and iPhones owing to their low power consumption for mobile uses. Since the Kindle depended on extending battery life, all hardware needed to be power efficient. Amazon settled on Gumstix as the low-power microcontroller, the main hardware interface between the processor and other chips, memory, and display. The choice would build on Gumstix's architecture for E Ink's displays rather than developing the interface between the architecture and operating system from scratch.[64] Other than reducing the overall size of the operating system by removing superfluous controller interfaces and introducing new power and display routines to suit the new technology, the Lab126 team made minimal changes to Linux 2.6.10 for the Kindle 1.

Delays marred the Kindle's launch. Some of the problems were logistical, as the shipping process for the electronic paper screens damaged the product because of atmospheric conditions during shipping.[65] Amazon was an unwitting bystander in takeovers and litigations that further delayed the device's production. Intel's announced exit from the mobile device processor market in June 2006 and sale of its XScale ARM series of processors, the Kindle's core architecture, to Marvell created a complex transitional period, causing delays in receiving the microprocessors.[66] The wireless modem, Qualcomm's AnyDATA, was also delayed after litigation by Broadcom threatened to stop the arrival of the modems in the United States.[67] Exacerbating these supply issues, Bezos encouraged Lab126 to constantly tinker with hardware specifications, which led to further delays in finalizing the device.[68] The early supply chain issues likely led to an understocking of the first-generation device, which sold out immediately at launch and remained out of stock for months afterward, missing out on a lucrative holiday season.

Since launching the first-generation Kindle in the United States in 2007, Amazon has unveiled a new generation each year except 2008, after substantial interest in the first-generation device in the United States led to troubles meeting demand. The Kindle has developed in four distinct phases (figure 1.2). The first two generations represent the *experimental* phase, where Amazon explored the device's optimal design. For example, the Kindle 2 (2009) introduced a four-direction navigation pad after the Kindle 1 trialed a one-dimensional navigation bar. The Kindle 3 (2010) marked a move to the *mature* stage, as Lab126 refined the hardware to

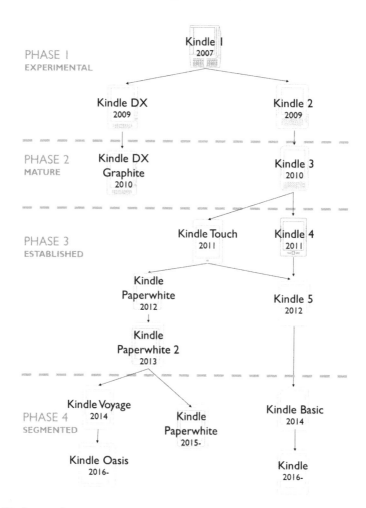

1.2 Kindle genealogy

mainstream acceptance. The third phase was the longest sustained period without major innovation after the introduction of Touch (2011) and Paperwhite (2012) as further enhancements of the original device and reflecting the dominant trends in touch interface design encouraged by the emergence of the iPad. The latest phase, *segmented*, was marked by the simultaneous launch of the Kindle Basic and Voyage in 2014, as Amazon sought to create a market for both budget and luxury ebook readers after the failed attempt to create a luxury ebook reader market with the Kindle DX (2009), which had initially been designed with a "fully quilted surface" to denote luxury.[69]

The Kindle 1 was never released outside the United States, but the Kindle 2 launched internationally in October 2009, eight months after its American debut, at an event during the Frankfurt Book Fair.[70] The launch was delayed by the complexity of negotiating roaming mobile data contracts across Europe, as well as Amazon's insistence on having a selection of 280,000 books at launch in the United Kingdom, its primary European market. Genevieve Kunst, Amazon's senior manager of digital media, addressed the Independent Publishers Guild UK conference in March 2009 to encourage independent publishers to digitize their back catalogs.[71] Six months later, Amazon's Kindle selection on launch day included books from many of the largest publishers, although Oxford University Press and Macmillan did not initially sign up. Random House abstained too because of an ongoing payment dispute with Amazon.[72] Similar struggles between large trade publishers and Amazon have been persistent during the Kindle's life span, but the international launch solidified the Kindle's dominance of the ebook market. E-readers, led by the Kindle, represented 25 percent of "reader device market share" in September 2009, second only to the desktop and printed PDFs with 42 percent share.[73]

The Kindle DX launched in April 2009, three months after the Kindle 2, to break into the Portable Document Format (PDF) market with a 9.7-inch screen, almost twice the size of other Kindle models.[74] The large screen allowed Amazon to target readers who wanted to keep the fidelity of PDFs, as well as readers who require larger font configurations. Rather than reflowing the page, the Kindle DX allowed users to view print media in facsimile. The device's marketing relied on PDFs rather than any of Amazon's proprietary ebook standards. Once native PDF reading was introduced on the DX, every subsequent hardware release featured the option. Specialized PDF e-readers have been a continuous desire for digital publishers, from EveryBook's collaboration with Adobe, EB Dedicated Reader, in the late 1990s to Sony's release of Digital Paper in 2014. The launch of the iPad took the market share instead.

Amazon designed the DX with higher education in mind, as the integration of a native electronic paper PDF reader at near US letter size would offer a clear advantage for reading journal articles and textbooks on-screen. Evan Schnittman, a vice president at Oxford University Press, claimed the DX was "a new holy grail" for electronic textbooks.[75] Bezos announced the device at Reed College as part of a pilot study into Kindle use in the classroom at seven universities, including Reed, Princeton, Washington, and Virginia.[76] The experiment failed, with the American Council of the Blind and National Federation of the Blind suing Amazon over a lack of accessible navigation controls.[77] The DX was not doomed to obscurity, however, as a second version, the Graphite, was launched in 2010, and the two models are among the most desirable collectibles for ebook enthusiasts because of their large screen size and PDF compatibility, with devices selling regularly for over $100 and up to $300.[78]

The Kindle 3, the beginning of the *mature* phase of Amazon's dedicated ebook readers, offered a significant overhaul of its design in response to the success of the iPhone in July 2009. The quirky elements of the original two generations were replaced with a straight QWERTY keyboard and symmetrical design. Amazon integrated well-received features from the DX, as the Kindle 3 introduced the ability to view PDFs and added voice-guided menus to address the accessibility concerns raised by the DX lawsuit. Having iterated on design, the Kindle 3 marked the moment where the subsequent generation stopped radically departing from the previous device.

Amazon's continual support for developing e-reading hardware was instrumental in establishing the viability of ebooks for publishers. After e-readers' brief period of dominance, hardware is no longer central to any ebook platform's business, as users are more likely to read ebooks on smartphones or multifunctional tablets, including the Amazon Fire, than on a dedicated device. The Kindle's rise mirrored the smartphone's ascent, fueled by the availability of wireless communication infrastructures and high-resolution screens that are more convenient to hold in transit than a book. Apple sold 1.3 billion iPhones between 2007 and 2017, creating a larger potential user base for ebooks than dedicated hardware, and Amazon would have been foolish to ignore the opportunity.[79] The company addressed four core challenges facing ebooks in designing the Kindle: (1) ensuring the platform included enough content to build a user base; (2) developing displays sophisticated enough for reading on-screen for a sustained period; (3) navigation; and (4) connectivity. The last three challenges marked the beginning of a new form of ebookness that extended the core principles developed throughout the history of the book and ensured a usable and efficient hybrid between digital and physical reading systems.

Content

John Maxwell argues that ebooks replicate simplistic web pages, but "the e-book privileges *content* where the web privileges *connection*. In doing so, the e-book adheres to an industry-era scarcity model where content experiences are relatively few and must be acquired at some cost, whereas the web assumes sheer abundance."[80] While ebooks do not emphasize the connectivity associated with websites, standards such as HTML and CSS allow the reader to change the formatting to their preferences.[81] Ebook formats are designed to be robust and encompass a wide range of genres from biography to poetry. Amazon prioritized content over connectivity as a core element of ebookness.

Amazon's ambitions required extensive digitization. Book conversion lags behind other creative industries, including film and music, as text is more laborious to digitize, requiring several stages from taking photographs of pages to optical character recognition (OCR), a process where an algorithm determines what text appears on a scanned page, and manual correction of errors. Transcribing a book manually can be more cost-effective than automated processes. Due to text's perceived simplicity but technical complexity, Van der Weel states that "paradoxically, text is both the first and the last of the medial modes that is to go digital."[82] Amazon created Mechanical Turk (MTurk) in 2004 to accelerate digitization for "Search Inside the Book."[83] As a corollary, the automation process offered a safeguard to prevent users from uploading pornography on the Kindle.[84] MTurk allowed Amazon employees, and later third parties, to set small tasks for completion in exchange for a nominal payment. MTurk's name references an eighteenth-century chess-playing "automaton" that actually featured a secret cabinet hiding an excellent human chess player.[85] Bezos described Mechanical Turk as the "guts of Amazon" alongside Amazon Web Services and framed the project as "artificial artificial intelligence" and "humans-as-a-service" for exploiting cheap labor to undertake menial tasks that one would assume that computation could easily automate, such as correcting scanned texts.[86]

Mechanical Turk continued Amazon's reliance on user-generated content that started when its professional editorial staff was replaced by an influx of volunteer-contributed reviews. Amazon's business strategy depends on commodifying humans both as contingent labor for its warehouses, delivery network, and small-scale tasks and as data points of consumption. Jeremy Antley describes our relationship to these platforms as "data serfdom," where users produce value for the data lords with little return.[87] Amazon's approach through MTurk is conspicuous owing to its framing. Lilly Irani argues that the service, and Amazon more broadly, rationalizes the contingent labor and data serfdom by "rendering it manageable through computing code."[88] The dehumanizing rhetoric of the exotic "Turk" (a name Bezos approved despite the negative connotations, noting that "he personally would bear the responsibility for any backlash")[89] and framing humans as "services" and "artificial intelligence" are emblematic of Amazon's attempts to mask the company's reliance on manual human labor. Other than Amazon Logistics, the company's delivery service, the vast labor force of over a half million workers is hidden from sight, with an emphasis instead on automated grocery shopping, drone delivery, and "artificial artificial intelligence."

Display and Navigation

Electronic paper was a significant factor separating the Kindle and Sony's 2004 launch of the Librie from earlier e-reading hardware.[90] Futurists had long predicted "smart" paper that replicated the dynamism of digital displays while maintaining the flexible materiality of print, but the technology's history starts in the 1930s with innovations in photocopying. Chester Carlson's invention of "xerography," or "dry writing," in 1938 not only led to Xerox's dominance of the photocopying industry but also created the "direct positive-to-positive operation" technology behind electronic paper.[91] Serious work to translate the principles of xerography to display technology began in the early 1970s, when researchers at both Xerox PARC in Silicon Valley and Matsushita in Japan developed electronic paper screens.[92] Neither research group was focusing on developing the technology for digital book publishing, as Nick Sheridon aimed to create Gyricon as a display screen for desktops coming from Xerox PARC, while Matsushita was interested in using the display for clocks. By 1997, "electric paper" reemerged as one of the top priorities for Xerox PARC to rebrand as the "Digital Document Company."[93]

Sheridon's vision was realized in the late 1990s, when the MIT undergraduates J. D. Albert and Barrett Comiskey, along with their professor Joseph Jacobson and investors Jerome Rubin and Russ Wilcox, founded E Ink. The team positioned itself as a disruptive force within publishing. An early profile in *Wired* highlighted the company's desire "to replace ink as we know it."[94] The start-up entered into an exclusive partnership with the Dutch company Philips Electronics in 2001 to create "radio paper" (the combination of electronic paper with wireless connectivity), with ambitions to launch in 2005.[95] When the device failed to materialize, Prime View International (PVI), a Taiwanese company, purchased the license from Philips in 2005, before acquiring E Ink in 2009.[96] Once Philips canceled its exclusivity contract with E Ink, companies were able to build on technology that had not yet fulfilled its potential.

The Kindle 1 used E Ink's electrophoretic display (EPD), the cutting edge of electronic paper technology by the mid-2000s. The screen renders text and graphics using "positively charged black particles and negatively charged white particles."[97] Electrode layers placed on either side of the electronic paper capsules foreground a ratio of black or white particles according to the shade of gray required. Figure 1.3 visualizes how six pixels are rendered through the electrode layers. Grayscale is more viable than full-color display, which requires an assembly of capsules in red, green, and blue.

Electronic paper extends battery life. Once a page is rendered on the screen, the text can be displayed indefinitely without requiring further power until a page turn alters the signals from the electrode layers. Additionally, the technology did not require back lighting, producing a more natural reading experience. The technology does involve some trade-offs: electronic paper can display static grayscale images, but colors and the refresh rate required for videos remain beyond the capabilities of electronic paper. Nonetheless, electronic paper is reliable for static images and remains the preference for a niche group of readers who continue to use e-readers. E Ink has improved its screen technologies significantly since 2007. The first update came with the arrival of the Kindle DX, which used E Ink "Pearl," reducing the image update time of text by 50 percent and images by 40 percent.[98] The Oasis, Amazon's flagship e-reader in 2017, used E Ink's updated Carta screens, which refreshed the image on

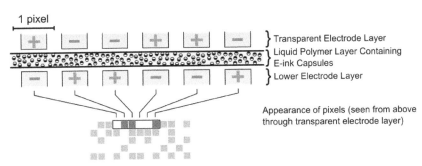

1.3 Electrophoretic display. Source: Run!, "File:E-Ink.Svg," Wikipedia, 2006, https://en.wikipedia.org/wiki/File:E-ink.svg.

a screen in 75 percent of the time of the previous generation, creating a smoother reading experience. E Ink Carta also increased the fidelity of images and text rendering to 300 pixels per inch (PPI), a measure for how visible individual pixels are on a display. This pixel density offered the equivalent of the first generation of Apple's Retina technology, which was marketed as the pixel density exceeding the input capacity of the human eye.[99] This clearly lagged behind the vanguard of mobile screens and came with a premium price, which has led to stasis in one of the most visibly important technologies in the Kindle's stack.

Amazon needed to adapt the Linux libraries for the Kindle to ensure that users could use the hardware's limited audiovisual capabilities through Advanced Linux Sound Architecture (ALSA) and the libraries for JPEG and PNG image formats. Audio and still images were peripheral to the first-generation device but enabled Amazon to offer an "experimental" MP3 player, and publishers could embed images at a low resolution and use up to four shades of gray for images. Despite its continual reliance on electronic paper, the dedicated Kindle e-reader has yet to be commercially viable with more than sixteen shades of gray. The introduction of E Ink Pearl with the Kindle DX upgraded the color palette to sixteen shades of gray, allowing more complex images to appear on the device. As an illustration, we can compare a screen saver image of Jules Verne, author of *Journey to the Center of the Earth*, that appeared on both the Kindle 1 and DX (figure 1.4). The limited palette of the original Kindle required optimization to be effective, an additional cost for publishers. The necessity to display PDFs on the DX required higher fidelity.

Electrophoretic displays remain the most common commercial electronic paper technologies despite continual investment in developing alternate technologies such as "electrowetting," a full-color, flexible "video-speed" form of electronic paper.[100] Amazon invested heavily in the technology and filed over 250 patents containing the keyword "electrowetting," but no commercial product has included the new displays. Companies have also attempted to introduce full color to electrophoretic displays, with E Ink's research and development team demonstrating a prototype in 2016.[101] A paradigm shift to full-color electronic paper will revitalize the e-reader market by offering more direct competition with tablets. The closure of Liquavista, Amazon's electrowetting display spin-off, in early 2018 painted a bleak picture for the future of the display technology.

To overcome the limitations of electronic paper during the production of the first Kindle, Lab126 engineers incorporated a narrow second

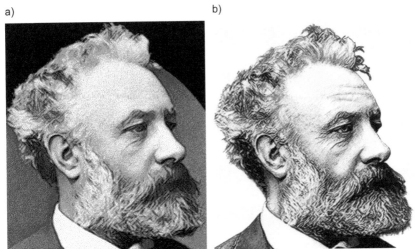

1.4 Comparison of E Ink displays of Jules Verne screen savers. Left: Kindle 1, four shades of gray. Right: Kindle DX, sixteen shades of gray.

screen using a polymer network liquid crystal display (PNLCD), a display technology similar to electronic paper that was not backlit and limited battery consumption to counter the slow refresh rate of the electronic paper (annotation 108 on figure 1.5).[102] The strip updates more quickly than the electronic paper to create a navigation aid so that users knew which line or menu option was selected without refreshing the primary screen. Lab126 hard coded the strip to feature a maximum of two hundred lines, restricting the total number of lines viewable on the Kindle at one time.[103] The navigation bar required constant battery power and thus did not persist once the user switched the display to standby.

While the PNLCD was the final compromise, the Lab126 engineers also investigated the potential of configurable keyboards where touch screen sensors were placed under a second electronic paper screen that could refresh different configurations according to the user's current navigation needs (figure 1.6).[104] Once the reader has opened an ebook, the keyboard is wasted screen real estate, when navigation is paramount. This option would offer more customization but would not solve the problem of finding one's position on the primary screen. The idea would eventually be implemented with the arrival of the Kindle Touch.

Electronic paper offered new opportunities for screen savers. Earlier implementations of screen savers for cathode-ray tube (CRT)

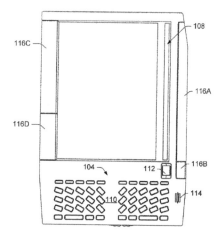

1.5 Navigation features for the Kindle 1 (adopted from patent). Gregg Zehr and Symon J. Whitehorn, Handheld electronic book reader device having dual displays, US Patent 8,950,682 filed March 29, 2006, and issued July 6, 2010, figure 1.

a)   b)

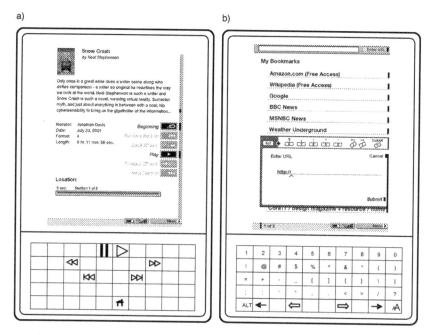

1.6 Configurable keyboards (adopted from patent). Source: Johnston and Zehr, Configurable keypad for an electronic device.

monitors were designed to avoid screen burn-in, where a static image would imprint a ghostlike permanent image on the display. Conversely, electronic paper is optimized for static use, albeit with the chance for ghosting if a hard screen refresh is not implemented periodically. Screen savers were instead developed for the Kindle to use the bistable properties of the screen. if the screen only draws power when the screen is refreshed, it is possible to display a static image indefinitely when the user turns off the device. The first-generation Kindle featured inspirational screenshots of prominent literary authors including Jane Austen and landmark text technologies including the Lindisfarne Gospels and Charles Babbage's difference engine. Amazon also used the screen saver to request feedback, pairing an image of George Grant's calculating machine with an email address soliciting feedback.

Navigation

The Kindle design team focused on emulating the conditions of print rather than creating something that pushed the limits of books. The Kindle was not too dissimilar from conceptions of the book-as-object: "The Pentagram designers [brought in by Amazon initially for external advice] began by studying the actual physics of reading—the physical aspects of the pastime, such as how readers turn pages and hold books in their hands."[105] The Lab126 team noted several significant properties of print required for ebooks: "It never becomes hot and is designed for ambidextrous use so both 'lefties' and 'righties' can read comfortably at any angle for long periods of time."[106] This lofty ideal was only half realized in the final design with book navigation buttons on both sides of the screen, albeit with a larger "next" button on the right-hand side, designed for the "righties."

Early ebook readers' designs reflect their awkward mix of book-as-object and the desktop computing paradigm, using wedges (e.g., Kindle 1, Rocket eBook) and two-page spreads (e.g., Sony Data Discman), accompanied by QWERTY keyboards, simultaneously upholding and challenging the historical design of books. The hardware keyboard on Kindle devices until 2011 was inspired by the dominant aesthetic of the BlackBerry in the mobile imagination before the launch of the iPhone. Bezos briefed the Kindle designers "to join my BlackBerry and my book."[107]

Ebook hardware launched since the release of the iPad in 2010 dedicates a large surface proportion to the screen with a minimalist interface, mimicking a tablet rather than a book. The appearance of ebook hardware has become homogeneous to reflect the popularity of tablets since 2010. Apple's introduction of both the iPhone and the iPad emphasized the screen over more diverse hardware interfaces. In following this trend, ebook reader design has shifted from modeling the book-as-object to a flat representation of a page.

Despite following trends in mobile hardware design, ebook reading software is unique among software packages dedicated to presenting text. Ebook software emphasizes reflowability—the concept that text does not have to be fixed to the size of the page but can be changed to fit the reader's preferences and exact screen size—and presentational aspects, beyond typographic formatting, are largely left to the software to interpret.[108] Reflowable text mitigated the problems of zooming and scrolling that burden formats such as PDF, which attempt to re-create the fidelity of a printed page on-screen. The Kindle's early hardware constraints continue to inform contemporary ebook design, where text should be optimized for reflowability with minimal consideration for tables or images. These requirements made ebooks with rigid formatting demands difficult to render on the screen, as reflowability prioritizes text over other elements. For example, word search ebooks and other language puzzle titles can feature errant line breaks if the reader chooses a larger font size than the author's default setup.

The ebook is defined by its relationship to print, particularly as a simulation of the book trade and print culture. For example, page numbers are an invaluable tool for academic citation practices, but the principle converts poorly in reading systems that allow users to alter the unit of the page on the screen. While Amazon has attempted to replicate page numbers through various algorithms including "Real Page Numbers," the introduction of a proprietary "location" mechanism introduced persistent identifiers across the Kindle, even if this does not translate to other ebook platforms. "Locations" are determined by a simple calculation:

$$\frac{\text{Compressed file size in bytes (excluding images)}}{150} + 1$$

The average ebook is divided into 4,000 to 8,000 locations. This allows for technical precision without becoming unwieldy outside of lengthy, text-heavy books such as dictionaries. Locations therefore strike the balance between percentages and byte-level references.[109] This is not entirely transparent, however, as the calculation includes markup and therefore cannot be rendered on a one-to-one basis with the contents visible to the reader's eye. Nonetheless, locations offer a compromise between the well-understood unit of the page and the lack of universal location standards in digital objects.

Amazon has constantly struggled with navigational structures beyond turning a single page. An early patent reveals that the company wanted to include a "tactile member" that allowed users to apply pressure and scroll rapidly through the text, akin to rapidly flicking through a book (figure 1.7).[110] Lab126 included the tactile member to mitigate the larger-scale navigation otherwise lost in the more straightforward single-unit-forward-or-back navigation system. The table of contents was the dominant midlevel navigational paradigm until the introduction of Page Flip in 2016, which attempted to rectify the lack of macro-level navigation through a "bird's-eye" view of the book.[111] The mechanism relies on a grid structure with the software interface rather than introducing a hardware solution.

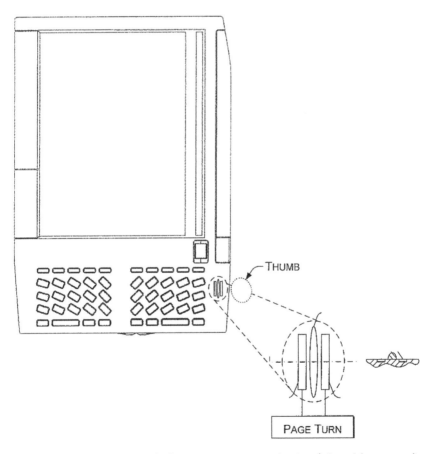

1.7 Detail of the "tactile member" as a page-turning mechanism (adapted from patent)

Connectivity

Amazon's service infrastructure was built around its Evolution-Data Optimized (EV-DO) network, Whispernet. The company partnered with Sprint to offer free data when accessing the Kindle ebook store, paying only for the content. Amazon absorbed the data fees into the cost of the device, as it defrayed the costs associated with subscription, something Bezos was keen to note when critics raised concerns about the high initial price.[112] His strategy revolved around these affordances to entice readers who would otherwise be hesitant to move away from physical books. The product page for the first-generation Kindle boasted: "System requirements: None, because it doesn't require a computer."[113]

Users would need to wait until the release of the Kindle 2 for Wi-Fi. This was the converse of the model established by Apple, where a Wi-Fi-only model was cheaper than the mobile data model, but the strategy allowed geo-blocking, as Amazon could determine exactly where its devices functioned. Users without access would need to use the USB transfer. The Wi-Fi-only model allowed users to choose their access options, skipping the subsidized contract with Sprint. Users who still have working first-generation devices have continued to enjoy the subscription-free service more than a decade after launch. Kindle 1 users still receive sporadic firmware updates. For example, when the company upgraded its Transport Layer Security (TLS) certificates from version 1.0 to 1.2 in March 2016, it pushed an update for the Kindle 1 firmware containing the new certificates, ensuring that users could still access the Kindle Store and third-party websites rather than denying support for the nine-year-old devices.[114]

The release of the Kindle DX and expansion into international markets presented fresh challenges for offering an internationally consistent mobile data network. Amazon upgraded the modem from EVDO to High Speed Packet Access (HSPDA) to offer faster speeds and functionality outside North America.[115] This increased access to over one hundred countries, far exceeding the number of regions where one can purchase a Kindle or natively access Amazon's services, so users could download ebooks while traveling outside their home region.[116] Access was treated equally across countries: a reader with a North American Kindle could use roaming data in all countries with contracts. The company's marketing emphasized the international reach of the Kindle 2's roaming data as "now with global wireless."[117] The move allowed Amazon to offer one of the strongest challenges to print's perceived supremacy, as users could now purchase books on holiday rather than having to plan in advance if traveling to markets with limited access to books in their native language.

Ebookness

Amazon's careful consideration and integration of the various levels of the ebook platform led to its success where other companies had previously failed. Shifting focus from product to service was instrumental in developing a mature ebook platform. Amazon developed a complex infrastructure in the decade preceding the Kindle's launch, easing the transition to the Kindle's services. Given Amazon's large market advantage, Bezos, Zehr, and Lab126's vision of ebookness is now emblematic of ebook culture. The connection between Amazon and ebooks has at times hindered the acceptance of the medium because of the perceived injustices inflicted by the company on the book trade, but Amazon's core strength lay in envisioning how contemporary developments in technology could be paired with some of the most accessible and useful elements from previous attempts at developing an ebook platform.

Computers, and by extension software, simulate other media environments, such as the book.[118] Ebook reading software designed for operating systems beyond the dedicated hardware are built on the restrictions of e-readers. For example, users of the Kindle for Mac engage with a second-generation simulation of the book that is bound by the rules of both the book and ebook hardware. "Ebookness" emerges from how Amazon has reshaped four principles of print culture: *discrete characters and words*, *mass reproduction*, *paratext*, and *sociality*. By prioritizing the reflowability of discrete characters at the expense of the unity of the printed page, the Kindle team developed a reading experience that could compete with print. Mass reproduction was expanded to include mass distribution made possible by Whispersync. Amazon constantly experimented with the final two elements to ensure the optimal reading experience, offering something supplementary to reading print. While popular narratives have framed a great struggle between print and digital modes of consumption, the two media complement each other, and Amazon's business interests depend on the success of both. As the company has maintained its position as the largest ebook platform, its vision of ebookness has become dominant, for better or worse, and an understanding of these developments must consider the complexities of Amazon's relationship with the book trade.

The Kindle occupies an awkward position in histories of mobile computing. It was not the first electronic paper device, and it was overshadowed by the launch of the iPhone seven months earlier in March 2007. The Kindle instead depended on Amazon's infrastructure to attract users. The company rapidly changed from a web retailer to essential infrastructure for a variety of first- and third-party services in its first decade. The company prioritized technologies and infrastructure to transform industries rather than replicate preexisting models. Take web retail as an illustration: in the mid-1990s, mail order was an established business model, but emerging web technologies offered vast improvements over the web's slower and less dynamic predecessor. Amazon took this approach to all new projects. Werner Vogels, Amazon's chief technology officer, argued that "Amazon is a technology company. We just happen to do retail. Everything Amazon does is driven by deep technology stacks."[1]

Danny Fortson and Simon Duke, journalists for *The Times* of London, describe Amazon's infrastructure as "the fourth utility—after water, gas and electricity."[2] The wires and protocols of the internet are far more important as a utility than Amazon (notwithstanding the company's entry into laying undersea cables in 2018), but the hyperbolic comparison gives us a reasonable starting point for thinking about infrastructure.[3] Utilities, roads, fiber optics, and Wi-Fi networks are all examples of infrastructure. Etymologically, the prefix "infra-" comes from the Latin preposition for "beneath." Susan Leigh Star and Martha Lampland extend this definition by noting that "infrastructure is something that other things 'run on,' things that are substrate to events and movements."[4] Electricity powers other tools rather than being an intrinsically valuable commodity. Others build on the infrastructure developed by utilities and internet services. Often the infrastructure is hidden in favor of the final service. For example, we are less concerned with how an email is transferred from California to Hong Kong than with its authorship and receipt, but a vast technical infrastructure of servers and protocols ensures the message's cross-continental delivery within minutes.

Large technology companies develop modular infrastructure to enable cross compatibility for engineers to rapidly build new internal projects.[5] Amazon recognized the value of these services to a wider audience and elected to allow third parties to access the infrastructure. The company diversified its business interests to ensure the maximum number of third parties used its services. The footer for Amazon's home page lists forty different enterprises ranging from Withoutabox, a service for independent filmmakers to submit work to film festivals, to Amazon Restaurants, a home-delivery service built on Amazon's delivery network. The company has further business interests in cloud computing and storage (Amazon Web Services, Drive), publishing (DPReview, Kindle Direct Publishing), film (Box Office Mojo, IMDb), fashion (Fabric, 6pm, Zappos), web analytics (Alexa), and video games (Twitch, Lumberyard, Games Studio). These diverse services are connected by providing infrastructure for others. Amazon's annual reports often highlight these successes. For example, in the 2015 letter to shareholders, Bezos states: "Used well, our scale enables us to build services for customers that we could otherwise never even contemplate."[6] Infrastructure forms "a gateway, permitting other systems to interact with [Amazon] to form a seamlessly interactive network."[7] Any technology company forming an integral part of the network will remain important as infrastructure even if its primary products or services diminish.

Amazon's infrastructure formed the basis of the company's plan for the Kindle's broad adoption. Sony and Cybook launched ebook readers with similar specifications to the Kindle in late 2007, but the competitors lacked Amazon's sophisticated infrastructure. Sony offers a useful illustration of the benefits of mature infrastructure, since the company failed to create a sustainable ebook business despite its resources and experience building hardware compared to Amazon, which had never released a device before the Kindle. We can think about media formats as a form of infrastructure. The physical medium of a CD or tape cassette plays a subordinate structural role to the content stored on it. Sony has a patchy history of introducing new formats, with Betamax and MiniDisc as just two of its high-profile failures. The company's investment in proprietary media formats highlights its main limitation in developing infrastructure: it focuses less on cross compatibility, leading to higher development costs.

Amazon instead followed Apple's road map for iTunes and the first-generation iPod by integrating its core services—web-based retail, a large cache of user-generated data, Amazon Web Services, Mechanical Turk—into the Kindle platform. Early commentary asked if this was the ebook's "iPod moment," although the *Wall Street Journal* counteracted this early hype by suggesting that the Kindle was having an "eight-track moment" as a temporary phenomenon.[8] This initial pessimism stemmed from previous ebook failures and framed Amazon primarily as a retail company in the mid-2000s. The popular press's reporting on Amazon drives its public perception. Profiles of the company viewed its history through the perspective of retail, indicated by titles such as *One Click* and *The Everything Store*.[9] For example, Brad Stone frames Amazon Web Services in terms of "the everything store" that "stocked Amazon's shelves with incongruous products like spot instances and storage terabytes."[10] Even in 2020, when global COVID-19 lockdowns boosted Amazon's share prices from $1,900 in January to almost $3,500 in September, the focus remained on the growth in terms of home delivery, ignoring how Amazon Web Services also saw a dramatic increase in traffic owing to the shift to working from home.[11]

Table 2.1 shows thematic words that appear frequently alongside "Amazon" in news reports indexed by Google News between 2010 and 2018. Journalistic accounts focus on the company's technology but emphasize its retail operations over developments in media and other markets. This is not atypical, however, as General Electric is still associated with hardware and Microsoft with productivity software despite the companies' substantial investment in other business models. Amazon is most

Table 2.1 Common themes in top 100 collocates of Amazon in the Brigham Young University NOW corpus

Theme	Frequency
Technology (e.g., "Google," "Cloud")	39,522
Retail (e.g., "Purchase," "Retailer")	30,185
Media (e.g., "Studios," "Netflix")	11,258
Meta (e.g., "Bezos," "CEO")	11,196
Other (e.g., "Peru," "River")	5,221

See appendix A for full details.

productively categorized as one of the five "technology giants" alongside Alphabet (Google's parent company), Apple, Facebook, and Microsoft.[12] Disparate interests across the companies can be tied together by a common use of technology.

Any attempt to summarize Amazon's complex and diverse historical trajectory will be reductive by nature, and others have already written detailed histories of the company.[13] My interest here focuses specifically on how Amazon the technology company's development of the Kindle shaped our popular understanding of ebooks. Nonetheless, several broader concerns are worth addressing first. Undercover investigations by newspapers including the *New York Times* revealed exploitative labor practices in Amazon's warehouses, head offices, and hardware-manufacturing collaborations with Foxconn in the Hunan Province of China, which, along with perceived tax evasion tactics, overshadow the company's dominance within retail.[14] The drip of negative articles about Amazon turned into a steady flow by the late 2010s, challenging the company's narrative. Brian Merchant has documented the problematic connections between Amazon and fossil fuel companies.[15] Caroline O'Donovan and Ken Bensinger revealed the extent of deaths connected to Amazon drivers.[16] It is no coincidence that these investigations emerged while Amazon consolidated its position as one of the largest technology infrastructure companies. As with similar platforms, including Cloudflare, a comparison to more traditional infrastructure such as roads allows these companies to plead neutrality when offering support for causes that would otherwise be deemed unsavory. These criticisms still frame Amazon as a retailer, ignoring expansion into other areas even if they are the primary focus of the article, such as a subhead for an article about streaming football matches describing the company as a "US online retailer."[17] The focus on expansion over profitability encourages this narrative, as it hides Amazon's interests in diversification and surprises pundits when, for example, the acquisition of Twitch did not fit into preconceptions of Amazon's strengths.[18] Retail wisdom suggests that scale is essential, but Amazon understood that, in the digital age, advanced technology trumps physical inventory. Amazon was an underdog to established retailers such as Walmart, Toys"R"Us, and Barnes & Noble, which had yet to exploit the technological and logistical affordances of online retail. Amazon's focus on technology and infrastructure for retail encouraged Toys"R"Us to partner with the company to boost its online presence in 1999.[19]

Amazon's origin story is well known: Bezos was working as an analyst for the Wall Street investment firm D. E. Shaw in May 1994 when he had a "eureka moment" about online commerce.[20] The web was changing from a utopian space of experimentation to a commercial juggernaut.[21] Bezos had an epiphany after reading that web use was likely to increase by 3,200 percent per year as users quickly adapted to web-based retail. He identified books as a suitable foundation for establishing an online retail business. International Standard Book Numbers (ISBNs) were widely adopted in the book trade and were easy to convert into a catalog. The materiality of print was also amenable to mail operation: books were nonperishable and could withstand manhandling while shipped.[22] After a beta launch in 1994, the website opened to the public in 1995 and was an immediate success. In 1996 the *Wall Street Journal* called Amazon an "underground sensation for thousands of book-lovers around the world, who spend hours perusing its vast electronic library, reading other customers' amusing on-line reviews—and ordering piles of books."[23] The novelty of Amazon's range of services helped normalize online retail and laid the foundations for a more extensive infrastructure.

Virtualization and AWS

Amazon Web Services (AWS), launched in 2004, was the catalyst for the company's transition from an online retailer to a cornerstone of internet infrastructure. The service was intended as a commerce application programming interface (API) for third parties to use the powerful infrastructure Amazon had built to date.[24] Instead Amazon built a "cloud computing" platform integral to the internet's infrastructure and the second part of what Bezos described as Amazon's "guts" in tandem with Mechanical Turk.[25] Its entry into cloud computing was a dramatic turnaround from Bezos's acknowledgment in 1999 that the company did "not have backup systems or a formal disaster recovery plan. . . . Computer viruses, physical or electronic break-ins and similar disruptions could cause system interruptions, delays, and loss of critical data."[26] Many large-scale web applications use AWS, most notably Netflix, a direct competitor of Prime Video. Brad Stone argues that this marked a turning point in the development of Amazon, as it expanded the scope of Amazon's products beyond tangible goods to infrastructure and services.[27] The company was an early mover with cloud computing in 2006, which allowed it to build capacity at scale. In turn, this profit could be turned into further investment in research to create new services that benefited external customers and, more importantly, Amazon's businesses.

The mythical origins of AWS recall that the service developed through selling spare server capacity that would otherwise only be used during peak demand. Amazon's need to survive the onslaught of purchases between Black Friday and Christmas led to surplus servers for the rest of the year. Rather than lease extra servers at a premium cost for the busiest period of retail, Amazon could purchase capacity for peak times and then rent the surplus for the remaining ten months of the year. Werner Vogels dismissed this narrative, stating that AWS was developed to provide Amazon employees with a suite of prebuilt network tools to avoid having to develop this infrastructure from scratch before undertaking new projects. Once Amazon introduced this service for employees, it was a short step toward selling this infrastructural service during the early hype around cloud computing.[28] Since Amazon pivoted earlier than its competitors, the company established itself as a leader when others, including IBM and Microsoft, took longer to scale up.

AWS's physical presence is hidden literally as commercially sensitive information, and metaphorically by the cloud's association with ephemerality and immateriality.[29] Amazon's public-facing customer-centric ethos requires the environmental and labor costs to remain hidden to drive the narrative. These centers are the counterpart to Amazon's distribution centers in enabling the Kindle's online infrastructure to prioritize areas according to socioeconomic affordances and limitations. AWS is one of Amazon's most profitable services. In 2019, AWS provided 12 percent of all net revenue, or $35.03 billion in total, for a profit of $9.2 billion. Conversely, despite revenue in excess of $170 billion, North American product and service sales returned a smaller profit margin of $7.03 billion, with estimates that costs from COVID-19 will further reduce profitability of the company's physical services during 2020.[30] Providing critical digital infrastructure is more profitable than retail, leading to further investment in cloud services at the expense of the perceived traditional strengths of Amazon, including bookselling.

AWS was instrumental to the Kindle's development and success because of its focus on virtualization and abstraction of the computational process. An IBM white paper identifies the virtual computer as "a logical representation of a computer in software [to provide] more operational flexibility."[31] The Kindle offers a similar logical representation of the book in software, extending beyond facsimile privileged by formats such as PDF. As a result, ebooks model books, while other formats model text or print. This logical representation requires additional features to differentiate a book from other digital written genres such as journalism or blogging. For example, EPUB extends the base HTML specification by introducing new tags including "spine" and font obfuscation to simulate the affordances of the book removed by text-oriented specifications. The Kindle was the first ebook platform to focus on virtualization rather than offering a flat representation of print, complementing its precursor. The flexibility of cloud computing, which moved ebook infrastructure from on-device to remote storage, also created opportunities for reading surveillance on an unprecedented scale. Virtualization services such as AWS are an essential component to the Kindle's success, as they encapsulate both the product and the process. The practice enables the complex modeling of the book trade and a way of integrating the structure of the book trade into a relatively underpowered computer.

The Rhetoric of "Innovation"

Beyond AWS, Amazon has invested heavily in new technologies. The five largest technology companies (Alphabet, Amazon, Apple, Facebook, Microsoft), known as the "Big Five," use the rhetoric of innovation to compete in the marketplace. This manifests in prizing start-ups and disruption over focusing on improving existing products and processes. Technology companies use research and development as a central strand of their marketing strategies. For example, in an interview on *60 Minutes* and a promotional website in 2013, Bezos revealed plans for "Amazon Prime Air," a drone delivery system, before the technology was approved for testing.[32] The announcement was a statement of intent designed to build excitement and increase share prices rather than demonstrate meaningful innovation. Seven years later, the company is still performing closed tests in Cambridge, England. Amazon faced greater barriers to entry into an increasingly restricted drone airspace, leading to further delays, but the reveal of speculative technology so far in advance of its implementation is highly unusual for a company like Amazon. Beyond this big marketing push, patent filings, acquisitions, and academic collaborations provide a more meaningful insight into how Amazon frames its role as a technology company, as such documentation provides evidence of unfinished and abandoned ideas. Alessandro Delfanti and Bronwyn Frey used Amazon's patent filings to explore how the company explores the future of work in an example of how this gray literature helps illuminate corporate ideologies.[33]

The company's famed secrecy prohibits engineers from producing material for academic journals and conferences in line with its main rivals.[34] Academic collaborations are often local and outside the company's main business interests. For example, Amazon maintains strong links with the University of Washington, endowing the computer science department with two chairs in machine learning, and running the general Amazon Catalyst research fund for any initiative looking for funding at the university.[35] The first rounds of Catalyst provided funding for projects as diverse as health, 3D printing, renewable energy, and robotics. Amazon Web Services offers an open credit scheme for educational projects to train future engineers.[36] Despite this gesture toward openness in the broader scientific community, this segmented access separates Amazon's core businesses from academic collaborations, unlike the open nature of Microsoft Research or Google and Facebook's interactions with universities. The company's collaboration with academics therefore offers little useful insight into Amazon's infrastructure.

Acquisitions are more fruitful for understanding Amazon's position in the technology marketplace. The company's first acquisitions in 1998 were PlanetAll, "a Web-based address book, calendar and reminder service," and Junglee, "a leading provider of Web-based virtual database technology, which allows visitors to access a variety of products sold by other merchants."[37] The two start-ups were acquired for infrastructure purposes instead of adding a flashy new service direct to customers. A year earlier, Bezos's first letter to investors gestured at this interest: "The Company's current strategy is to focus its development efforts on creating and enhancing the specialized, proprietary software that is unique to its business and to license commercially developed technology for other applications where available and appropriate."[38] Acquiring businesses to license technology was the first shift in the company's priorities from retail to providing infrastructure for third parties.

Amazon's patents are its most public statement of intent regarding technological and infrastructural innovation. The company was one of the top twenty most successful patent applicants in 2018 in a list dominated by hardware manufacturers including Samsung, Qualcomm, Intel, and Taiwan Semiconductor.[39] Lab126's focus on hardware increased the rate of patent filings, but Amazon also continued to protect algorithms and software. This diversity reveals what kind of hardware the company is developing, as well as many of the processes underlying these developments. Patents therefore are useful markers of Amazon's technological progress.

Bezos's early patent filings were controversial, particularly "Method and system for placing a purchase order via a communications network," filed in September 1997 and granted exactly two years later.[40] The innocuous title belies the much-contested patent's claim that Amazon was first to develop the one-click payment option for web-based retail. The technology allows users who have entered their personal details and credit card information to choose to buy something without requesting confirmation. Users would not have extra steps to confirm their purchase and reconsider the decision, thus replicating impulse purchases in brick-and-mortar stores. The patent caused immediate concern within the technology community, drawing criticism from Tim O'Reilly, an influential computer guide publisher, and Richard Stallman, an early free software advocate, who viewed the patent as an implementation of preexisting HTTP cookies rather than a substantially new idea.[41] While cookies were originally designed for Netscape Navigator, David Kristol and Lou Montulli's Internet Engineering Task Force Request for Comments (RFC) "HTTP State Management Mechanism" proposed an interoperable standard for articulating "stateful sessions with HTTP requests and responses."[42] In other words, cookies enable servers to identify returning visitors along with limited information about their previous visits. The initial RFC mentioned web retail as a possible implementation alongside personalized journalism recommendations. Paul Barton-Davis, an early Amazon programmer, opposed the patent, which he believed was contradictory to the principles of open technology driving the web's early development as well as Amazon's early ethos.[43] Bezos rejected the claims, stating that "the vast majority of our competitive advantage will continue to come not from patents, but raising the bar on things like services, prices, and selection," but he agreed that software patents should be protected for a shorter time and agreed to fund a prior art database that never materialized.[44]

The controversy did not slow Amazon's patent-filing policy, as it has been granted over eleven thousand applications since 1997, revealing a gap between ideology and practice in the company's technological development. For example, Lab126 filed seven patents related to the Kindle 1 simultaneously in March 2006, more than eighteen months before the device was launched. The seven patents feature the same context and diagram but diverge in the claims made, outlining separate processes and innovations from the shape of the device to its cloud-based delivery. As an illustration, "Handheld electronic book reader device having asymmetrical shape" reveals Amazon's interest in ebooks in 2006 and how this was reshaped by the attrition of the application process in its final iteration in 2016.[45] The original application made seventy-one claims, which were whittled down to twenty in the accepted application. The delays revolved around contentions over the similarities between the proposed wedge-shaped reading device and a patent filed by Nokia in 2002.[46] In response, Zehr and Whitehorn emphasized the media specificity of the invention by focusing on ebooks rather than the original claims for "electronic media," as well as the specific hardware configuration of four screens in nonparallel structures and the wedge's specific angle, which replicates a folded-back paperback. Zehr and others at Amazon sought to claim the design was unique among mobile computers, but this was narrowed to outline how the Kindle was distinct from competitors including the Sony Librie, which did not feature four screens or a wedge shape. From the outset, Amazon was thinking beyond e-readers to position itself as a media hardware producer by using the language of "media" rather than "books" in these early patents. An e-reader was just the logical starting point, as Amazon was well established as a bookseller.

Patent applications are expensive, but Amazon does not implement all granted techniques, such as the abandoned "tactile member" page turner discussed in the previous chapter.[47] The company is renowned for investing profits into growth: investment in "technology and content," which also included the cost of AWS and Prime Video, topped $29 billion in 2018.[48] While patents may not offer the greatest return on investment, the company's patent filings explore new opportunities without committing to launch. As a result, the patents are scattershot rather than focusing on one facet of Amazon's business. For example, on June 27, 2017, the US Patent and Trademark Office granted Amazon thirty-seven patents in its weekly update. Most of these applications were submitted between 2013 and 2015, with four applications dating back to 2011–2012. The four older applications featured contentious broad claims. For example, "Public-domain analyzer" was filed in December 2011 as part of Amazon's drive to offer free access to titles with expired copyright terms. Copyright law changes, particularly since the late twentieth century, have made discovery of these titles challenging. The patent outlines a method of identifying relevant titles through consulting metadata and generating a "confidence level whether work is in [the public domain of] a country."[49] The published patent is commonsensical, since the public domain analyzer relies on Amazon's metadata and proprietary algorithm, it primarily claims territory. Other patents granted on June 27, 2017, are more detailed and span the range of Amazon's current service interests, including improvements to its data centers,[50] Alexa,[51] and the backbone of its emergent drone technology.[52] The applications were in process for variant amounts of time, so any connections are serendipitous, but the volume and scope indicate the extent of Amazon's experimentation in different industries.

Amazon's patent filings accelerated during the Kindle's development cycle as the 1,000 patents filed before 2007 were dwarfed by 6,000 awarded in the decade afterward (figure 2.1). Examiners and inventors work together to classify patents into standardized categories to position the invention within broader technological trends. Patent offices continuously update the classification system, but it lags behind innovation in digital media.[53] As a consequence, the most frequently occurring classification number remains the default "1/1" option, which appears in

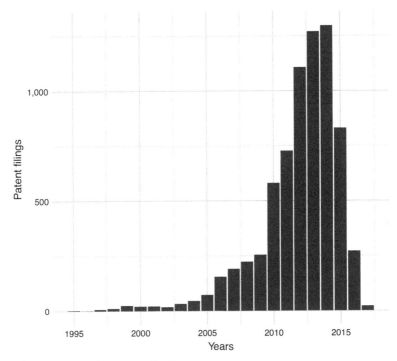

2.1 Amazon's granted patent applications, 1995–2017

1,600 applications, albeit often with other numbers. A closer examination of classification patterns offers a clear overview of Amazon's R&D interests: it has over seven thousand classifications in the data-processing range (700–715), including "data processing: financial, business practice, management, or cost/price determination" (705) and "multicomputer data" (709), reflecting Amazon's strengths in retail and cloud computing respectively. Eighty percent of all classification numbers come from the 700 range, which encompasses computational innovations, but the company also filed 14 percent of its patents in the 300 range, used for general hardware and electronics. Many of these patents focus on optical and image analysis, which is not traditionally seen as one of Amazon's strengths, but the patents outline optical character recognition (OCR) techniques and approaches to improve the visual sensors for devices such as Echo Show.[54] The hidden layers of Amazon's infrastructure are more expansive than the visible. In mid-2018, the optical recognition technologies documented in the patents were highlighted in Amazon's controversial collaboration with US police departments in Florida and Washington using Rekognition, its facial recognition technology.[55] Likewise, the patents related directly to the Kindle represent only part of the broader set of technologies that underpin the device.

Amazon's modular infrastructure becomes clear when we look at the connections between classification numbers in its patents. Figure 2.2 shows a network of classification numbers for the company's patent applications between 1997 and 2011. Several themes—security, data, and wireless—emerge as important across Amazon's services. AWS and online retail have a fingerprint in patents clustered around networking and retail respectively. As the company's public image depends on retail technology, this can be seen as "offensive and defensive weapons in legal struggles with their competitors," or a way to stake Amazon's territory.[56] Even with the densely connected clusters of classification numbers, patents tie together disparate elements of Amazon's infrastructure, reinforcing the

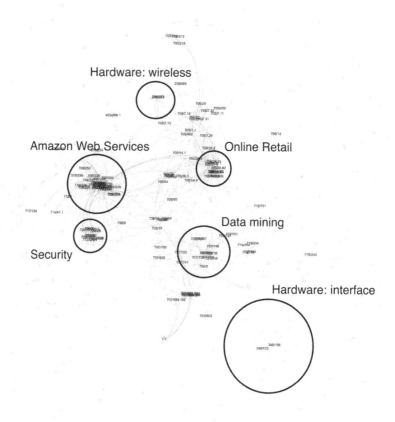

2.2 Network of patent classifications

modularity of the company's interests. Engineers working on drone delivery and groceries do not work in silos but build technologies that reinforce the company's overall strengths. The Kindle benefited from this approach, as it combined expertise in networks, wireless, retail, and data mining. The mass connections between separate classifications indicate a modular yet interconnected approach to technological innovation.

Table 2.2 maps Amazon's trajectory from a web-based retailer to infrastructure provider through identifying the most prominent words in patent filings over three-year intervals. The patents diversify over time and offer a narrative of the company's development. Amazon's first patent application, "Secure method for communicating credit card data when placing an order on a non-secure network," filed by Bezos alone in March 1995, reveals the lack of trust in web-based retail at the time.[57] The patent cites publications such as "Perils and Pitfalls of Practical Cyber-commerce" that outline a range of obstacles for online retail, including cryptography, impersonation, and growth management.[58] It describes a transitional system between telesales and online retail to instill trust by separating the order and payment systems. Users would submit an order online and then "during a subsequent telephone call to the remote merchant location [enter] the complete credit card number." The information would be automatically processed on a secure internal server.[59] The idea appears quaint two decades later, but this early patent signaled Amazon's

Table 2.2   Three-year moving average keywords in Amazon's patent filings

1995–1997	1998–2000	2001–2003	2004–2006	2007–2009	2010–2012	2013–2015
card	auction	pay	task	computing	device	inventory
credit	search	content	storage	network	data	producer
associate	gift	marketplace	embodi-ments	virtual	session	second
data	items	fulfillment	configured	device	storage	holder
order	recipient	page	data	module	gateway	first
said	bid	inventory	WS	can	power	crypto-graphic
telephone	item	product	traffic	communi-cation	blob	electro-wetting
point	terms	image	tasks	DNS	antenna	parsed
purchaser	category	listings	path	address	element	leasing
confidential	facility	plan	mobile	execution	NCC	fluid

See appendix A for further details.

ambitions to build trust in online retail by revising the dominant model of retail for a web-based environment.

Just three years later, customers were comfortable enough to use Amazon. The technological arms race shifted toward developing auction technologies such as the 2002 patent "User interfaces and methods for facilitating user-to-user sales" to compete against the emergence of eBay, which began applying for patents in 1998. In the patent, Roseman et al. emphasize Amazon's strengths in using metadata to generate recommendations for users and speculate about asking customers to "pre-order" items by indicating the maximum they were willing to pay.[60] Outside the more outlandish claims, the illustrations demonstrate how little third-party retail services have developed over the last two decades, since the design matches the marketplace today.

The third phase in Amazon's patent filings was more substantial as the company began to file patents relating to ebooks and other hardware, including tablets, phones, and voice-activated assistants. The terminology shifted from "ebooks" to "digital content." This is emphasized in patent applications such as "Method and system for providing annotations of a digital work," which forms the basis of Amazon's Kindle Popular Highlights system and was further expanded into the X-Ray service for ebooks, films, and music.[61] As Amazon built a reputation as a media technology company, its patents began to reflect the company's interests in media beyond books. Patents aimed to cover film, streaming, video games, and ebooks, leading the company to adapt the term "digital works." For example, "Playlist-based detection of similar digital works and work creators" lists "music files, video files, [and] electronic books" mediated through sources including "web sites" and "physical CDs."[62] Amazon's move into other creative industries encouraged cross-fertilization of media metaphors, as the patent was an extension of one filed in 2001 called "Recommendations and services based on works played or stored on user devices." Amazon's infrastructure treats the book as one medium among many interacting with its systems. The company does not privilege the book above other commodities but treats it as another product to sell and accumulate data from. This approach exemplifies what Shoshana Zuboff calls *surveillance capitalism*, which "unilaterally claims human experience as free raw data for translation into behavioral data." These data can be converted into "prediction products" but have increasingly been "traded in a new kind of marketplace for behavioral predictions [called] *behavioral futures*."[63] The speculative nature of this project ensures that Amazon collects all possible data from bookselling and consumption with the aims of monetizing it later. Mark Davis describes this overreach as Amazon bringing the act of reading into the market.[64] As I have argued elsewhere, premature marketization of reading data can only be as effective as the analysis, which has yet to result in clear benefits for Amazon, publishers, or readers.[65]

Retail Infrastructure

Amazon's early development relied on a mixture of retail innovations and leveraging new logistics and warehousing technologies. The company's logistical strength led to the development of its Prime service and the erosion of waiting times to Prime Now (one-hour shipping in select cities in the United Kingdom and United States). While it has an extensive network of warehouses in strategic locations, this physical infrastructure is underpinned by the company's data-processing capacity to ensure that items are in the right warehouses to meet tight delivery schedules. Amazon's recent interest in drones and warehouse robots reflects a natural progression to focusing on automating the retail process. The outward-facing emphasis of progress in automation masks the vast network of contingent labor working to meet the tight deadlines of deliveries in less than forty-eight hours.

Before Amazon built a sophisticated warehouse and distribution network, the company relied on an artificially inflated catalog to give the appearance of a large bookstore. At launch, it needed to attract Borders and Barnes & Noble customers without having a comparable warehouse. While the start-up did not have the same brand recognition, Amazon developed advanced supply chain technology to become far more efficient than its brick-and-mortar rivals.[66] For example, the layout of its warehouses changes to meet the demands of changing customer orders rather than remaining static. Bezos initially decided against warehousing stock but preferred to list titles as available and order books from wholesalers on request, passing part of the savings onto customers.[67] This approach was unsustainable, and as Amazon grew, it began building warehouses for popular items to reduce waiting times. By 2017, the company amassed an extensive international warehouse network of almost 200 million square feet.[68] Amazon's vast footprint has a large environmental impact for the sole benefit of faster shipping. Prime delivery worked through stocking goods in strategic locations, although its data-driven approach to rolling out shorter shipping times reinforces racial and class divides in major US cities.[69] Amazon Prime was initially seen as a risky proposition, since shipping fees can be lucrative, but it reaped $1 billion in membership fees during the first year of operation.[70] Prime was a Trojan horse for Amazon's broader plans to turn retail customers into users of the full suite of Amazon services. Subscribers soon gained access to premium Twitch, music, and video services while receiving discounts for specialist retail operations including Pantry, a home delivery grocery service. In the 2016 report to shareholders, Bezos describes Prime as one of the three pillars of Amazon alongside Marketplace and AWS.[71] All three services form the blueprint for Amazon's "walled garden," where users can access the majority of services required on the internet.[72] Schemes like Prime invoke a fear of sunk cost, where customers are more likely to purchase something via Amazon to make the most of the membership fee even if the product is cheaper elsewhere.

By encouraging users to see Amazon's ecosystem as an interconnected suite of services, Prime has become central to the company's business-to-consumer offerings. In this sense, Prime functions as a service infrastructure, offering a common base for consuming Amazon services that discourages users from moving to another platform. The subscription service permeates all parts of Amazon, including the Kindle. Two subscription services are available for the ebook platform: Prime Reading and Kindle Unlimited. The latter offers a fuller library at an additional cost, but Prime members gain the benefits of the former. Both schemes aim to change readers' consumption habits so that they remain Kindle-only readers. If many exclusive ebooks cost only a couple of dollars, and Unlimited costs $9.99 to access the same content, users are encouraged to read up to five books a month to make the most of their membership.

Amazon invested in online retail infrastructure to build a reputation in an underdeveloped niche. The company was keen to shift to a service-oriented business model early in its development. While Amazon struggled through the malaise of the dot-com bubble in 2000, Bezos suggested that the company might become "an incubator for e-commerce companies that can start companies at lower costs and more quickly than any other company in the world."[73] The rhetoric was toned down in future press releases, but the ethos remained throughout the development of third-party retail services starting with zShops in 1999. The service provided the blueprint for today's third-party marketplace by allowing merchants to "offer a vast array of popular or hard-to-find items" on the web store.[74] The storefront merged with Amazon Auctions, a failed attempt to compete with eBay, to form the current marketplace.

Traditional retailing wisdom suggests that allowing third parties to sell direct to consumers undercuts sales, but Amazon understood the importance of transaction logs as a commodity. Businesses have taken advantage of its infrastructure for third-party retail. For example, Thriftbooks sells books for under a dollar and sells up to twelve million books a year via Amazon through rescuing "landfill-bound books, sight unseen, for around 10 cents a pound."[75] The most successful operations employ data scientists and financial analysts to find the most profitable books. Amazon benefits from the data to enhance its recommendation algorithms, identifying older titles to bring to the Kindle and pocket transaction fees without the need to warehouse items. In 2006 the company launched Fulfillment by Amazon (FBA) to allow third parties to use its warehouse and delivery infrastructure.[76] FBA reflects Bezos's focus on scale: Amazon warehouses are larger than any third-party start-ups' storage facilities, so both parties will mutually benefit by using this scale to market to a large user base. The scheme also allowed Amazon to recoup the shipping costs lost through Prime subscriptions, as third parties pay the company to store and deliver the items. The ability to target both end users and businesses as customers was replicated in the development of the Kindle, as Amazon could use its large customer base to encourage publishers to digitize books that remained out of print but interested users. FBA is just part of Amazon's shift from service provider to service infrastructure, where scale and volume are more important than limiting direct competition. In his 2017 letter to shareholders, Bezos noted that over half of all products sold through Amazon were sold by third parties, cementing the company's importance as web retail infrastructure.[77] Ben Thompson argues that Amazon is interested in developing an infrastructure for all retail activity and transactions rather than focusing on one business model, no matter how contradictory those motives might appear externally.[78]

The introduction of Amazon Pay in 2007 to compete with PayPal expanded the company's transaction log data beyond the confines of its own retail website to gather further evidence of consumer habits across the web.[79] Aiming to leverage the company's reputation for secure payments, Pay never reached the same customer base as PayPal, despite Amazon's substantial market share in retail. PayPal is a direct competitor, and its user base may support it instead of Amazon and may boycott the company. The so-called Everything Store is designed to be comprehensive, so loyal customers have little need to shop elsewhere. Amazon Pay shows that the company's infrastructure has its boundaries and outside of the hidden use of AWS, it is less likely to succeed outside of Amazon's core service infrastructure.

The internal retail operation was far more successful. Bezos capitalized on the fact that brick-and-mortar bookshops would never be able to compete with Amazon's ability to cater to the demand of the "Long Tail," the model that 90 percent of all interest comes to the top 10 percent of most popular items, while the final 10 percent of interest is spread thinly through the remaining 90 percent of items.[80] In bookselling, this is the distinction between best sellers—titles that sell large quantities in a relatively short period—and the backlist, older titles that sell steadily if left visible in a store. Brick-and-mortar bookstores traditionally chase best sellers rather than selling older titles, which can only feature limited stock, as booksellers must ensure all books will sell in a reasonable period. Brick-and-mortar retailers rely on "core stock" such as *The Highway Code* and *The Hobbit*, which are likely to sell consistently over time. Conversely, Amazon's extensive warehouse network and online catalog allow the company to profit from obscure titles hidden from traditional bookshops' customers. A store with over four million unique titles can be unruly unless tamed by a search bar. The runaway success of best sellers such as a new *Harry Potter* title allows Amazon to offer such books at a heavy discount, thus attracting more new customers. Amazon's catalog of sixty-five million other books props up discounting practices even if each only sells a single copy a year.[81] The company's data collection practices allow it to profile networks of users' interests in niche genres and provide recommendations from the end of the long tail.

In 2016, Amazon transitioned from online to physical retail by opening its first bookstore in Seattle, followed by other branches across the United States. Ironically, it wished to avoid another company undercutting its physical retail and filed a patent in May 2012 describing a method for blocking customers' access to competitors' prices when physically in a store.[82] The company had previously benefited from this phenomenon, as browsers refer to Amazon's app for price comparisons when in the competitions' shops, and the patent is a defensive tactic for ensuring other retailers did not develop similar technology. Amazon Books' aesthetic revolves around the importance of user-generated data and replicating the technology of online retail in a physical space. For example, Prime customers received in-store discounts, while those without the premium service pay full list price for in-store purchases.[83] Curated displays drew on user-generated data, with shelves dedicated to esoteric categories including "4.8 Stars and Above" and "Most-Wished-For Books." Rather than work with traditional product categories, Amazon wished to experiment with new models of discoverability, drawing attention to its data structures rather than broader trends within publishing.

Amazon's entry into physical grocery sales with the launch of Amazon Go in December 2016 and acquisition of Whole Foods in June 2017 marked a broader commitment to brick-and-mortar retail. The Whole Foods acquisition provided Amazon with a large and loyal grocery customer base, as well as the preexisting infrastructure to intervene in grocery home delivery. Whole Foods' distribution network would provide the foundation for Amazon to enter the notoriously difficult grocery market and pivot away from strengths in nonperishable goods. Amazon Go's launch demonstrated the extent of Amazon's ambitions in physical retail through a provocation about the future of grocery shopping with the emergence of the internet of things, or a new wave of technology with native network functionality. Amazon Go is marketed as "a new kind of store with no checkout required."[84] The generic title belies the fact that the company's first checkout-free store focused on food rather than books. RFID (radio-frequency identification) technology is pervasive in libraries, which lessens the perception of checkoutless book shopping as "magic." Amazon Go's food retail operation mixes AWS, internet of things, and knowledge of users' purchase history to create a digital experience in a physical retail space. A *New York Times* report on the first location's launch noted the abundance of cameras present on the store's ceiling, indicating the importance of facial and product recognition over a more convoluted internet-of-things solution.[85] While Amazon has expanded far beyond its original bookstore, the company continues to explore the role of digital infrastructure in retail as both a service for other businesses and a method for data collection.

The launch of AWS in 2006 marked a consolidation of Amazon's philosophy for virtualizing infrastructure even if doing so undermines the company's previously profitable ventures. The approach allowed Amazon to shift from being a retailer to a retail platform, letting third parties use its extensive warehouse and delivery infrastructure. The launch of the Kindle saw the equivalent shift in Amazon's approach to books. Before 2007, Amazon was a major online retailer through its reputation for books, but this model was unsustainable. Since the Kindle had no major competition in the mid-2000s, it offered the opportunity to create *the* infrastructure for digital book distribution, mitigating any potential drop in physical books sales from Amazon. After an initial push with hardware, a move toward emphasizing infrastructure has made the Kindle vital to the future of screen reading, reflecting its position in digital and off-line cultural more broadly.

Within Amazon's warehouses, there is no distinction between a cloth copy of Jami Curl's *Candy Is Magic*, a variety box of Skittles and Starbursts, or a Peppa Pig plush doll. All three items are stored, organized, and shipped in the same fashion.[1] Despite this ambivalence, books remain central to Amazon's retail operations. Books, and specifically ebooks, accumulate and return a greater volume of data than other products. Amazon uses both distribution and consumption to monitor the ebb and flow of the book trade to predict future trends, working with well-established industry standards including ISBN, Online Information Exchange (ONIX), and machine-readable cataloging (MARC) to create a conceptual model of the book and the publishing industry. The Kindle built on the core pillars of Amazon Web Services' virtualization tools detailed in the previous chapter and the company's commitment to model the book based on the wealth of internal and external data it had accumulated.

Warehouses of Metadata

Bezos faced an uphill battle to compete with Barnes & Noble but used the publishing industry's long-standing collaboration to develop ISBNs to Amazon's advantage. F. Gordon Foster, a professor at the London School of Economics, developed the British Standard Book Number (SBN) in 1966 to manage the needs of WH Smith at the request of the British Publishing Association. The standard was quickly adopted by a range of booksellers and publishers for cataloging and warehousing, with the International

Organization for Standardization (ISO) ratifying the standard as International Standard Book Numbers (ISBNs) in 1970.[2] Publishers now use ISBNs as the backbone of spreading metadata to distributors, retailers, and libraries.[3] The metadata standard provides information about a book's publisher and region in a human- and machine-readable format.[4] This data structure also distinguishes between different editions of the same book. For example, the 1991 Picador paperback copy of Alastair Gray's *Lanark* has an ISBN of 0-330-31965-5. The first number indicates the publication region, with 0 representing the Anglophone market. The number 330 refers to Picador as the publisher, with the following five digits noting the specific book in Picador's list. Each ISBN concludes with a check digit to ensure the number was correctly entered through "an elegant and rather ingenious system since it guards not only against inaccurately recorded digits but also against the apparently more common error of transpositions."[5] ISBNs can identify specific editions of books with complex bibliographic histories. In the case of Gray's *Lanark*, my search on Amazon.co.uk in July 2015 returned two Canongate Classics editions published in 2002 and 2007, and the original hardback from 1982 on sale for £87.47. Conversely, Amazon.com records the two Canongate titles, the original, an American edition published by Harvest Books, and the Picador edition. Amazon's search function privileges local and new editions, but as it integrates ISBNs into product page URLs, it is possible to bypass this navigation system to locate specific editions. Book collectors can use the system to ensure they receive the expected version of a book rather than purchasing the latest reprint.

The World Wide Web of 1994 at Amazon's launch was vastly different from the contemporary web, where all information is assumed to be online. Data about the book trade appeared in sources such as Bowker's *Books in Print*, which was available to retailers in print or on CD-ROM and contained a catalog of ISBNs for books still available to purchase from publishers and wholesalers. Retailers used *Books in Print* to supplement their in-store holdings and as a data source for preordering books. Customers could request titles from the database through the retailer, but the information was not publicly available without purchasing access. Information about forthcoming books was only available through trade sources, the popular press, or bookshops. Amazon challenged this informational monopoly by building its online catalog from the *Books in Print* data set to demonstrate the large catalog of titles they *could* order from wholesalers rather than what was currently in stock.

Amazon used *Books in Print* to inflate the number of titles available on its website to make its selection appear larger than that of other retailers.

The boast that Amazon was the "world's largest bookshop" drew a lawsuit from Barnes & Noble in 1997, which was settled later that year when the companies agreed "they would rather compete in the marketplace than in court."[6] Amazon's sleight of hand opened an industry data source for public consumption to allow users with niche interests to discover relevant books. Brick-and-mortar bookshops need to stock books they are confident will sell within a reasonable time frame to justify the shelf space at the expense of discovering more obscure titles. Ordering directly from distributors and warehouses at the point of customer order while displaying a large stock rewrote these rules. Readers who did not feel represented by the limitations of brick-and-mortar retailers saw the extensive database as catering to their tastes.

Amazon reshaped ISBNs as web-based metadata that were discoverable rather than an identifying number for warehousing and distribution, turning an industry standard into a broader public good. Product pages turned ISBNs into searchable entities on the web, acting as unofficial URIs for the book trade. Book metadata were no longer obfuscated through standards such as ONIX or MARC. Others have built on this process, including Daniel Green, the cofounder of CamelCamelCamel, a website that tracks price fluctuations on Amazon, which launched in 2008.[7] This is vital in the world of algorithmically mediated pricing, since automated systems can rapidly increase the cost of a book beyond its actual value, as with Michael Eisen's example of a $23,698,655.93 copy of Peter Lawrence's *The Making of a Fly*.[8] External services including Google Books link to Amazon as a centralized repository of book metadata that would only exist in a more authoritative form on individual publishers' websites. The company's ubiquity across book trade platforms is equivalent to Facebook's integration of "likes" across the web, establishing the company as bookish infrastructure.

In April 1998, David Risher, then lead of product development for Amazon, launched an investigation into selling music, with the new product shop opening later that year.[9] The music industry had no equivalent for ISBNs, so Amazon created a broader cataloging standard. The company decided to issue every item a ten-digit Amazon Standard Identification Number (ASIN), which uses the full range of alphanumeric characters to identify nonbook items.[10] Currently every nonbook ASIN (including ebooks) begins with B. This practice can catalog up to three thousand billion unique items. The development of ASIN runs counter to the widespread use of Universal Product Codes (UPC), a barcode standard featuring thirteen or eighteen numbers to identify items from various countries.[11] UPCs integrated a superset of ISBN called ISBN-13, formally introduced in January 2007, although the format had a longer history starting with the inclusion of barcodes on books in the 1980s.[12] ISBN-13 contains no additional metadata, as the first three digits, usually 978, refer to the country, which in the case of books is represented by the fictitious "Bookland."[13] Preexisting ISBNs could be used with the new prefix and a recalculated check digit. Bookland was also given the prefix 979, doubling the possible number of ISBNs. ISBNs prefixed with 979 are not used in Anglophone markets as of 2018 but have already been adapted by the French ISBN authority, L'AFNIL (Agence Francophone pour la Numérotation Internationale du Livre).[14] French books with ISBN-13s starting with 979 receive an ASIN to identify the product page, and the ISBN is only visible in the "Détails sur le produit."[15]

While ISBNs and ASINs can identify unique editions, Amazon uses a higher-level metadata structure to connect separate editions to reuse valuable data internally. Christopher Weight, a member of Kindle Special Ops, led research on "title sets," which connect similar books based on a probabilistic model of both metadata and textual similarities.[16] Strategic reuse of data also links relevant metadata across regions regardless of the local publisher. For example, reviews are shared across editions to boost the number of voices commenting on a product, although this creates problems when criticism of a poorly edited version is carried over to a more carefully produced edition. The English-language edition of Emily St. John Mandel's *Station Eleven* is available to purchase from nine Amazon regions, with shared data despite the novel's publisher varying between the United States (Vintage / Penguin Random House), Canada (Harper Perennial / HarperCollins), and United Kingdom (Picador/Macmillan). Most often, blurbs and professional reviews will be linked, but if a lower threshold for reviews has not been met, reviews from a more popular edition will be pulled through. It is common practice in book retail to use data sources such as Nielsen BookData or Bowker's *Books in Print* to populate online catalogs. Data will appear consistently across Waterstones, AbeBooks, and Bokus, but Amazon expanded this approach by extracting subsets of its data for different markets and formats.

Although ISBN was an early international identification standard, the book trade struggled to agree on other metadata standards. Bad practice is still common within the trade, encouraging Karina Luke, executive director of Book Industry Communications (the British publishing supply chain organization), to publish a statement condemning superfluous title metadata such as the introduction of "Man Booker Prize winner" or "The explosive next book from . . ." in the subtitle of product pages for Amazon and other online retailers.[17] The disparities between identifying books and authors have remained an open problem, as author metadata can be inconsistent and frequently requires disambiguation for common names such as John Smith or generates multiple records attached to transliterated names such as Fyodor Dostoyevsky. Projects such as Open Researcher and Contributor ID (ORCID) attempt to create consistent standards for authors in academia but rely on contributors signing up, limiting its appeal as a universal standard.[18] Amazon extended the ASIN standard to include persistent identifiers for both authors and customers, flattening the hierarchical relationship between the objects. For example, George R. R. Martin has an author ASIN of B000APIGH4, whereas the Kindle edition of his novel *A Storm of Swords* is the product number B004PIJEWD. Amazon integrated authors, bibliographic objects, and consumers into a single conceptual model that favors relationships over hierarchies of production. Amazon prioritized connectivity over authority when constructing its computational model of the book trade.[19] When everything is treated as a relational entity, it can be difficult to find meaning. For example, Paul Ford struggled to find patterns in the complexity of Amazon's reviews and product information, since he did not have access to the full relational data underpinning Amazon's data collection and analysis processes.[20] Since Amazon alone has access to the full data structure, it can offer public access to individual elements without jeopardizing its complex data surveillance system.

ASINs are flawed due to the lack of external oversight. The system privileges books as a central part of Amazon's infrastructure, but third parties might not use due diligence to correctly enter metadata. If third parties create an incomplete or faulty listing for a print book, additional records are tied to new ASINs. For example, a search for Ian Bogost, Simon Ferrari, and Bobby Schweizer's *Newsgames* in July 2017 produced nine separate product pages for the title despite the need for only two official product pages relating to the cloth and paperback editions.[21] The remaining seven product pages feature incorrect metadata about authors, titles, and publication date, with some listing the seventeenth century, and the addition of the publisher to the book's title. These product pages are created by automated vendors, which set prices according to other offerings. Most of these prices exceed the cost of purchasing directly as a consumer from the MIT Press, which suggests the merchants do not currently stock the title but will purchase at point of order. The introduction of ASIN as an all-encompassing structure requires tight control on Amazon's part to avoid such duplicitous efforts, but the evidence from faulty *Newsgames* metadata is replicated with other titles. The company does not collaborate with librarians or other information professionals who also work on similar metadata issues. As a consequence, little consistency exists between metadata fields beyond ASIN. While BIC requires metadata about availability, territorial rights, and a cover image for books published in the United Kingdom, third parties can circumvent this rigor when uploading product data. Retail is less profitable than AWS, so Amazon has little interest in substantially overhauling these systems. These weaknesses are frequently exploited, particularly given the scale of the Amazon marketplace. For example, in 2018 it emerged that CreateSpace was used to launder money by creating fake books for real authors and using their social security number.[22] Just as with roads, electricity, and the internet, the Amazon infrastructure is designed to be used by all with little oversight on *how* it is used until problem cases emerge.

ASINs do not offer human-readable information about products, and no public documentation exists. Nonetheless, we can identify patterns in the standard. For example, Bella Forrest's monthly releases of books in the *A Shade of Vampire* series conform to a sequential pattern of the first four digits of the ASIN. *A Shade of Vampire 10* begins with B00S, and *11* starts with B00T, indicating that numbers are assigned in order but not sequentially. The first ebook editions of J. K. Rowling's *Harry Potter* series begin with B019PIOJ, indicating that they were uploaded nearly simultaneously, although the final two digits are not sequential. There is no check digit, since the ASIN for *The Philosopher's Stone* and *Chamber of Secrets* differ only by the final digit. Unlike ISBNs, publishers cannot register a cluster of ASINs so there is no continuity between publications. For example, one of the later Pottermore publications, the playscript for *Harry Potter and the Cursed Child*, has an ASIN of B073P9348D. There are also clusters around genres: the ASINs of Amazon-published public domain titles begin with B004 regardless of publication date. ASINs reflect Amazon's general commitment to data: volume and obfuscation override fidelity and legibility. Any patterns are circumstances of coincidence rather than the meaningful data points embedded in ISBNs.

Amazon's digitization projects offered further data points in the company's understanding of the book trade. Converting print is complicated by the asymmetric representation of a photograph of the page and the text it contains. As discussed in chapter 1, Amazon prompted publishers to digitize their backlists as part of the "Search Inside the Book" scheme that formed the basis of the Kindle's large launch catalog, and Mechanical Turk was an early attempt to improve the quality of digitized texts. Users will only buy high-quality scanned ebooks, so Amazon invested in accurate modeling of print initially to increase adoption. Texts reported as having bad formatting as a result of poor-quality OCR are removed from the storefront for review. Teresa Elsey notes that 69 percent of books flagged on the Kindle storefront are the result of users reporting typos.[23]

Gathering data on common mistakes in conversion techniques allowed the company to reuse the textual data of ebooks in other ways. Amazon explored machine learning approaches to digitization through modeling contemporary language use across publishing. Early retail experiments led to the development of Statistically Improbable Phrases, an algorithm that scoured digitized material for phrases that only appeared in a single title. When a user searched for that phrase, it would appear as a result even if the phrase did not appear in the book's title. For example, searches for "nadsat" or "droog" are likely to relate to Anthony Burgess's *A Clockwork Orange*. Amazon engineers in the Digital Products group led by Sonjeev Jahagirdar also focused on using contextual learning information to improve the quality of an initial scan.[24] The patent offers an example of a Mexican restaurant menu, where a probabilistic model can determine that "taco" is more likely than "baco." Such experiments show how data from one part of Amazon's services are often reused in a different context, affirming the company's ambivalence to the book as a unique cultural object.

Amazon: Twenty-First-Century Book Historians?

Amazon's infrastructure, which now encompasses many aspects of the production and reception of books, recalls Robert Darnton's model of the book trade as well as library science models such as the Functional Requirements for Bibliographic Records (FRBR).[25] Darnton argues that it is impossible to consider the book outside of the wider context of its production and reception, which takes the form of a network of relationships between objects such as the printing press and human producers in roles such as the author or smuggler.[26] We can trace parallels between Darnton's theoretical model of the book trade through countless years of research in the archives of the Société typographique de Neuchâtel (STN) and how Amazon has accumulated and analyzed a mass of data related to the industry. For example, Darnton's visualization of the relationship between bookshops and literary demand maps distribution in a similar manner to Amazon's profiling of warehouse locations and next-day delivery priorities. Both models analyze the needs of local markets and sociopolitical constraints such as taxation and policy.[27]

FRBR complements models of the book trade by outlining the relationship between the idea embedded within text and its containers. The model emerged from the challenges of cataloging a "book" that might exist in various forms (audio, electronic, print) and editions (hardback, EPUB, PDF). For example, Margaret Atwood's *The Handmaid's Tale* is available as a hardcover, paperback, ebook, and audiobook, as well adaptations as an opera, television show, and film. These different formats can take a different approach to Atwood's work but are unified by the central idea of her original novel. The underlying logic of ASINs and title sets runs parallel to FRBR, as Amazon links various editions across regions and formats. The purpose of each project is different: Amazon uses "title authority" to maximize the marketing potential for a single text, while FRBR attempts to tackle ontological issues around preservation.

The Kindle pushed Amazon toward addressing traditional bibliographic problems such as linking different editions of the same book internally, called "title authority," and delivering errata to copies of a book already downloaded on readers' devices.[28] Both problems are central to the bibliographic impulse to map the development of a book and discrepancies in editions that can lead to different interpretations of the same text. Amazon's interests were more pragmatic, as the ability to map text across editions and corrections would enable consistent popular highlights to appear across editions and other Whispersync functions to act seamlessly regardless of updates or variation in regions. Janna Hamaker and colleagues on the Kindle's Reading Experience team conceptualized title authority in terms of "similarity" and "alignment."[29] An algorithm would first consider whether the books are similar, and then check the "alignment" of the text word by word on a global and local level. The algorithm produces a granular list of changes within individual editions that shows the development of a book over time that can otherwise be lost. These changes can be significant yet go unnoticed, such as Martin Eve's discovery of the discrepancies between the British and American editions of David Mitchell's *Cloud Atlas*, where Mitchell made different corrections between the two editions owing to changes in the publishers' staff.[30]

Documenting changes in content is simple compared to the potentially more intrusive effort of issuing errata. In *Merchants of Culture*, the sociologist of publishing John Thompson lauded the ability to update ebooks in digital publishing models, which could immediately correct any mistakes by altering titles on users' devices.[31] While texts can be updated automatically, users need to opt in to the scheme; otherwise Amazon deprioritizes updatability and allows readers to elect if and when to update their content. This produces ancillary files specifically containing errata, the equivalent to the print practice of errata slips if the errors were identified before the end of the production process. Amazon's default approach to errata and title authority demonstrates a commitment toward the authenticity

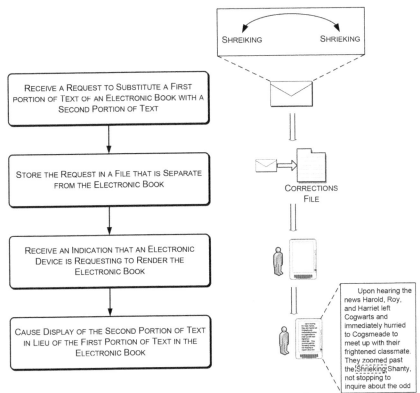

3.1 A flowchart detailing Amazon's process of removing errata from an ebook (adapted from patent filing). Source: Ward et al., Selecting content-enhanced applications, 9.

of documents. The book is a discrete object that can be supplemented by other files but largely exists as an individual entity. Although Amazon's data collection practices flatten relationships between objects, producers, and consumers, the actual object is still treated with reverence.

User-Generated Data

Amazon benefits from connecting bibliographic data with empirical evidence of reception. The company's methods unintentionally tested the most contentious point of Darnton's model of the book trade: the feedback loop between readers and authors. Since the company used Bowker's *Books in Print* to extend its catalog in 1994, others have followed the same steps of curation. User-generated data, including diachronic patterns in purchases, reviews, and search inputs, are more valuable commodities than bibliographic records, as they are generated by the interaction between user and platform. Information about the book trade such as the ISBN standard has a finite boundary and can be relatively easy to capture, share, and analyze. The implicit data of consumption generate a larger data set: each book format is allocated a single ISBN, but thousands of people can purchase, read, and review that edition via Amazon, creating a substantially larger volume of data. Shoshana Zuboff has described this form of data as "behavioral surplus," which is collected and mined by large technology companies to extract value from otherwise free or cheap services.[32] Bezos understood the data's value and considered selling premium memberships to third parties in exchange for access to Amazon's cache of data. Nonsubscribers would be at a disadvantage, as Bezos stated they "wouldn't have access to Amazon's rich data and whizzy technology."[33] The scheme was pure rhetoric, and the company elected to instead keep most of its data private to build its own analytical services without sharing results with the producers.

Nonetheless, Amazon's valuable user-generated data sets exist in a semipublic fashion. Individuals' browsing histories are hidden, but recommendation engines show users how algorithms connect products for recommendations.[34] The company's services highlight some of the forms of data they are analyzing and offer a level of insight into trends in contemporary publishing. For example, the Amazon page for Neil Gaiman's *Norse Mythology* offers three data points: "frequently bought together," "customers who bought this item also bought," and "what other items do customers buy after viewing this item?" This granular recommendation engine exploits a multidimensional data set that accounts for time of purchase and confirmed or potential interest. The *Norse Mythology* recommendations demonstrate that users will likely buy bundles of Gaiman's books simultaneously, but if they do not purchase the book, they are still likely to buy similar titles by different authors as determined by Amazon's recommendation algorithm, including Graeme Macrae Burnet's *His Bloody Project* or Louise Doughty's *Apple Tree Yard* in February 2017. These recommendations constantly shift, prioritizing newer releases with high relevance as Stephen Fry's rendition of Greek mythology, *Mythos*, which appeared as the second-highest recommendation. Ed Finn concludes that "taken in aggregate, the recommendations offer a way to read Amazon's best guesses about literary desire at a given point in time, and as they are also potentially subject to influence from marketing campaigns, movie tie-ins, and the like, they operate in a feedback loop involving publishers and booksellers as well as consumers."[35] Nonetheless, the rhetorical framing of the recommendations engine is visible through the publicly available suggestions. Users can purchase more books by the same author based on strong tie recommendations, while titles with weaker ties are noted through the looser affiliation of having been bought "after viewing this item." Amazon's focus on one-click purchasing and other methods to reduce the number of clicks to purchase is reflected only in the prepackaging of titles that have been bought together previously. The other recommendations require users to visit each page individually before adding the titles to their shopping basket, ensuring some users will not follow through with the joint purchase.

Ed Finn has documented recommendation networks for individual authors including Junot Díaz, Toni Morrison, and David Foster Wallace, but Amazon's recommendation engine at scale has largely eluded scholarly attention.[36] Julian McAuley et al. produced a data set featuring recommendations for over 600,000 Kindle titles produced in 2014 that demonstrates widespread exploitation of Amazon's clear recommendation categories for ebooks.[37] Three-quarters of the books feature at least one recommendation, with a third receiving over eighty. An asymmetry characterizes the links, however, as some books have thousands of recommendations, whereas most books are only recommended on one other product page. Most Kindle titles in the sample are loosely connected, but there remains a highly connected inner core of books linking to one another up to a thousand times, showing an instance of a group of titles frequently purchased together during 2014.

The uneven distribution pattern is typical of a network of this size.[38] The specific titles with the most recommendations (table 3.1) are more surprising, since the list does not correlate with *Publishers Weekly*'s best sellers for 2014, including a list dedicated to Kindle sales.[39] All the titles were published primarily for the Kindle, and many of the titles were self-published. Amazon is responsible for this insular view of recommendations, as only seventy-one references to ISBNs link to Kindle manuals and "how-to" guides, reinforcing the ebook marketplace as distinct from print. The algorithm is hard coded to ignore convergence between print and ebook purchases, thus favoring digital-only titles at the expense of legacy strongholds. Moreover, the frequent appearance of books produced by Mark and Aaron Shepard suggests a level of algorithmic gaming to increase their visibility in recommendations. By naming recommendations lists with their process of generation, Amazon allowed producers to focus on specific techniques to increase their visibility. A marketing campaign can request that users view pages together or download free copies of texts together to increase the likelihood the two titles will appear in mutual recommendations. The data can only reveal inherent truths about Amazon's data collection and analysis processes rather than trends within

Table 3.1 Frequently recommended titles

ASIN	Title	Inbound links
B005F9ZLD2	Mark Shepard, *Simple Sourdough* (Simple Productions, 2014)	6,831
B0057XK230	Jason Edwards, *Will Allen and the Great Monster Detective* (Rogue Bear Press, 2013)	4,212
B00CHTEMUG	Aaron Shepard, *The Legend of Lightning Larry* (Skyhook Press, 2013) [no longer available]	3,940
B00CYPKEN2	Aaron Shepard, *Pictures on Kindle* (Shepard Publications, 2014)	3,672
B005FG163Y	Aaron Shepard, *From Word to Kindle* (Shepard Publications, 2014)	3,220
B00BMHUDP2	J. S. Scott, *The Billionaire's Obsession* (Kindle Direct Publishing, 2013)	3,122
B00APM2K5Q	Earl Nightingale and Robert C. Worstell, *How to Completely Change Your Life in 30 Seconds* (Midwest Journal Press, 2012)	2,893
B00B56PP26	Steve Scott, *How to Write Great Blog Posts That Engage Better Readers* (Kindle Direct Publishing, 2014)	2,745
B00BSG4LXW	Steve Scott, *61 Ways to Sell More Nonfiction Kindle Books* (Kindle Direct Publishing, 2013)	2,651

the book trade itself. The company's dominance ensures some collapse between the two categories. Timothy Graham separates recommendations between "popular" in views and "best-selling" with the example of Veronica Roth's *Allegiant*, which averaged three stars from 8,241 reviews while sitting at the fourth best-selling Kindle spot.[40] The recommendations network in table 3.1 reflects how popularity can be gamed with the goal of improving sales, although this tactic favors short-term gain.

Amazon uses its "p13n" (personalization) data structure to generate information on elements such as titles "frequently bought together." These recommendations often come with restrictions: my account will only show items available in the United Kingdom and will prioritize products available directly through Amazon (tagged as A1F83G8C2ARO7P). Further conditions influence the display of recommendations: "frequently bought together" will only display a title if "has_seller_difference" and "has_diff[erent]_avail[ability]" are both false, restricting recommendations to books in Amazon's inventory rather than third parties. The focus on user-generated reviews demonstrates the company's commitment to producing large volumes of data over traditionally authoritative sources. Bezos hired James Marcus and other reviewers to contribute expert opinions and suggested that the general philosophy of hiring reviewers and editors was "to seem smart and authoritative—to become not just a store but a *destination*."[41] The editors also curated the home page to highlight titles in a similar manner to the tables at the front door of a brick-and-mortar bookshop. This editorial team was later dismissed as Amazon began to focus instead on user-generated content. Bezos wanted reviews to reflect the honest opinions of customers rather than appear to be filtered, so he allowed both positive and negative reviews on the site. The current Amazon home page balances these two extremes by mixing personalized recommendations with generic advertisements. Editorial content still appears at the fringe of the front page through blogging insights such as Amazon Chart's Week in Books. Amazon's incursion into brick-and-mortar shops accelerated the trend through curating categories according to user-generated data, including "Most Wished For Cookbooks" and "Highly Rated: 4.8 Stars & Above."

Unfortunately, Amazon's popularity and the high stakes of getting good reviews on its websites led to an influx of fake or paid reviews, which Amazon is constantly battling to remove.[42] Amazon created mechanisms for user feedback to facilitate a greater curation of reviews. These include rating reviews if they are useful—which then affects a review's visibility—and the ability to respond to reviews. This has become a potent battleground in recent years, with readers using the reviews to attack authors' ideologies. For example, the release of Hillary Clinton's *What Happened* garnered a flood of 1,500 reviews within twenty-four hours of release, with a high proportion of one-star reviews coming from unverified purchases, which suggested the users were reviewing the book out of spite rather than having read the content.[43]

Daniel Allington argues that this plurality of opinions reflects "popular" rather than "literary" taste in titles like *The Inheritance of Loss*.[44] Users talked about the aesthetics of an edition or other tangents rather than focusing on the textual content. Occasionally the focus on the materiality of an edition, mixed with Amazon's enthusiasm for reusing content, can have an adverse effect on a book's product page, as criticisms of a poorly bound hardcover can translate to an additional poor score on the Kindle edition. Conversely, a poorly scanned text can have a negative impact on a luxury high-production print copy. Despite these limitations, Ann Steiner argues that the Amazon review systems "enhance [users'] feeling of belonging to a global community of readers with similar daily problems and desires."[45] This community spirit is not always apparent in review data. For instance, only 9 of the 218 reviews of Mark Levinson's *The Box* received more than ten recommendations. Down-vote data are not publicly displayed but are evident from the position of the final two reviews, which are displayed outside the usual set of "verified purchases." User engagement is low, as only twenty comments were left for nine reviews. The most popular reviews were 745 percent longer than the mean review length and were posted early in the book's life cycle, authored by prolific reviewers in the "top 1,000" or otherwise mocked for stating "I though it would be about using Cargo Containers as homes but it was not I waisted money on this book." The prioritization of reviews by verified purchases and "Vine voices" outweighs user ranking of reviews, and the algorithm also promotes longer reviews. It is unclear whether the recommendation algorithm drives low user engagement or if the community issues emerge from knowledge that unless one is part of the several elite clubs, a review is unlikely to be promoted. Amazon reviews do not encourage extended social interactions but archive changes in taste postpublication, as early reviews are supplanted by more critical reappraisals of material later. Individuals more interested in substantial engagement with peers use websites such as LibraryThing or Goodreads that encourage more extended interactions rather than the superficial call-and-response system of Amazon's review service.

The review data therefore reveal the biases of Amazon's data collection and processing more than contemporary literary tastes. Although Amazon is the largest book retailer and clearly drives the culture, it still is insular, and much of the public-facing infrastructure reflects the company's practices rather than broader issues within publishing. The book trade exhibits an underlying distrust of the data-driven analysis of publishing trends emphasized in accounts such as Jodie Archer and Matthew Jockers's *The Bestseller Code* in doubling down on the concept of taste as a "gut instinct."[46] This gulf leads to exaggerated claims on both sides and conversations that are not productive for both parties, and as a result, the book trade is not geared for tackling the challenges presented by large technology companies. As Amazon has taken control of much of the bookish infrastructure and forced companies to adopt certain workflows, these new methods have created a degree of distrust. Mark Davis argues, "e-books can be understood as an important strategic site in a wider corporate struggle over the digital commons, and for information ownership and control, taking place among large digital corporations, and as a corporate tool in that battle."[47] Amazon has managed to increase the volume of data available for internal analysis while closing off the information from publishers, resulting in a divergent marketplace where ebooks designed for the Kindle Store succeed above those that have been developed for print distribution.

File formats are an essential part of digital media consumption. A software package requires instructions for how to present and interpret the data compiled in a media file. Despite their significance, formats often receive less attention than other aspects of media and platforms. Jonathan Sterne argues that format is too often conflated with medium, which only reveals itself during moments of competition: Betamax/VHS, Blu-ray / HD DVD, MiniDisc/MP3. Format encapsulates "a whole range of decisions that affect the look, feel, experience, and workings of a medium. It also names a set of rules according to which a technology can operate."[1] Within the confines of contemporary computing, the file extension is the most prominent signifier of format and demonstrates the fluidity between software and format. A word processor document can have multiple extensions (.doc, .docx, .odt), which in turn can be opened by various software packages (Microsoft Word, OpenOffice, Google Docs). Despite this fluidity, each of the formats has different material limits and structures.

Ebooks require an understanding of digital format theory *and* the substantial history and conventions of print bibliography, as a clear continuity exists between the two. In the study of the transmission of printed texts, the format refers to a work's wrapping, which signifies a book's role. For example, cloth-bound academic publications are a marker of prestige designed primarily for libraries, while the subsequent paperback reflects the economic or cultural success of the initial publication. Formats are ingrained in book history: from Aldus Manutius's development of a Renaissance "paperback" to the distinctions between folio, quarto, octavo, and other bindings.[2] These formats referred to the binding and were an important indicator of a title's prestige: a cheap edition featured more sheets of paper stitched together in a single gathering, while the most important titles comprised many single folded sheets of paper stitched together into a large volume called a folio.

The digitization of the book has reshaped our understanding of format. Matthew Kirschenbaum argues that, rather than existing as a single finished object, "a book is an assemblage of digital assets, consisting, in practice, of multiple files and formats collected in a digital asset management system, or DAM. These files contain artwork, fonts, style sheets, metadata, and of course the text. A book is thus also a network, since these digital assets must be orchestrated to interact with one another in structured and predictable ways in order to generate desired outputs, such as an EPUB or an XHTML file."[3] Even so-called plain text, displayed without any formatting attributes through a command line or editor interface, is mediated through format by character maps and font families. Character maps translate hexadecimal numbers into the letter or symbol to display. The "map" in the name is literal: specifications include a grid with coordinates to locate specific characters. For example, the ASCII character map represents a capital A with the hexadecimal number 41 (column 4, row 1), and its lowercase equivalent is represented by 61. ASCII does not dictate how a character should be displayed, which is handled by font rendering systems such as TrueType and PostScript that take the number and convert it into a recognizable shape. Users can then choose a font family to display their text according to individual preferences. Text display therefore requires several processes before a single character is rendered as a series of pixels on a screen (table 4.1).[4]

Table 4.1 Layers of text display

Layer	Format	Output
Style sheet	h1 {color: gray;}	a
Markup	<h1>	**a**
Bitmap	a	a
Font renderer	Times New Roman	[instructions for drawing a lowercase a in Times New Roman]
Hexadecimal character map	0 x 61 (column 6, row 1)	a (lowercase)
Binary	110001	110001

Markup languages such as HTML enable further presentational differences. Software packages interpret extra text surrounding content to be displayed to present headings, bold text, and other visual differences. For example, in HTML, <h1> is the tag for displaying a heading with the highest priority (designated by the number, which notes a hierarchy down to <h6>, the smallest subheading). CSS determines how headings are displayed through additional markup: "h1 {color: gray;}." In this instance, the heading will be in gray, but further markup may include font size and alignment. Markup only offers recommendations, however, since readers may choose to increase the font size or change the color to suit their own preferences. While HTML and CSS are powerful tools for tinkering with presentation, the additional text can greatly increase the size of an uncompressed ebook.

Developing the Kindle Format

In *Memory Practices in the Sciences*, Geoffrey Bowker compares the Earth to a vast geological archive; similarly, the Kindle is a palimpsest that reveals earlier iterations if you just scratch below the surface.[5] This approach to formats ensures consistency but also makes it difficult to change things. As Daniel Pargman and Jacob Palme argue, "The most common solution is to patch things and hobble along. Any deviation from that solution requires potentially large alterations of the existing information infrastructure, and such alterations are *expensive*."[6] As a result, examining the origins of the Kindle file format is essential to understanding the platform's current limitations.

Amazon designed the Kindle during a period of relative stability within the ebook industry. In the early 2000s, an industry group initially called Open Ebook, spearheaded by Dick Brass of Microsoft, had agreed on a set of standards.[7] Over forty publishers, booksellers, and technology companies collaborated on the Open eBook Publication Structure (OEBPS), the precursor to EPUB, an interchange specification designed to allow publishers to easily convert files to various proprietary formats.[8] No reading system interpreted OEBPS directly, so technology companies could create proprietary formats derived from the specification. For example, Sony developed BroadBand eBook (BBEB) for its first-generation Librie in 2004, before committing to EPUB with the launch of the PRS-505 hardware in 2007. Likewise, Amazon's acquisition of Mobipocket, discussed in chapter 1, included the popular MOBI format, another derivative of OEBPS. The reliance on Mobipocket technology two decades later brings significant archaeological baggage to the platform. Amazon's commitment to backward compatibility (ensuring new titles are still readable on older devices) while ensuring new devices have enough flagship improvements *and* ensuring broad cross-hardware support places a substantial strain on format specifications.

Amazon's cumulative approach to format created a series of geological layers visible within each ebook. Each successive upgrade to the file format moved further away from the original design but still accounted for its genesis as Palm Resource Code (PRC), a database language designed for Palm OS in 1996. Amazon's commitment to backward compatibility ties the company to this lineage to avoid obsolescence update cycles that have defined Apple's business model during the 2010s. Apple's yearly upgrade cycle primes customers for depreciated apps with major operating system updates, but the realities for text-oriented software are different. Without flagship hardware improvements or significant security vulnerabilities, it is more difficult to justify breaking access to content for users who continue to use older devices. Since static text appears to be simple to render, any changes will be met with greater resistance.

The first Palm hardware was released in 1996, the same year the XML 1.0 specification was published. Rather than adapting an emerging open standard, Palm built PRC and Palm Database (PDB) for text reading in the popular C programming language. These formats have little formal published documentation but provide the foundations for the contemporary Kindle ebook. The technical limitations of Palm OS determined how PRC files were processed on derivative devices.[9] The Palm Pilot 1000, one of the first Palm devices, released in 1996, handled an upper limit of twelve megabytes of random-access memory (RAM) and four megabytes of read-only memory (ROM). As a result, all documents were precompiled before transfer to Palm devices to reduce storage and memory costs. This asymmetrical structure was attractive to publishers hoping to protect intellectual property, and Kindle formats never deviated from this model. Until the development of KF8, all new Kindle file formats were renamed MOBI files, and devices would still process PRC ebooks. Amazon's file formats are based on archaic standards from 1996 rather than EPUB3, which derives from modern web specifications such as HTML5 and CSS3. Several of the Kindle's quirks emerge from this historical divergence and Amazon's later attempts to reconcile the expectations of users for contemporary ebook design. Newer file formats integrate features from EPUB3, but the geological layers of the original format remain. PDA users who wanted to read ebooks in the 1990s had different needs from ebook readers in 2007. PDAs featured small, low-resolution screens, so reflowable text, a central part of "ebookness," was more user-friendly than attempting to create print facsimiles.

MOBI in turn was built on Memoware, an amateur ebook production community launched in 1996 after the release of the first Palm Pilot. Once established, the community changed focus to create an early ebook store.[10] Memoware's name links to Palm's "Memo" software, as users wished to create ebooks for their Palm Pilots before reading systems were available for Palm OS. Early adopters focused on creating computer manuals for Memoware, which influenced the design of the MOBI format specification, which includes basic linking and interactive features required for the genre. The initial transition from MOBI to AZW was straightforward. For security reasons, Amazon's development team removed the ability to use JavaScript, extended the DRM protection, and changed the file format's name from MOBI to AZW. This early rebranding allowed publishers working outside of Amazon's service infrastructure to provide DRM-free Kindle-ready titles. If readers change an ebook's extension from MOBI to AZW, reading systems will interpret the file identically. While newer formats deviate from this model, newer devices still read legacy formats.

Amazon's choice of MOBI in 2005 was pragmatic. EPUB was not established as a consumer-facing format, and all proprietary formats derived from the best practices of OEBPS, HTML, and CSS. EPUB developed traction simultaneously to the Kindle, and without the momentum from the Kindle's high-profile launch, it is likely that EPUB would never have seen widespread adoption. Google Books focused on facsimiles; Apple would not launch iBooks until the reveal of the iPad in 2010. Other than Sony, the ebook market depended on a diffuse network of bookstores and had not gained critical mass since substantial investment in hardware earlier in the decade.

Since 2007, Amazon has developed several format specifications to meet the conflicting needs of dedicated hardware and third-party software, summarized in table 4.2. These sociomaterial constraints result in several contested aspects of the Kindle format's perceived pitfalls. Criticisms are often based on typographic issues that remain challenging for other ebook file formats.[11] If we move beyond these common ailments, the format ecosystem contains the geological layers that can be peeled back to reveal a broader history of displaying text, from precompiled databases to cloud-assembled files.

No public documentation for Kindle formats is available, but Amazon provides "best practice" advice for publishers preparing HTML or EPUB content for conversion to a Kindle ebook.[12] Instead, to understand the Kindle's formats, I reverse engineered available source code and DRM-free publications. Publishers can use a command line tool, KindleGen, or a graphical user interface wrapper, Kindle Previewer. These tools offer an

Table 4.2 Summary of Kindle file formats

File extension	Year released	Features
.prc	1996	Palm Resource Code. Database files containing on-screen reading documents.
.mobi	2000	An ebook format based on PRC and developed to display HTML-like attributes.
.azw	2007	The original Kindle format, based on MOBI. Speculated acronym: Amazon Word.
.tpz	2008	Topaz. The primary format for Kindle files downloaded for iOS devices.
.azw3/.kf8	2011	A transformation of AZW to bring it more in line with EPUB standards. Launched alongside the Fire tablet range.
.azw4	2014	A wrapper for PDFs.
.kfx	2015	Completely rewrote the format logic and rules. Marketing through "enhanced typography."

approximation of what the final output will look like on a range of devices to avoid any errors that can occur during the complex conversion process. Self-published authors can use Kindle Create, which converts Microsoft Word documents into Kindle files, alleviating the requirement to understand markup languages to produce a basic ebook.[13] Amazon's documentation shows disregard for publisher autonomy through comments such as "publishers do not need to define a start reading location because Amazon does this during the upload process."[14] Amazon asserts control over the Kindle ecosystem by keeping the internal workings of its file formats secret and stripping unwanted HTML tags from the conversion process. This approach ensures Amazon's dominance by creating an environment resembling Jonathan Zittrain's metaphorical use of "walled gardens" to describe "sterile appliances tethered to a network of control."[15]

On the other hand, due to the World Wide Web Consortium's dedication to open standards, EPUB is thoroughly documented. The industry standard forms the basis for many Kindle files at the production stage, but its cloud-based conversion process reshapes these data. Kirschenbaum warns that "programmatic computational environments [apply] some particular logic—a certain formal materiality—to the string of bits in question."[16] The differences in the "formal materiality" of Kindle files and EPUB stem from divergent ideologies in the production and consumption of digital content. Both formats have the same building blocks derived from open web standards including HTML, CSS, and XML. The standards depart at the point of processing the raw materials. The most important differences are compression and data storage. While EPUBs use ZIP compression, which maintains the original file structure, Kindle files are delivered in binary format, which obfuscates the structure of the original file. This shift ensures Kindle formats are more difficult to preserve. Amazon changed its data-storage practices with the introduction of KFX, which changed the underlying format from XML, the standard for EPUB, to JSON. For our purposes here, the two markup languages are nearly identical beyond syntax differences. Let's take a name as an example:

```
XML: <person>
         <firstName>John</firstName>
         <lastName>Smith</lastName>
     <person>
JSON: {"person" : {
         "firstName" : "John",
         "lastName" : "Smith"}}
```

Beyond minor technical and syntactical differences, the choice between the two standards comes down to developer preference and what systems the content needs to interact with. Nonetheless, Amazon's choice to move away from XML, the industry standard, introduces an additional conversion process that can increase corruptions while also reducing publisher autonomy.

The shift away from XML-based standards was part of a larger move toward a broader typology of ebooks. Amazon introduced multimedia ebooks with the launch of the Fire tablet range, leading to the development of KF8, an extension of AZW that incorporated elements of EPUB3 rather than resurrecting older aspects of the MOBI specification. While many of these new web technologies feature in the Mobipocket specification, Amazon intentionally restricted them when launching the initial Kindle to avoid the possibility of malicious JavaScript or SQL injections and to suit the restrictions of an electronic paper screen. The new format allowed for the development of new genres, including digital comics, that were not covered in previous iterations of AZW. KF8 introduced "app-amzn-magnify," a JavaScript library that allows publishers to locate areas to magnify on images rather than relying on the pinch-and-drag metaphors common on smartphones and tablets. These incremental improvements focused on balancing the needs of new genres with ensuring the security of the format.

KF8 enabled the publication of PDF-like content without simulating the flexibility of print. For example, in Doug Dorst and J. J. Abrams's *S.*, napkins and bookmarks appear nestled in predetermined pages in the print version. In the Kindle edition, the fixed layout determines where annotations and ephemera appear, but the actual ephemera have to be represented as photocopies with a note that the page is a "[found object]."[17] The Kindle file format explicitly forbids more extensive interaction, although the iBooks version allows users to move the found objects across the page they are initially displayed on.[18] This deferral to a facsimile-level fidelity was only possible on higher-resolution screens, and both smartphones and dedicated ebook readers lack the screen capacity to display the content accurately. Nonetheless, this was an intentional decision that negatively shapes the reader's experience. Dedicated e-readers that launched before 2011 are unable to open KF8 titles, marking the first substantial break in backward compatibility. The format is largely relegated to displaying fixed-layout and interactive titles, and other ebooks that use the format strip any unnecessary elements to ensure a version of the text can be displayed on all dedicated hardware.

The launch of KFX in 2015 marked a break from the conventions of both EPUB and PRC and allowed the Lab126 Application Framework team to explore alternate layout engines, leading to the design of XYML.[19] As the quaint name suggests, the markup language is based on XML and describes the x- and y-coordinates of text and images. The Application Framework team designed XYML as a lightweight alternative to CSS.[20] Using this proprietary format, Amazon can strictly control how content appears on the platform. Electronic paper presents unique challenges for rendering content, since a single screen must load simultaneously when the user refreshes the page, whereas a web page using HTML and CSS can afford to load from top to bottom. The solution? Encourage a nonlinear approach to layout rendering. XYML breaks from the Western tradition of left-to-right, top-down presentation in favor of a nonlinear approach according to the needs of specific publications.[21] As a result, the Kindle can now render more complex comic book layouts and render more languages, including Arabic and Japanese. Rather than using CSS, this proprietary solution obfuscates page layouts, ensuring Amazon's control over the sort of content available on its Kindle Store.

Amazon also introduced KFX to correct some long-standing issues with formatting through what was termed "enhanced typography." The new rendering engine built on "hyphen," a Linux package that replicated the digital typography pioneer Donald Knuth's TeX engine's implementation of automated hyphenation, where a set of rules determines if and where line breaks should be introduced in justified formatting. Amazon marketed the revised layout engine as a revolution in formatting, but as Guido Henkel has argued, it has often detracted from the primary content.[22] He criticizes KFX for glossing over some of the long-running issues in the Kindle formatting process in place of superficial aesthetic improvements. Henkel attacks the Kindle's inability to offer transparent images in either JPEG or PNG, which are both accepted Kindle image formats. Instead Henkel notes that "Amazon is now converting all images in an eBook into JPG XR format, including all GIF and PNG images, as well as SVGs."[23] Converting images to a single format ensures consistency in delivery even if doing so alters the images. JPG XR is not a lossless format and can introduce new visual artifacts into images.[24] Henkel's focus on transparent images is misguided compared to the semantic and character mapping issues embedded in the format discussed in the "Accessibility and Internationalization" section. In fact, transparent images would run counter to Amazon's deference to user choice, as it is possible in some Kindle configurations to alter the background color, rendering some transparent images illegible. Amazon attempt to navigate the fine balance between using more flexible standards and ensuring the platform runs efficiently across user configurations.

The use of Cairo, a graphics-rendering package, reveals how Kindle engineers have navigated issues around displaying images, as the source code reveals that the Lab126 engineers removed Scalable Vector Graphics (SVG) compatibility from the library despite dedicated devices having the capability to display SVG.[25] The company emphasizes conservative aesthetic principles to avoid unforeseen bug exploitation. For example, in the Kindle format ecosystem, it is impossible to layer objects, as demonstrated by shifting the ephemera in S. across pages. SVG allows designers to draw objects on top of other text or images, and the oversight required to manage this feature is undesirable for Amazon, which restricted SVG's use. Recent guidelines have relaxed the ban on SVG with the introduction of enhanced typography, but publishers can only use a limited set of tags.[26] The design conservatism puts a clear focus on the primary object—most commonly the text, but also images in comic books—and ensures that content can be rendered on any Kindle hardware.

Autonomy and Control

The introduction of KFX allowed Amazon to assert its authority over the rendering of ebooks, counter to the more open approach taken by other platforms. KFX stores ebooks in a company-designed version of JSON called "Ion" designed in 2009 and deployed across Amazon's services. The company emphasizes readability in the format specifications: "Because most data is read more often than it is written, Ion defines a *read-optimized binary format.*"[27] Beyond the obfuscation potential of the specification, dictating a transition from EPUB to JSON allows Amazon to control features embedded in the content available via the Kindle. Jiminy Panoz, an ebook designer, notes that Amazon processes EPUBs through a command line simulation of a web browser, also known as a headless browser, to check the HTML before rendering the content in Ion. Preprocessing offers Amazon control over unwanted features, including "removing drop caps or floats when the user reaches a font-size ceiling," but at the expense of the autonomy of both the consumer and producer.[28] The inherent tensions between publisher and Amazon control within the Kindle platform ensure that the reader cannot expect the affordances of contemporary reading platforms without the full palette of open web standards.

Ebook formats are designed to meet the needs of publishers and technology companies rather than users, resulting in criticisms of the presentational aspects of the format. The ability to compress data to protect proprietary elements of both the main text and the algorithmically generated aspects of an ebook was vital for publishers' comfort in adopting open standards. The World Wide Web Consortium (W3C) designed open web standards such as HTML and CSS to work in the broadest possible context, while the book trade had specific intellectual property and metadata requirements. For example, ebooks need to contain identifiable information about authors or editors, and most titles are linked to ISBNs. When users visit web pages, they download a copy and can "view source" to see how they work; publishers wanted to protect their content through use of digital rights management (DRM). The Kindle DRM system is based on eBookBase, a collaboration between Mobipocket and Franklin Electronic Publishers in the early 2000s to create a cross-platform DRM database for ebooks.[29] Copyright reform advocates such as Cory Doctorow lobby against DRM as anticonsumer, but the technology offers conservative publishers reassurances about the unauthorized transmission of their intellectual property.[30] Ebook formats err on the side of publisher control over user autonomy. Formats thus extend beyond logical representations to consolidating power within relationships. While reassuring publishers hesitant about digital distribution, the Kindle format's black box positions Amazon as dominant in the hierarchy. As Kirschenbaum notes, this problem extends beyond the Kindle to much of contemporary publishing, where "no publisher has as much oversight of their workflow as they might like. Much happens through contractors and third parties."[31]

The mixture of Amazon's DRM, the Kindle file ecosystem, and the demands of different operating systems has a clear effect on generating unique ebooks. A user's hardware determines the format type of an ebook (see table 4.2). This can be as minor as a different file extension for identical files, as in the case of Touch and Kindle for Mac ebooks, which have different extension names (figure 4.1). Greater differences occur at the forensic level, where each file header includes a DRM payload to determine if an ebook is loaded to the authorized hardware device. Every Kindle download is identified by a unique number generated with reference to the ebook's ASIN and the reading system software package as part of its social DRM protection (that is, embedding the ability to identify where a pirated file originated). If a user downloads the same book twice, each copy will contain a unique identifying number. Amazon uses this number to authenticate an ebook with an associated hardware serial number to stop users from sharing content.[32] The resulting encrypted text differs between copies, but the files remain the same size.

Beyond DRM and strict metadata requirements, ebook specifications are flexible and open for interpretation by the reading system, which in turn depends on the hardware and software available to the end user. This affords the user limited autonomy over aspects of the presentation within the publisher's and technology company's constraints. Formats offer recommendations rather than dictate rules to enable user customization through fonts and layout. Reading systems are inconsistent in their support for features, so the format cannot mandate elements unavailable for certain software without breaking backward compatibility. For example, due to the interpretive differences between platforms—an Android mobile phone does not have the same screen real estate as Kindle for Mac displayed on a forty-inch screen—the same content will not be displayed consistently across the Kindle platform. Dedicated hardware displays have variable requirements: the original Kindle had a six-inch screen, the DX featured a nine-inch screen, and the recent Oasis range settled on seven inches. The format must be rigorous to provide a standardized "Kindle aesthetic" but also allow for ample variation between devices and reading preferences. Despite the introduction of comics and fixed-layout and media-rich ebooks, the "text-heavy" reflowable ebook remains the most common format. The genre of Kindle content is optimized for the

Women in Love [Amazon Fire].azw3	505 KB
Women in Love [Kindle 2]	644 KB
Women in Love [Kindle 3]	644 KB
Women in Love [Kindle 7].azw3	505 KB
Women in Love [Kindle for Mac]	505 KB
Women in Love [Kindle Touch].azw3	505 KB

4.1 Logical similarities between copies of D. H. Lawrence's *Women in Love*. Screenshot by the author.

limitations of dedicated e-readers rather than designed to showcase the more complex rendering capabilities of desktops and smartphones.

The technical details and choices made about the format specification have an impact on the structure and typography of specific texts. In Walter Isaacson's *Steve Jobs*, the Kindle's ability to mark the entry point of the text as separate from the beginning of the main body means that the ebook initially opens on the "Characters" page rather than the table of contents.[33] Brian Abel Ragen acknowledged this structure with regard to Junot Díaz's *The Brief Wondrous History of Oscar Wao*.[34] Both titles feature preliminary materials that shape interpretation, so this decision alters the reading experience. The Kindle Publishing guidelines reveal that the process is algorithmic rather than editorial, which leads to inconsistencies. The algorithm does not open the book at page 1 by default. While Isaacson's biography of Jobs opens before page 1, *Oscar Wao* starts with the main body, ignoring the front matter. A 2016 patent filing by Sravan Babu Bodapati and Venkatraman Kalyanapasupathy, two members of the Machine Learning team, captures how the algorithm worked that year. First, titles were scanned for keywords in titles deemed either relevant ("chapter 1," "prologue," "introduction") or irrelevant ("copyright," "acknowledgments"). If this process fails to produce a clear cutoff point, the algorithm compares a "bag of words" from any introductory matter and compares its similarity to the main text with the assumption that any "relevant" text will bear similarity to the main body. When the algorithm fails to determine an appropriate Start Reading Location (SRL), a "manual review operator" from the publisher makes the decision.[35]

Accessibility and Internationalization

Pargman and Palme introduced the concept of "ASCII imperialism" to discuss internet and platform governance's Anglocentrism, highlighted by the dominance of ASCII across computational systems.[36] The Kindle's file format contributes to this phenomenon despite its origins. Thierry Brethes and Nathalie Ting designed Mobipocket to be used internationally. The MOBI specification offered publishers a choice of two character maps: UTF-8, which features over one million unique characters from global languages; or Windows-1252, designed by Microsoft, emphasizing the Latin alphabet with a limit of 256 characters.[37] To extend the map metaphor, UTF-8 offers a detailed map of the globe, while Windows-1252 documents a province. Publishers could choose between the limited palette of Windows-1252 to decrease the file size or use the richer character set of UTF-8 to publish non-English language content. When revising the MOBI specification for the Kindle, Amazon engineers restricted access to Windows-1252, reducing support for non-English languages and nontraditional typography.

Publishers worked around this early constraint by inserting images of characters not available in Windows-1252. Figure 4.2 shows a JPEG used to display ō (014d in the Latin Extended-A Unicode character map) in Walter Isaacson's *Steve Jobs*. The solution is incompatible with the core tenet of reflowability, as the image does not scale with the font sizes, leading to unreadable text. The workaround also affects the algorithmic reading paratext, including text-to-speech, definitions, and Word Runner, which cannot parse the images as part of the word, rendering the text as "S [obj] t [obj]." The white background draws the reader's attention to the character's absence. The restriction ironically mirrors the Unicode Consortium's insistence that text without a visual representation in a text-rendering engine should instead appear as an empty box (□) to signify an absence. Newer hardware offers support for Unicode, which could fix this error, but older devices without UTF-8 support cannot display the text correctly. Publishers would need to create multiple unique versions of the same text to be optimized for the different devices. Since this would only benefit Amazon, it is difficult to justify the expense.

Formatting errors extend beyond the integration of characters incompatible with Windows-1252. As with the use of images in place of text, these issues that appear to be minor inconveniences can affect the broader accessibility of the ebook. Isaacson opens his book with a dramatis personae, where Little, Brown decided to format individuals' names with small capitalization (the first letter of each word is larger than the remaining characters, although all letters are in uppercase). Publishers achieve this effect through tagging, but the implementation is inconsistent across ebook platforms. For example, in a simplified version of ebook formatting, "H<small>ELLO</small>" would be rendered as "Hello." Small capital letters are parsed separately from full capitalization when KindleGen converts EPUB to AZW, which was only fixed with the launch of "enhanced typography" with the Voyage. As a result, "Kobun Chino" is presented in text as "KOBUN CHINO," a minor typographic difference, but the <small> tags are interpreted as spaces, so the software reads the

KOBUN CHINO. A Sōtō Zen master

4.2 Detail of JPEG for diacritics in Walter Isaacson's *Steve Jobs: The Exclusive Biography*. Source: Walter Isaacson, *Steve Jobs: The Exclusive Biography* [Kindle for iPad 4.10], AZW3, B005J3IEZQ (Little, Brown Book Group, 2011), loc. 200.

text as "K OBUN C HINO," which affects the quality of its text-to-speech and Word Runner conversion. Choosing Windows-1252 by default and stripping tags without context may create a consistent presentation, but the changes to accessibility and semantic access can adversely affect readability.

Amazon engineers have developed various technological solutions to what remains a social problem. For example, Anubhav Kushwaha, a software development manager at Amazon, experimented with compressing ebooks by using an index dictionary. Each unique word received an identifying number in a dictionary that is then recalled in text rather than repeatedly spelling out words (figure 4.3).[38] The method has a historical precedent in early ebooks implementations developed for the US Navy to increase the efficiency and speed of reading reference manuals.[39] Pertinent strings can also be compressed into dictionary entries, reducing commonly used markup such as <h1> for headings or navigational elements to a numerical string far more compact than the original markup. The technique was initially designed to circumvent the expense of storage memory in the 1980s, but Amazon recast the technique for obfuscation of content in the constant arms race with users who were reverse engineering the Kindle DRM to transfer ebooks to other platforms.

Kushwaha's work mirrored earlier research into character-level dictionary indexing. Amazon headhunted Eric Menninga, a typography veteran of nineteen years for Adobe, to work on improving the layout of Kindle ebooks and "solve the problem of authoring complex documents for display on devices with varying capabilities."[40] Menninga worked with Lokesh Joshi, another typography expert, to expand the Kindle character map to be compatible with UTF-8 while restricting access to exploits within the system.[41] Building on Kushwaha's work, Menninga and Joshi focused on generating indexed dictionaries of characters in an ebook rather than words, allowing for a customized character map for each title. Each ebook features a compressed version of UTF-8 rather than offering access to the complete character map, with a customized map that includes only the characters present in a particular title.[42] A new character map with just an index of characters present in the text further obfuscates the content and adds an extra layer of security to the DRM. Just like Amazon's approach to converting EPUB to AZW through JSON, the character map conversion introduces an additional risk for creating unintended errors that can be difficult to troubleshoot given the obfuscation process. As figure 4.4 shows, this represents clear progress for better internationalization support, but the approach is constrained overall by Amazon's extensive use of proprietary solutions based on available open technologies.

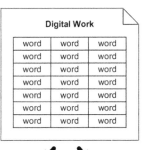

4.3 The user dictionary approach to compressing ebooks

a)

b)

1

1

В начале июля, в чрезвычайно жаркое время, под вечер, один молодой человек вышел из своей каморки, которую нанимал от жильцов в С-м переулке, на улицу и медленно, как бы в нерешимости, отправился к К-ну мосту.

Он благополучно избегнул встречи с своею хозяйкой на лестнице. Каморка его приходилась под самою кровлей высокого пятиэтажного дома и походила более на шкаф, чем на квартиру. Квартирная же хозяйка его, у которой он нанимал эту каморку с обедом и прислугой, помещалась одною лестницей ниже, в отдельной квартире, и каждый раз, при выходе на улицу, ему непременно надо было

Loc 18   1%

1%   Locations 18-27   14347

4.4 Comparison of how a Kindle 2 (left) and Kindle Touch (right) render the same MOBI file of Фёдор Достоевский (Fyodor Dostoyevsky), *Преступление и наказание* (*Crime and Punishment*). Source: Федор Михайлович Достоевский, *Преступление и наказание* (Russian Edition) [Kindle Touch 5.3.7.3], AZW3, B00KHRXSMI (Общественное достояние, 2014), loc. 31.

This approach ensures that a reader can access the same ebook title on a Kindle 1 or Voyage and it will be optimized for that hardware, not to mention the array of secondary platforms Amazon supports. The hardware and software will also create fluctuations in the naming conventions of a file. For example, the same title will be branded "AZW" on a Kindle 3 but appear as "PRC" on a non-Amazon-branded Android device. These minor deviations appear through the longitudinal development of platform-specific workflows that lead to different results even if the output is nearly identical. The formatting of several editions of Walter Isaacson's *Steve Jobs* biography shows a consistency between file types, but also format differences in variants. The ebook is not a single file, however, as several services are sideloaded through separate files (table 4.3).

Steve Jobs is a technically simple ebook with occasional images, but otherwise no complex formatting. Nonetheless, the biography is made up of many distinct files: outside of the main ebook, we find over thirty different files sideloaded with metadata (table 4.3). Many of these files are optional services available only on certain devices, but in several instances, the Kindle offers a unique interpretation of formatting choices owing to its archaic roots. The available sideloaded content can be grouped into four primary categories:

1. *Bibliographic metadata* about the length of the book, the author, and other aspects often found on the opening pages of a printed book

2. *User-generated metadata* pertaining to reading time and the collation of popular highlights

3. *Generative paratext* created through algorithms packaged with the ebook to interact with other elements of the Kindle platform, including page numbers, indexing, reading speed, and vocabulary building

4. *Metrics and logs*: local files compiling information about the user to be sent back to Amazon

The ad hoc assembly of files server-side has clear consequences for the platform. While users have the flexibility to view the same title across a spectrum of hardware and software configurations, with a range of additional features, the structure of the text as a material object is permeable and prone to error. Each download is unique and offers a narrative of both its production and consumption through metadata traces. The platform focuses on scale and variety, which can adversely affect the quality of products that have not been optimized for the Kindle.

Table 4.3 Folder structure for various active Kindle versions of Walter Isaacson's *Steve Jobs*

File	Description	Touch	Kindle 8	Android	Fire	Mac
AZW	Base ebook file in most advanced format available for each device					✓
AZW3		✓				
KFX			✓	✓	✓	
SDR	Folder containing relevant metadata	✓	✓			
AuthorProfile.ASC	Popup boxes in JSON about the author, and to appear at the beginning and end of the ebook	✓				
StartActions.ASC				✓	✓	
EndActions.ASC		✓	✓	✓	✓	
AZW3F	Encrypted reading metrics data	✓				
TICR				✓	✓	
YJF			✓			
MBP	JSON reading metrics data					✓
AZW3R	Annotations / page number data	✓				
APNX	Page number algorithm					✓
PHL	Popular highlights XML	✓	✓	✓	✓	✓
MF	A log of server requests		✓			
LanguageLayer.kll	SQL database for Word Wise, Amazon's vocabulary builder		✓			
XRAY.db	SQL database containing the index information for the X-Ray system			✓	✓	
XRAY.asc			✓			
amazn1.drm-voucher.ast	DRM information			✓	✓	
kfx.luci	A series of 11 encrypted metadata files				✓	

Kindle ebooks are created on Amazon Web Services to optimize titles to work with new features while remaining backward compatible with older devices. Over the Kindle's first decade, the company introduced new formats while maintaining support for older devices. The resulting infrastructure supports an ecosystem of formats rather than a single file format that has been developed alongside hardware and software innovations in an incremental fashion. The Kindle file format is not a stable object until a user downloads the file for a specific hardware-software combination. The results are closer to the letterpress era, where print runs could be varied according to their production rather than a seamless and standardized process. Since 2012, Amazon has processed a stack of "source ebook data" including "text," "graphics," and "font data" through a server to produce "modified ebook data" personalized for individual users.[43] The shift from storing compiled ebooks on a server to generating personalized copies on the fly offers extra DRM protection through identifying specific copies circulating in the wild while also allowing publishers to provide a single "master copy" that is then converted to suit specific hardware configurations by stripping out or adding content where appropriate.

The complexities of the Kindle's formatting process are difficult to reconcile within the usual confines of format, as the Kindle exhibits a greater fluidity emblematic of Amazon's algorithmic control of the process. No archetypal Kindle file format exists, and even though newer formats derive from older specifications and remain stable based on the hardware-software configuration of a particular user, the notion of a prototypical Kindle format is difficult to formalize in practice. It is closer to the complex multiserver assemblage of Google Docs than the more straightforward single-file PDF. The combination of sideloaded paratext and vastly different file formats for the primary content, as well as the generation of data and content algorithmically through first and subsequent use, makes the Kindle file format difficult to pin down as a single conceptual unit. Jiminy Panoz describes the equivalent EPUB phenomenon as a spectrum, since reading systems are not required or able to interpret all aspects of a common format.[44] This courtesy also extends to developers to adapt the standards to best suit their platforms. The common principles that emerge across format iterations are more important than the differences, as this is what defines the contemporary ebook.

Amazon is unlikely to switch to the status quo of EPUB. The decision to implement JSON on top of keeping elements of PRC allows the company to maintain control over the features available to the title and protect publishers' intellectual property. An asymmetrical process allows the company to only include white-listed elements rather than experience unwanted behavior. As a consequence, the most accurate representation of a Kindle file exists not in publishers' archives or on readers' devices but in the databases containing JSON to be converted to a title when requested by a user. From the perspective of creators, it is impossible to ensure that the carefully designed ebook will be preserved through the upload *and* download processes according to the latest, or historic, software demands. Users—and researchers—will not necessarily have an identical experience on any two devices, and finding consistency is difficult.

Through Amazon's continual expansion of the platform, and its long history embedded in older computing traditions, the format has remained one of the most complex parts of the Kindle infrastructure. Amazon's commitment to backward compatibility while simultaneously attempting to diversify into tablets and encourage a small number of readers to upgrade on a yearly obsolescence cycle has led to a complicated ecosystem of file formats that are distinct yet similar. As the Kindle platform has grown, quality control has become more difficult to maintain, leading to differences in the display of titles between a Kindle 1 and iPhone X. Simultaneously, each new iteration of the Kindle file format has introduced new proprietary and divergent rules and logics, ensuring that Amazon maintains control over what is allowed on the platform. While this initially came at the cost of accessibility and internationalization, newer devices have struck the balance between control and access.

Once Amazon started to build its extensive warehouse network, Bezos envisioned "Project Fargo," a reference to the 1996 Coen brothers' film, where the company would have at least one of every product in stock.[1] Early Lab126 mission statements echoed the sentiment for ebooks, with the desire to have a copy of every book ever published available for download.[2] The US Kindle Store boasted over 5.5 million titles in September 2017, but Amazon faced an early hurdle to offer a more modest catalog of 88,000 titles at launch. The technical barriers of digitization were insignificant compared to the social challenges involved in persuading publishers to create ebooks. Publishers were comfortable with producing books digitally, but they remained skeptical of digital distribution before the Kindle's launch. The gamble paid off, and Amazon boasted a large catalog in November 2007 "including more than 101 of 112 current *New York Times* Best Sellers."[3] The combination of best sellers and a range of older titles built a critical mass for the Kindle's launch and encouraged consumers that publishers were serious about ebooks.

Ebook publishing divides into four main segments: *frontlist, backlist, public domain*, and *digital-only / self-published* works. The frontlist and backlist are mainstays of legacy publishing. Publishers release new titles, called the frontlist, aiming to sell them in high quantities and create a best seller. After the peak window for sales, thought to be as short as twelve weeks for most books, titles move to the backlist, where they remain in print if they continue to sell enough copies to justify a reprint. For publishers with a rich history, such as Penguin, Faber & Faber, and Oxford

University Press, the backlist represents a valuable revenue stream, as readers continue to consume historically significant titles still protected by copyright. As of 2020, books published before 1924 are in the public domain in the United States and can be published without prior permission or for free on the Kindle. Ebook platforms' infrastructure bypasses the workflows and timescales of legacy publishing. Start-ups have taken advantage of these new freedoms, including digital-only publishers such as Canelo and self-published authors who choose to circumvent the gatekeeping function of publishers entirely. Recent journalism prophesying the demise of ebooks focuses on print-oriented publishers' difficulties in adapting to the demands of digital publishing with new titles, and the expenses of digitizing the backlist, while ignoring the rise of digital-only publications owing to their association with vanity presses.[4] There are a few exceptions: Mills & Boon, a romance publisher, has pivoted toward digital publications to satiate its audience's demands. Other publishers focus on print first with ebooks remaining an afterthought, outside of a few publishers who continue to hire digital-publishing advocates. The long-term success of ebook platforms such as the Kindle depends on a fine balance of these four segments. Kindle Direct Publishing and the promotional value of Kindle Unlimited built new audiences for born-digital content, but this increased readership exists in a symbiotic state with more traditional publishing, which drives readers to the Kindle Store before discovering new genres and experiences.

Despite initial optimism, print-oriented publishers now contest any challenge to the orthodoxy. For example, in 2008 Frankfurter Buchmesse participants agreed that digital sales would overtake print by 2018, and Dick Brass, vice president of technology development for Microsoft, predicted that "the last paper edition of the *New York Times* will appear in 2018."[5] Nonetheless, popular Kindle titles still correlate to the whims of print. From June 2010 to November 2011, Amazon maintained the Kindle Million Club, a list of authors who had sold over a million ebooks.[6] In the eighteen months this list was active, fourteen members were inducted. Stieg Larsson was the first inductee in July 2010, followed by other fiction heavyweights such as James Patterson, Lee Child, Suzanne Collins, and Michael Connelly in the following twelve months. Two Million Club members, John Locke and Amanda Hocking, were self-published, offering an early indication of the changes afoot. Contrary to the perceived phenomenon of "mommy porn" in the years since the release of *Fifty Shades of Grey*, this list reveals a convergence toward crime fiction and thrillers, with the occasional science fiction and young adult title. Many brand-name authors only entered the club with the release of a film or television adaptation of their works. For example, George R. R. Martin sold over a million copies of his works after the popularity of the first season of *Game of Thrones* in September 2011, and Stephenie Meyer's appearance on the list in November 2011 coincides with the penultimate *Twilight Saga*'s release date in cinemas.

The club has several notable absences, including heavyweight authors such as Stephen King and J. K. Rowling. Both decided against publishing ebooks owing to skepticism about the format. King's hesitance was born out of the failed attempt to serialize *The Plant* in 2000, although his books had continued to be available for sale as ebooks, on Amazon no less, before the Kindle's launch. The success of the first-generation device persuaded King to pen a promotional story, "UR," released with a cover adorned with his custom pink Kindle 2, to mark the launch of the device. King joined Bezos for the device's launch in New York City's Morgan Library in February 2009, fully endorsing the device. Nonetheless, in the two years after King's entrance to the Kindle market, he had not sold a million copies despite having forty novels in print at the time. Rowling was another high-profile abstainer and resisted the Kindle's siren call until 2011, when she launched Pottermore to challenge Amazon's ebook dominance. Pottermore was initially designed as an interactive version of the seven core *Harry Potter* books featuring several gamelike features but evolved into the exclusive ebook distributor for the series. Rowling elected to distribute ebooks directly via Kindle Unlimited in 2015 to promote the subscription service. Readers who wished to purchase the titles were instructed to visit Pottermore, allowing Rowling to sidestep the Amazon infrastructure and dictate terms of access. Rowling's position was unique, as the *Harry Potter* series had greater cultural and economic clout than other authors, and she could dictate terms to Amazon: Nielsen BookScan data show that Rowling sold 1 percent of all books sold in the United Kingdom between 2001 and 2018. Rowling and King raised the potential for an alternative ebook ecosystem, disconnected from the whims of Amazon, but as the market has consolidated, even the refuseniks have fallen into line. Without a concerted effort from major publishers and high-profile authors, it is unlikely that Amazon's grip on the ebook market will slip.

The Frontlist and Best Sellers

The best seller is an enigma in publishing studies, as it is one of the only metrics embraced by an industry that otherwise shuns quantification. Best sellers are editorialized and depend on algorithms with clear human biases. For example, when the *New York Times* publishes its best-seller list, the data are collected from a range of self-reporting sources filtered by "standards for inclusion that encompass proprietary vetting and audit protocols, corroborative reporting and other statistical determinations."[7] The *Times* keeps the exact list of bookshops secret, to discourage mass purchasing from suspected reporting stores, but its precautions do not stop authors from gaming the system. Lani Sarem's young adult novel *Handbook for Mortals* was dropped from the best-seller list in August 2017 when bookstores reported suspicious bulk-buying patterns in an early draft of the list circulated to trade members.[8] Further levels of curation exist. Cookbooks often outsell other trade nonfiction but remain conspicuously absent from best-seller lists. The newspaper also created a separate list for children's books after the *Harry Potter* series became a perennial fixture on the trade fiction list. Amazon challenged this orthodoxy from its early categorization of best sellers. Readers could find the most popular title within microgenres, with the expectation of real-time updates rather than offering a snapshot of the previous week.

Amazon adopted its familiar strategy of discounting best sellers to attract users to the Kindle. *New York Times* Best Sellers available at launch were capped at $9.99, leading to discounts as high as $20 for hardcover nonfiction titles to establish trust in a new format and counter early skepticism toward buying digital books. The value of a digital version of a newly published hardcover remains hotly contested by major publishers and Amazon over the last decade after this initial reduction in value despite publishers' earlier trials of the scheme, including Random House's launch of $9.99 titles for the AtRandom imprint in 2000.[9] After these skirmishes, agency pricing is the current paradigm for big publishers. Agency pricing fixes an ebook's cost, with a note from Amazon that the price was publisher mandated. Under this model, "the retailer acts as an agent of the publisher, which itself sets the retail price of the ebooks, with the retailer taking a commission" of 30 percent.[10] Titles protected by agency pricing can cost more than their print equivalents. For example, Philip Pullman's *La Belle Sauvage* had a recommended retail price of £20 but was available in hardcover for £9 and Kindle edition for £9.99 when published in October 2017. Likewise, Elena Favilli and Francesca Cavallo's *Good Night Stories for Rebel Girls* (£16.99 RRP) was £8.49 in print but £9.99 for the Kindle.[11] Ebooks in the United Kingdom were subject to a 20 percent value-added tax until May 2020, while print is exempt, accounting for the higher price, but the distribution costs of ebooks are substantially lower.[12] In recent years, the industry has therefore favored price matching to ensure a robust hardcover market by fixing the prices of ebooks. The higher cost of goods clashes with the public's perception that an ebook should be relatively inexpensive compared to the print edition. Increasing the costs of new books shrank the potential size of the market, but ebooks could still be useful for developing the backlist. Conversely, the gold rush of Kindle Direct Publishing (KDP) was predicated on cheap titles, hollowing out the potential for titles that sit between cheap digital-only publications and the more expensive releases of print-oriented publishers.

Digitizing the Backlist

The backlist presented a greater opportunity for publishers that might have a treasure trove of older titles that might be profitable if sold at low cost in high volume. Although publishers had used digital tools to produce books for decades, material created before the introduction of digital workflows remained inaccessible. Since the 1980s, early innovators such as Coach House Press used Standardized General Markup Language (SGML), the precursor to HTML, to aid typesetting. This practice is now widespread, and print books start their lives as "born-digital" objects, easing the transition from print to ebook versions.[13] Titles published before the 1990s were difficult to convert to an appropriate format, as no digital typescript existed for many titles that had not enjoyed enough success to merit a reprint.

The public domain was a known quantity. Organizations such as Project Gutenberg, Early English Books Online, and the Oxford Text Archive started digitizing public domain books in the early 1970s. The projects' investment in digitizing public domain titles created opportunities for publishers to produce ebooks for a low price or free, which led to several start-ups focusing on public domain titles, including Aegitas, Bartleby.com, and Enhanced Media Publishing.[14] Public domain ebooks are low cost with little risk, as any further editorial work is optional, and these works come with a preformed market. Jacob Flynn, Rebecca Giblin, and François Petitjean's analysis of copyright terms reveals that books in the public domain receive more investment than those under direct ownership of a single publisher, especially as competing ebooks can be published, thus incentivizing higher quality.[15]

Amazon removed editorial oversight from the publication of public domain titles, and as a result, there has been an increase in poor-quality editions that have not been edited to clean up the scanned text or otherwise create a high-quality edition. For example, Whitney Trettien has traced a zombie print-on-demand (POD) edition of John Milton's *Areopagitica* from an Internet Archive digitization of a University of California Libraries copy through to unedited digital and print version.[16] The Kindle's scale precludes thorough quality control. Amazon temporarily removes any reported low-quality editions, but this approach relies on free labor from customers who have purchased a copy of the text rather than Amazon manually or automatically identifying poor-quality digitization before publication. The automation of publication from archive to Kindle also produces books not intended for the audience. For example, on June 29, 2017, Project Gutenberg published the August 21, 1858, edition of *Stephen Branch's Alligator*, a regional newspaper focused on New York politics.[17] Prabhat Prakashan, a company specializing in Hindi literature, published a Kindle edition of the text, with clear attribution to Project Gutenberg, on September 16, 2017, for $4.81.[18] No evidence indicates that anyone has bought the book, as it is available for free elsewhere. Amazon's commercial imperative runs counter to the ideology of other digitization projects— even for-profit organizations such as Early English Books Online (EEBO) and other UMI publications—as other initiatives value the archive as a unit over single texts. The values of Amazon's digitization efforts instead focus on offering already plentiful texts in a new format.

Amazon's digitization strategy differed from Google Books in two important ways. First, Google Books focused on quantity over quality, as most users would not see the underlying text and it formed the basis for a search engine, while Kindle users would purchase titles to read and expect a much higher quality. Second, Google Books' scope was necessarily wide to generate the most data, while Amazon needed to target titles that were feasible to sell. Eighteenth-century religious tracts and agricultural manuals enrich Google's search engine and draw users to the database but are unlikely to be commercially viable in bulking up an ebook store, especially once the expense of digitization is taken into consideration. In 2007, during the great push to convert materials for sale at the Kindle's launch, Levy reported that Amazon's cost for digitizing and correcting each book was roughly $200 per title.[19]

In 2012, users could no longer download free editions of public domain texts but could access the same material through a Kindle Unlimited or Prime Reading subscription. Amazon's release of "Kindle in Motion" in 2017 attempted to distinguish Kindle public domain ebooks from other brands by adding animations and advanced typography and formatting to select public domain titles. Publishers could integrate animated GIFs into their books using the new feature. For example, Anna Sewell's *Black Beauty* is available as a Kindle in Motion edition through Two Lions, one of Amazon Publishing's imprints, to demonstrate the viability and power of the technology.[20] Pottermore is the only other publisher to produce Kindle in Motion editions to replicate the animated newspapers in *Harry Potter and the Philosopher's Stone* and *Fantastic Beasts and Where to Find Them*. Amazon used public domain titles as a purchased proof of concept for the format rather than circulating for free. The strategy was unsuccessful, as no new Kindle in Motion titles were published after 2018. As discussed in chapter 4, Amazon's attempts to differentiate its format ecosystem have been met with publisher apathy without investment from the technology company, as publishers need to produce multiple copies at the lowest possible cost rather than optimize for each platform.

Beyond public domain titles, digitizing backlists of authors still protected by copyright represented a lucrative opportunity for those who held the rights. A legal distinction exists between copyright and rights. The former term refers to the exact expression, or the order of the words, while rights protect the idea in specific forms. For example, an author may transfer the rights to hardcover and paperback editions to different publishers. Adaptations, territories, and translations are all covered by separate rights, as well as different media, including audiobook and ebook. Each of these rights needs to be transferred in a contract. Sensing a gap in publishing contracts, Rosetta Books licensed ebook editions directly from authors such as Kurt Vonnegut and William Styron in 2001. Random House responded by suing the company in 2002.[21] The district court rejected these claims because the contracts did not specifically state "ebooks" but rather focused on physical rights.[22] The move was mirrored by Andrew Wylie, a prominent literary agent representing authors and estates including Chinua Achebe, Vladimir Nabokov, and J. M. Coetzee, who argued that since publishers had not negotiated for the rights for digital publication, he was able to publish these works through his own digital imprint, Odyssey Editions. Random House challenged Wylie in 2010, who settled the lawsuit. After the dispute, publishers began adding digital rights into contracts by default and quickly moved to ensure audio rights were included in contracts with the rise of Audible.[23]

Beyond recognized perennial sellers, the Kindle could amplify the discovery of obscurer titles and the backlists of authors to ensure a robust ebook marketplace without the costs of physically warehousing, printing, and keeping older titles in print. Cheap best sellers and free public domain ebooks attracted readers, but a healthy backlist ensured they stayed. Amazon introduced a "request this book" button on product pages not associated with a Kindle title to put pressure on publishers to convert popular print titles into an ebook. As many major authors were not instantly willing to offer their backlist on the Kindle Store, Amazon made announcements about major acquisitions, such as a deal with Penguin to publish Tom Clancy's backlist starting with *The Hunt for Red October* or the arrival of Danielle Steel's back catalog, both in 2009.[24] As the platform matured, the announcements reduced in frequency with the expectation that authors' titles would be available by default.

The backlist is a central part of publishing business models. It is unusual for a reader to *only* consume new titles. The 80,000 titles available at the Kindle 1's launch were only a fraction of titles in print in November 2007: the Publishing Association estimated the number of new titles released in North America per year to be 150,000, almost double the titles available at the Kindle's launch.[25] The quantity was not exceptional, however, as competitors such as Microsoft Reader, a software package for personal digital assistants (PDAs), featured a library of sixty thousand titles in 2011. Ebook stores historically built catalogs on the new titles published as ebooks, and any titles already digitized from the public domain. This leaves the period between 1922 and the 1990s, which Rebecca Rosen has called the "missing twentieth century."[26] Out-of-print books protected by current copyright legislation can be difficult to find even from retailers such as Amazon. These sixty years represent a vibrant body of literature that many readers would like to revisit. The books remain in limbo, as the digitization costs would be borne entirely by publishers. Investment in the back catalog only pays off with titles that sell. Despite the risk, ebooks are useful for testing the potential audience for a backlist title before investing in a full print run.

The digitization of the missing twentieth century is understandably patchy. Google Books and HathiTrust digitized many twentieth-century publications without permission from the rights holders. Copyright challenges prevent the data from being shared. Beyond intellectual property issues, the cost of digitization creates a barrier for many. Publishers including the MIT Press often rely on external funding from bodies such as Arcadia and the Internet Archive to incentivize digitization projects.[27] To determine the extent of digitization for the Kindle, I compared titles listed in the British National Bibliography as published in 1989 (30,490 books) with the Amazon store. These books' availability on the Kindle and, more broadly, the Amazon store reveals stalled progress in digitizing a cross section of the backlist. The year 1989 is significant in the history of digital books, as it marked the launch of Project Gutenberg's first ebook. The year is recent enough for books to potentially be topical and remain in print, yet distant enough that publishers were still shifting to digital workflows, so that most new publications would involve a hybrid of traditional and digital techniques. Amazon uploaded the data from the 1995 edition of *Books in Print* for its initial catalog, which was kept separate from *Books Out of Print 1995*, which contained 1989 titles that were out of print six years later. The product pages therefore indicate the proportion of titles still in circulation on the secondhand market and how many of those titles have appeared in a digitized form as a Kindle edition.

Table 5.1 breaks down the availability of titles published in 1989, where fewer than 10 percent of all titles have received a Kindle edition, with only 1 percent present in the Kindle Unlimited scheme, indicating that the service's exclusivity clause discourages publishers from sharing their backlist in the scheme. Amazon stocks more books in physical inventory than are available through the Kindle, and this is far surpassed by the availability of the books by third-party retailers. The third-party retail economy ensures the continual circulation of these out-of-print titles. Used copies of books from libraries are sold through Amazon, but if titles are no longer in circulation, we have no clear evidence the books may sell.

The overall volume of "Look Inside the Book" titles outweighs the number available on the Kindle, which automatically includes the feature on product pages. Almost two thousand titles—the equivalent of 80 percent of the volume of titles available for the Kindle—are available to browse online but are only sold in print via either Amazon or third-party retailers. These titles are digitized and shared with Amazon but have not been made available to sell on the platform, indicating there are social rather than technical issues for excluding the titles from the platform. Two main reasons exist for this gap. First, as discussed in chapter 1, the "Look Inside" function predates the Kindle and was used as an incentive for marketing,

Table 5.1 Digitization progress for books published in 1989*

Availability	Frequency
Kindle	2,697
Kindle Unlimited	201
First-party print	3,332
First-party print with Look Inside	1,142
Third-party print	21,974
Third-party print with Look Inside	642
404 error	60
No available copies	5,574
Total	30,940

*The sixty 404 errors come from books published by small independent publishers and individuals as well as ISBNs that were reused for several books by large academic publishers such as Elsevier that are not easily compatible with the ASIN infrastructure.

and publishers may not have granted Amazon the additional permissions to convert the book to a Kindle edition. "Look Inside" reproduces a facsimile rather than requiring the costlier step of extracting the text via optical character recognition to create a publishable ebook. Second, the genre of many books available exclusively via "Look Inside" reveals variations in digital distribution, as large academic publishers such as Springer Nature and Elsevier used the marketing potential of "Look Inside" but elected to not sell the books via the Kindle. Scholarly publishers invested in digital workflow technologies earlier than other publishers and gain more benefits from digitizing the rest of their back catalog owing to the additional merits of print-on-demand business models for the scale of print runs in academic publishing. The sector set up alternate infrastructures for disseminating ebooks on platforms such as ScienceDirect. As the library subscription model is the primary revenue stream for academic publishers, they rely less on the availability of titles for the Kindle.

The historical and geographical specificity of publishing also affects the availability of ebooks from 1989. While readers still consume classic works, most publications remain forgotten. The Cold War, the HIV/AIDS crisis, and futurist speculations on the 1990s were popular topics in 1989 publishing. Some of these titles may remain appealing, but the majority are unlikely to generate sufficient sales beyond curiosity to be profitable enough to digitize. The long tail of publishing uncovered by analyzing a slice of all books published in a single year also reveals a body of local-history titles that would not have a large-enough scale of interest to prompt a digitization campaign.

In a talk at Ebookcraft 2016, Teresa Elsey, then digital managing editor at Houghton Mifflin Harcourt, contextualized the lack of progress with the backlist by demonstrating the pressures of maintaining a backlist that remains perpetually "in print." Elsey calculated her group's workload for 2015—a total of 1,400 ebooks—of which only 20 percent were new titles. The remaining titles were books that had never received an ebook edition (10 percent) and new editions of preexisting ebooks (70 percent).[28] As more titles are introduced as ebooks, the burden of updating becomes a large proportion of the workload, leaving the older titles less likely to be digitized. Elsey attributes this constant churn to two factors: (1) the initial digitization gold rush, and (2) the shifting demands of ebook production and the anachronistic connection between ebook titles and reading systems. The digitization gold rush in the mid-2000s, facilitated by Google and Amazon, emphasized quantity over quality, and consequently an abundance of OCR errors, uncorrected print-based hyphenations, and other conversion artifacts remained in the process; in today's mature ebook marketplace, these errors are noticed by retailers and readers and need to be corrected. Elsey also notes the importance of the legal issues regarding permissions for digital editions that have emerged with a more substantial effort to digitize the backlist. The shifting demands of ebook production affect all backlist titles, including those born digital. Older titles need maintenance according to updated standards, and the conventions of ebook design shift, so even working titles may require updating to reflect the market. This is exacerbated by the anachronistic connection between titles and reading systems, which show no sign of aging, unlike their print counterparts.[29] Maintaining a backlist with the pressures of updatability remains an open challenge a decade after the Kindle's launch, decreasing the resources available for publishers to digitize more of their backlists.

The Emergence of Digital-Only Publishers

The now-infamous *Fifty Shades of Grey* trilogy challenged orthodox conceptions of publishing success made possible through developments with ebooks.[30] E. L. James, the pen name of Erika Mitchell, presented a mythical "rags-to-riches" narrative highlighting the potency of self-publishing. The novel started as fan fiction of the *Twilight Saga* posted on fanfiction.net, published in weekly installments for a rapt audience. Once James found a large audience, she published a revised version of the fan fiction as *Fifty Shades of Grey*, using print on demand before Vintage Books acquired the rights. James initially found success without the support of a traditional publisher, but her biography reveals that this is not a straight-forward narrative. Before the publication of *Fifty Shades*, James worked in television, and her husband, Niall Leonard, remains a screenwriter. James had appropriate connections to media industries and understood the nuances of contemporary publishing when choosing to self-publish the work.

Given the book's origins as fan fiction, it could not be published in its original form. James's media-savvy marketing through fanfiction.net built an audience that an author taking the traditional approach would struggle to replicate. The blurring of the lines between best seller and self-published work that *Fifty Shades of Grey* pioneered reveals the blueprint for entrepreneurial authors willing to start with the Kindle. The ability to read "mommy porn" inconspicuously was immaterial compared to its use of self-publishing, as the success of *Fifty Shades* depended equally on the print edition and its appearance in various gendered locations, including supermarkets. For example, in Norway, 96 percent of 177,000 total sales for the *Fifty Shades* trilogy were print rather than digital.[31] *Fifty Shades* sold over eleven million paperback copies in the United Kingdom in its first five years, according to Nielsen BookScan, further solidifying the series' best-seller status. The third title, *Fifty Shades Freed*, was the weakest seller but still sold twice as many copies as the fourth most purchased book from 2012 to 2017, *Harry Potter and the Cursed Child*. *Fifty Shades* was a phenomenon across formats that revealed the scale of the ebook market during its ascent. Regardless of the authenticity of James's underdog narrative, *Fifty Shades* demonstrated the marketing potential of fan fiction forums and self-published books to build loyalty before embarking on a more traditional publishing model.

The rise of self-published authors reverses twentieth-century trends but fits into more historical trajectories of publishing. The publisher has not always been separated from the author; for example, Samuel Richardson was the author, publisher, and printer of *Clarissa* in the 1740s. It was only with the professionalization of the printing press and publishers that Richardson's do-it-yourself mentality became abnormal. Self-publishing was tarnished as vanity publishing, since if a traditional publisher deemed a book unworthy, it was unlikely to be worth the money. Vanity publishing required authors to subsidize the cost of production and place advertisements at the end of the book to ensure a financial return for the printers.[32] Predatory vanity publishers, particularly in academic publishing, generated a stigma around self-publishing that presented a hurdle for the legitimacy of services such as Kindle Direct Publishing.

Kindle 1 promotional material heralded its extensive range of *New York Times* Best Sellers and backlist titles, but the launch of Digital Text Platform (the original name of Kindle Direct Publishing) marked a more substantial transformation. Amazon did not want to reveal its self-publishing ebook platform before the launch of the hardware, but the Digital Text Platform page launched on the same day as the Kindle and encouraged users to join up with Amazon. The splash page was accompanied by an FAQ that sold Amazon's ability to act as an intermediary in place of the publisher because "the Kindle Store provides the business, marketing, and vendor support you need to maximize your sales. Titles published on the Kindle Store are eligible for automated merchandising and personalization, Search Inside, Amazon.com's excellent Customer Service and order fulfillment services, and much more."[33] The FAQ, though not publicly released until the November launch date, was written in May 2007. KDP represented a strong backup plan for Amazon if print publishers were unwilling to publish digital publications.

Despite the term "direct publishing," authors using Kindle Direct Publishing benefited from association with the Amazon brand. Rather than releasing a MOBI file to a web page and hoping for the best, self-published titles were boasted by Amazon's full-service infrastructure and discoverability platform. While traditionally published and self-published works largely remained separate, authors could leverage the benefits of Amazon as de facto publisher in the process. Kindle Direct Publishing was not just another place to sell a few ebooks; it offered a new way for authors to make a living without relying on traditional publishing structures. The company's role as publisher is clear from how it shapes pricing: while authors can charge whatever they like, in 2015, authors only enjoyed a 70 percent royalty if they priced their title between $3 and $10.[34] Incentivizing lower prices encouraged the production of material deemed viable at that cost. KDP is not self-sufficient, however, as it relies on the prestige of legacy publishing to ensure that readers use the platform. The size of the market attracts users and authors to the platform, but without the prestige of a publisher's imprint, the Kindle platform would compete with start-ups like Wattpad and Archive of Our Own that offer similar services for free. These two divergent markets have been the subject of intense trade scrutiny, as official figures from the Publishers Association noted a 17 percent drop in sales of consumer ebooks in 2016, resulting in joyous articles about the downfall of ebooks.[35] The figures exclude two large segments of the market: digital-only publications and the entirety of Kindle Direct Publishing.

Early success stories shaped Kindle Direct Publishing's impact. John Locke capitalized on his fame as the first self-published author to sell over a million books. Locke was fortunate to be the first author to hold the top two slots in most-purchased Kindle titles.[36] His book covers reference the large volume of titles that have been sold, and a sense of bravado permeates his author brand. Locke signed a distribution deal with Simon & Schuster in mid-2011, allowing him to continue self-publishing new works.[37] This unusual deal marked a transition point where self-publishing was now seen as a viable career option, shedding its historical association with vanity publishing. Locke was later implicated in paying reviewers to secure a five-star rating for his titles and furthering the tactic by encouraging reviewers to purchase an Amazon-verified copy of the book to both increase his sales ranking and game Amazon's review algorithm.[38] The investigation raised important questions about the ethics and sustainability of self-published best sellers, which would often have to be priced at less than a dollar to be considered, compared to the higher price points expected from print-oriented publishers. After this negative publicity, and after the initial lucrative flurry of sales diminished, Locke stopped publishing new material in 2012.

The Locke model for self-publishing relied on the early Kindle marketplace, and as it has matured, so has the role of self-published and digital-only publications. The arrival of Kindle Unlimited, and more recently Prime Reading, is bolstered by the presence of these types of publication. Select popular legacy publications like the *Hunger Games* trilogy and *Harry Potter* series pepper a catalog of over a million titles. The tactic worked for Suzanne Collins, as the *Hunger Games* books were revealed as three of the top five most purchased fiction titles in the Kindle's first decade, alongside the first two *Fifty Shades* titles.[39] Collins outperforms Rowling because the latter entered the platform later and sold books via a third party. Licensing conditions for Kindle Unlimited require publishers to publish exclusively via the Kindle platform, optimizing the scheme for Kindle-exclusive titles available via KDP while remaining a barrier for traditional publishers.[40] The subscription service offered a revenue kitty to be shared according to volume of pages read. In August 2017, the KDP Select Global Fund was $19.4 million, although the payout per page was 0.4 cents, indicating that subscribers viewed more than 4.6 billion "pages" per month.[41] In this competitive attention economy, authors moved from Locke's scheme of paying for reviews to using underhanded tactics to encourage readers to skip to the end of the book or otherwise increase the visibility of a title.

Locke's early exploitation of Kindle Direct Publishing's fragility has been usurped by more flagrant abuses in recent years, including accusations of money laundering through selling extremely expensive fake books using authenticated authors' credentials.[42] David Gaughran, an author and advocate for self-publishing, has documented a litany of algorithmic gaming practices and errant punishments to authors who follow the rules to crack down on unscrupulous behavior. The Kindle Unlimited royalty pot has led to a common fake book scam, where content is stolen and rendered in large 2,500-page volumes, offered for free, and then added to Kindle Unlimited once its visibility is high to capture a larger proportion of the KDP royalties that month.[43] Authors and publishers of original content have also sunk to the same lows of click farming, or paying for third parties to download, "read," and review a book to increase its visibility.[44] Amazon's response has been to punish these unusual behaviors, but with the unintended side effect of harming authors who use third-party services such as BookBub to advertise their books.[45]

The benefits of self-publishing for groups underrepresented by print-oriented publishers have been overshadowed by automatically generated content that floods the Kindle Store.[46] Despite various schemes to undermine the credibility of self-publishing via Amazon, several authors have set an example of the new careers available in the digital age. Amanda Hocking, the second self-published author on the Kindle Millions Club, was one of the forerunners of the second wave of self-publishers. Hocking released her first book, *My Blood Approves*, in March 2010, and by the time she had sold a million books, she had published two series: *My Blood Approves* and *The Hollows*. The second book in *The Hollows* series was published a day before her induction into the Kindle Million Club, indicating a surge of sales related to this title. St. Martin's Press signed Hocking in 2011, but before that point, she was selling an average of nine thousand books a day.[47] Hocking's success demonstrates that self-publishing ebooks could lead to sustained print sales, as her most recent book series, *The Kanin Chronicles*, was published in 2015 by St. Martin's Press, four years after the start of the relationship. Self-publishing platforms such as Kindle Direct Publishing allowed authors such as E. L. James and Amanda Hocking to launch their careers, but both authors chose a more traditional route once they had established track records. These success stories have encouraged others to self-publish, with many authors electing to stick with self-publishing because of the autonomy and royalties unmatched by legacy publishers.

The rise of digital-only publishers like Canelo, a team who drew on experience from print publishers including HarperCollins and Bloomsbury, shows a sustainable approach to the development of separate print and digital reading audiences. The ebook marketplace has matured around the expectations of value from a consumer perspective. While readers may spend up to $25 or £20 on a newly released hardback book, the equivalent ebook's value proposition is far trickier. The perception that ebooks should be cheaper has led to more agile publishing models for digital-only titles, where publishers and self-published authors use newly created spaces within the ebook market. For example, ebooks can be much shorter than print equivalents, which makes it viable to charge as little as a dollar for a single book. Canelo's mission statement lists what it considers to be viable digital markets: crime, commercial women's fiction, action fiction, and "what we call 'geeky crossover,' such as horror, or historical fantasy."[48] The company focuses on genres it believes will thrive at a low and affordable price. Canelo expanded its offerings by opening Abandoned Bookshop as an imprint in 2016, with a mission statement to "uncover the best books we've forgotten about, lost sight of, or never even knew existed in the first place."[49] Focusing on recovering forgotten titles—orphaned works, titles out of copyright, or simply books that were not paid attention by their original publisher—approaches the backlist as an opportunity rather than a risk. Abandoned Bookshop leverages the credentials of publishers as curators to differentiate the venture from companies that have loaded portions of their backlist to the Kindle Store without a clear focus, and the mass of self-published work that defines digital-only publishing today.

Amazon's role in the distinction between self-publishing and digital only is complex. Since Amazon provides many services associated with the publishing process, can Kindle Direct Publishing be called self-publishing rather than traditional publishing, albeit with little editorial intervention? Amazon published 1.6 million titles through Kindle Direct Publishing in 2016, which would make the company the largest publishing company in the world.[50] It has run various schemes that fit into legacy publishing models, but with a digital twist. In 1999, "the company quietly leased the rights to a defunct imprint called Weathervane, and repackaged . . . creatures from the black lagoon of the remainder table."[51] The project was short-lived and erased from Amazon's institutional memory. The company returned to the idea while gearing up for the launch of the Kindle with the 2005 launch of Amazon Shorts, later retitled Kindle Singles. The program offered authors the ability to publish "short-form work (2,000–10,000 words, fiction or nonfiction)" that would be "available to customers via PDF, HTML, plain-text e-mail, and they are stored in customers' Digital Lockers forever."[52] The unfortunate mention of permanence in the marketing of an obsolete product demonstrates the precarity of the Kindle within Amazon's ecosystem. The company invested in the scheme in the signature Amazon style of commissioning exclusive content for the launch of the Kindle 2: Danielle Steel penned an exclusive autobiographical essay, "Candy for the Soul," for the launch of Amazon Shorts. In a 2012 editorial for the *New York Times*, Dwight Garner praised the series as "probably the best reason to buy an e-reader in the first place" as the home for "works of long-form journalism that seek out that sweet spot between magazine articles and hardcover books."[53] Enthusiasm for the format led to 1,248 publications in the series, but production slowed in recent years from a peak of 242 titles in 2015 to just 109 in 2017.

Since the Kindle's launch, Amazon launched a further fourteen imprints, ranging from Waterfall Press, a specialist Christian publisher, to Amazon Crossing, which specializes in translations. The imprints that focus on popular trade fiction, including most prominently Thomas & Mercer, a mystery and thriller imprint (911 titles since 2011), and Montlake Romance (1,378 titles since 2011), have had the greatest impact on publishing. Amazon publishes print copies of these texts as part of the promotion, although other retailers have hesitated to stock a book published by their fiercest competitor.[54] Through all these imprints, Amazon has published eight hundred books per year since 2009, making the company one of the twenty largest publishers in the United States.

Coda: Amazon Charts

May 2017 saw the launch of Amazon Charts, a weekly update on the most read and purchased books across the US Amazon web store, the company's latest attempt to disrupt trade publishing orthodoxies. The *Washington Post*—owned by Jeff Bezos, albeit independently of Amazon—included the data in its best-seller lists in January 2018 to provide the first list to account for the largest ebook retailer.[55] Amazon Charts data did not come with any figures but offered an inclusive definition of "book," which encompassed print, ebooks, and Audible. The latter two categories provided observable data for the "Most Read" charts. Kindle Unlimited books were counted "once a customer has read a certain percentage—roughly the length of a free reading sample,"[56] offering a surprising degree of transparency regarding methodology compared to the *New York Times* Best Sellers. The list also includes other features, such as tidbits about the authors' agents, that are unlikely to interest nonindustry members, as well as facts about the books based on the data, including tagging books as "unputdownable" if readers had generally finished the book in a single session, an honor that Sarah J. Maas's *A Court of Wings and Ruins* received in the first week.[57]

The separation of "Most Read" and "Most Sold" reveals the limitations of focusing on sales, which might not map over to what readers consume. I analyzed Amazon Charts' first eighteen weeks between May and September 2017 to show how the two categories work in parallel. Unsurprisingly, both reading and purchasing habits are strongly tied to film and television adaptations: Margaret Atwood's *The Handmaid's Tale* was omnipresent in both lists due to the television show's run from April to June and its availability on Kindle Unlimited. Negative reviews of a film have a chilling effect on Amazon users' purchasing and reading habits. For example, Stephen King's *The Gunslinger* appeared on the "Most Sold" list between May and July 2017 in anticipation of the film's launch on August 20. The book appeared on the "Most Read" lists for four weeks between July 30 and its cinematic release, when interest immediately dissipated. The influence of Kindle Unlimited is stronger for fiction than nonfiction. For example, the *Harry Potter* titles frequently appear in the "Most Read" section, but as the series is exclusively available via Kindle Unlimited, this does not register as purchasing the title. The data demonstrate a distinct split between hype cycles and marketing campaigns fueling purchases and what readers are actually interested in.

Amazon Charts provide a useful counterpoint to the *New York Times* Best Sellers list, a barometer of taste and frequent reference point for Amazon during the development of the Kindle. Thirty-nine percent of fiction and 43 percent of nonfiction that appeared on the *New York Times* Best Sellers list also appeared on Amazon Charts. More books appear on both the *Times* list and Amazon's "Most Read" books (47 percent of fiction titles, 51 percent for nonfiction). Readers are drawn to the same big books—Atwood's *The Handmaid's Tale*, Neil deGrasse Tyson's *Astrophysics for People in a Hurry*, Trevor Noah's *Born a Crime*—but differences emerge in the titles that hover farther down the charts. Some of these variations may be a matter of sampling. For example, Stephen Covey's *The 7 Habits of Highly Effective People* would be classified as a perennial seller by the *New York Times* and would be ignored even if it outsold other titles. Elsewhere the differences show how agency pricing has warped the market. Stuart Wood and Parnell Hall's *Barely Legal* debuted at number 5 on the *New York Times* Best Sellers list on August 13, 2017, but it did not appear on Amazon Charts. In September 2017, the Kindle edition was priced at $17.54, a mere fifteen cents cheaper than the hardcover. Since consumers value digital goods less than the equivalent physical artifact, the lack of discount has boosted print sales at the expense of ebook growth in mainstream publishing.[58]

Amazon released the best-selling Kindle title for each of the first ten years to celebrate its first decade (table 5.2).[59] The international launch of the Kindle in 2009 leans toward a convergence with the print marketplace, but the first two years are more intriguing. The 2008 best seller, *The Complete User's Guide to the Amazing Amazon Kindle*, outsold Khaled Hosseini's *A Thousand Splendid Suns* and Patricia Cornwell's *Book of the Dead* as users wished to learn more about the new platform. The inclusion of Ken Follett's *The Pillars of the Earth*, a novel first published in 1989, is more intriguing. Follett's sequel, *World without End*, was published in October 2007 and was one of the featured $9.99 *New York Times* Best Sellers on the first-generation Kindle's launch page. The prequel outsold the original, as it was both cheaper ($6.39) and longer (1,000 pages), demonstrating the volatility of ebook pricing from the start of the Kindle's life span.[60] The ability to read a dense novel from the backlist for cheap without carrying it around marked a landmark moment for the early adoption of the device as users began to see its advantages over print.

The Kindle's first decade has seen a wave of experimentation and the divergence of print and digital marketplaces. This shift has not necessarily

Table 5.2 Kindle year-by-year best sellers*

Year	Kindle best seller
2007	Ken Follett, *The Pillars of the Earth* (1989)
2008	Stephen Windwalker, *The Complete User's Guide to the Amazing Amazon Kindle* (2008)
2009	Dan Brown, *The Lost Symbol* (2009)
2010	Stieg Larsson, *The Girl with the Dragon Tattoo* (2008)
2011	Kathryn Stockett, *The Help* (2009)
2012	E. L. James, *Fifty Shades of Grey* (2011)
2013	Dan Brown, *Inferno* (2013)
2014	John Green, *The Fault in Our Stars* (2012)
2015	Paula Hawkins, *The Girl on the Train* (2015)
2016	Paula Hawkins, *The Girl on the Train* (2015)
2017	Margaret Atwood, *The Handmaid's Tale* (1985)

*Wheat, "10 Years, 10 Books."

democratized contemporary publishing, as predicted by early advocates of self-publishing. As indicated by the presence of the legacy publishing heavyweights in the "Most Read" section of Amazon Charts, the industry still depends on hype cycles, perennially popular titles, and best sellers. The initial promise of digitization and the backlist did not materialize into substantial new business for legacy publishers. While legacy publishers continue to engage with digital publishing, albeit with the caveats of agency pricing or with other concessions from retailers such as Amazon, the self-publishing and digital-only models will continue to thrive; but if the scaffolding from legacy media companies is removed, there is less evidence to demonstrate that this community is self-sustainable, and much of the cultural record may disappear with the planned obsolescence cycles of digital media. The ebook marketplace exists in a precarious state, still reliant on print-oriented publishers that resist committing to digital publishing. Amazon's infrastructure is essential to maintaining a strong presence for ebooks, but the lack of trust between publishers and Amazon continues to erode public interest in ebooks. The Kindle Store requires both continued investment from print-oriented publishers and the encouragement of digital publishing start-ups to become sustainable.

Books come in a variety of shapes and formats, from large, glossy cookbooks with full-page photos to cheap paperback reprints of classic literature and US letter–size sheet music. Readers form expectations from a book's materiality. For example, a large cookbook will be hardy enough to withstand contact with wet ingredients in the kitchen. Even if a book is blank, its materiality shapes our understanding, as Don McKenzie demonstrated by asking students to determine the contents of internally and externally blank books.[1] Conversely, ebooks are flat representations of a page on a screen and come with no embossed cover or pristine binding. The connection between material and content is broken. Even the most expensive ebook looks the same as a free public domain text. Early excitement about digital publishing suggested a grand revolution with enhanced multimodal books, but such promise could be fulfilled only with an exceptional level of investment. Attempts to build "enhanced" ebooks have been short-lived. Touchpress released critically acclaimed iOS app editions of Shakespeare's *Sonnets* and T. S. Eliot's *The Waste Land* in 2010, but after this success, the company decided to sell off its publishing-related portfolio and rebranded as Amphio in 2016 to focus on "culture, video and tech."[2] Examples like Touchpress reveal the tensions between the perception that digital books should be interactive multimedia packages and the demand from audiences more comfortable with reading linear text.

Amazon approached the challenge of "enhancing" books from a different angle. An individual Kindle device is not just an ebook reader but a single node in a densely connected network.[3] Amazon designed the platform as a service rather than a product, transforming the book from a discrete object into a networked entity. Publishers have remained faithful to the unity of individual books in their transition to digital products, so networks could only be formed as paratext rather than the erosion of barriers between titles proposed in earlier models of digital publishing such as Ted Nelson's Xanadu.[4] In response to these constraints, Amazon developed *paratext services* or features around the text that draw on different APIs (application programming interfaces) and data sources to construct ad hoc information about the book when a reader downloads it. The formulation of paratext services draws on both automation to create paratext and the encapsulation of the kind of fannish activity that Simone Murray calls the "digital literary sphere" within the Kindle ecosystem.[5] The vast range of curated and automated services available mirrors what Paul Benzon terms the DVD's "paratextual 'aesthetic of more' through special features."[6] Prompts to share the book, purchase similar titles, and remain online are pervasive throughout the interfacial paratext, often breaking the act of reading to encourage broader modes of consumption. Rather than building on the openness of the web as a global metatext or the closed models of the early 1990s wave of hypertext fiction and multimedia CD-ROMs, Amazon instead connected Kindle titles to its walled garden and selected third-party sources. This allowed a curated network rather than challenging the fundamental principles of the book trade.

To address ebooks' new features, Ellen McCracken extends Gérard Genette's concept of paratext to categorize the new genres created by ebook platforms through metaphors of gravitational force. McCracken reshaped centripetal and centrifugal forces to define paratext that encourages readers to escape from and remain in the ebook respectively. Centripetal paratext includes "formats, font changes, word searching, and other enhancements," while centrifugal paratext allows readers to "easily engage with blogs, other readers' comments, or an author's web page without putting aside the e-device."[7] While centrifugal paratext is considered the basis of any ebook, centripetal paratext is unique among formats and is often used for marketing purposes. The metaphor of centrifugal force suggests that readers *feel* as if they are leaving the platform, even while they remain within the bounds of the Kindle application. This has been a strength for Amazon, which achieved this balance by developing paratext services to introduce new updatable and dynamic features.

Paratext services can either *input* or *output* data. Input services include the integration of ancillary data sets for X-Ray; Amazon-owned services such as the Kindle storefront, Goodreads, and historically Shelfari; and third-party data from Wikipedia. Output services include integration with Facebook and Twitter, popular highlights, Flashcards, and editing Goodreads. Both input and output paratext services rely on a combination of user-generated content from first- and third-party sources and algorithmic generation. The automation process replaces the work of editors, indexers, and other outsourced workers. While these services cut potential costs for self-published authors, industry professionals are hesitant to develop Kindle-exclusive paratext, as this would create a precedent of creating extra content for individual ebook platforms. Automation potentially solves this impasse, but without an adequate level of quality assurance across the five million titles available, any automation will inevitably lead to an inferior product.

All paratext services are opt-in. The popular highlights and Word Wise, an interlinear definition service, are the only two features that intrude in the framing of the main text, with the remaining features only accessible through pop-up menus. Kindle engineers explored fixing this separation in 2010 with a second electronic paper screen that provided a range of paratext information including progress indicators, navigational aids, cover art, and promotional information (figure 6.1).[8] Paratext is framed as separate from the page, which remains unified outside centripetal forces. Recent software updates have converged toward a minimal interface: Kindle for iPhone 6.7 allows users to view just the main body, and the Kindle 7 discreetly displays the location information in the footer. The ability to layer and separate paratext distinguishes the ebook from print, where running titles, page numbers, and reader annotations are all flattened on a single two-dimensional plane. Amazon introduced new services with each hardware generation to encourage users to upgrade to newer devices, but the core content has remained stable. Partially this is a symptom of feature creep, where the company needs to create new paratext for the sake of demonstrating the innovations of a new device or software.

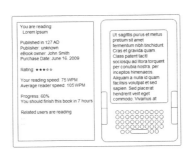

6.1 Service paratext on second screen (adapted from patent)

These new features, such as Page Flip, hide the text behind overwrought navigational interfaces. Page Flip evokes the ability to identify pages by layout, but when the Kindle layout is in flux and is often rendered at point of refresh, the connection between recognition and previously read materials is disconnected. Conversely, Kindle for Amazon Fire expanded the metaphor of the page with the introduction of "Page Turn," animated feedback of a page turning patented by Apple after developing the design for iBooks.[9] Johanna Drucker criticized the iBooks equivalent of Page Turn, arguing that "a too-literal misapprehension of what constitutes the distinctive features of a material form can give rise to a misconceived model of what it should be when redesigned in another media environment."[10] The aesthetic flourish of page turning loses all semantic information about progress or the perceived value of the book.

Despite Bezos's initial claim that you "can't outbook the book," the Kindle Oasis's product page listed paratext services under the title of "and goes beyond the book."[11] Readers can access external information "without losing your place in the book" or calculate how long it will take to complete the book. None of these features offer a significant improvement over print, but combined, they increase the accessibility of a book and offer further chances to engage with fellow readers when compared to the flattened representation of the page emphasized by PDFs. Amazon continuously experimented with how to "outbook the book" with additional automated paratext. For example, Walter Tseng and colleagues from the Reading Experience team experimented with generating word games such as crosswords and anagrams from Kindle titles to improve comprehension and literacy (figure 6.2).[12] The games depended on the integrity of other Kindle paratext services such as Shelfari, X-Ray, dictionaries, and Wikipedia. The reliance on both automation and the affective labor of Shelfari and Wikipedia for Kindle users mirrors the importance of Amazon Web Services and Mechanical Turk to the broader Amazon infrastructure. Both automated and affective labor are contingent and can break down, as my examples in this chapter demonstrate.

Amazon shapes the Kindle's paratext services through the acquisition of companies such as Shelfari and Goodreads and the internal development of services like X-Ray. Tully Barnett argues that these features allow "online friends, acquaintances, and strangers to co-inhabit a book with the reader and can co-construct a reading with more layers and nuances than was available for the printed book."[13] The Kindle Touch marked a transition from early service paratexts to more advanced integration of X-Ray and Goodreads, which Amazon acquired in 2013. Recent e-readers introduced further services including Word Wise, an option for interlinear glosses

a)   b)

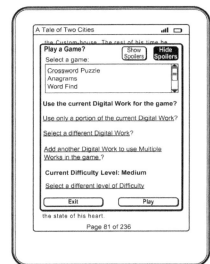

6.2 Tseng et al.'s prototype for automatically generating word games from Kindle titles (adapted from patent)

related to the most difficult words in a book.[14] Amazon marketed X-Ray on the ability to quickly navigate the book through a visual concordance of characters, themes, and locations, and Goodreads is now the primary form of social interaction on the Kindle, replacing custom-built offerings. The shift to Goodreads flattened Amazon's embedded social media from a diverse collection of tools and resources into a social book-shelving site. The consolidation of service paratext restricted how readers interacted with one another on the Kindle but foregrounded an already established reading social network masking a history of failed experiments.

Shopping in the Ebook

By 2014, Lab126 revised its mission statement, indicating an ambition "to make available in less than 60 seconds every book, ever written, in any language, in print or out of print."[15] Delivery in a minute is impossible without integrating the Kindle Store into the reading software. Apple introduced the iPod to complement iTunes and allow seamless integration, but early iPhones could only connect to the iTunes Store via Wi-Fi. The Kindle replicated the iPhone's always-on model by integrating both 3G and Wi-Fi networks but restricted access to a substantial bookshop in exchange for offering broader fast access to the web without charging for data transfer. An always-on bookshop removed several obstacles for continual consumption in app. Amazon even began to sell books from within other titles, although readers can opt out. For example, when readers complete Suzanne Collins's *The Hunger Games*,[16] a pop-up appears that encourages them to purchase *Catching Fire*, the second book in the trilogy. James Petts and colleagues working on the Personalization Platform developed an algorithm to further monetize reading through identifying references to books in a title and introducing links to their product page in the ebook.[17]

The technology team never implemented the algorithm due to the sanctity of the page, but it transformed other parts of the Kindle app to include personalized advertising. Kindle e-readers' home page libraries from the Kindle Touch onward feature a bar of recommended titles by default, with only three of the reader's owned books appearing until the reader clicks through to their full library. Free titles are conspicuously absence in these recommendations, even if a reader primarily consumes this material. Daily deals and best sellers are prominently displayed and can fill up to a third of the screen on dedicated devices. In the default setup for the Kindle Touch 5.3.7.3, the advertised books outnumber the titles in a user's library in volume, although proportionally, owned books take up most of the screen space. Nonetheless, users are constantly reminded that they are only a click away from purchasing new titles.

The Kindle 5 extended the logic of always-on consumption by integrating "special offers," or advertisements on the sleep mode screen, in exchange for a small reduction in the cost of the hardware. Users could purchase the subsidized device for $10 cheaper than full price, with the opportunity to pay $30 to remove the advertisements from the device at a later date. Many advertisements delivered to my devices displayed offers exclusively related to Kindle accessories and purchasing books via the store, but Amazon provides the opportunity for third parties to advertise products (books or otherwise) on the platform.[18] The shift from culturally significant to commodified screen savers demonstrates that Amazon's self-reported customer-centric approach can instead be seen as an attempt to monetize all areas of the Kindle platform.

User Labor

Beyond the storefront, Amazon relies on user-generated content to increase the appeal of its ebook catalog. This is most prominent in Kindle Popular Highlights, discussed in detail in the next chapter, but there are further examples of the company repurposing user labor to create metadata for books through Shelfari. Josh Hug and Kevin Beukelman, two former employees of RealNetworks, an early audio streaming service, founded Shelfari as a social network for bibliophiles in late 2006. Hug and Beukelman wanted to compete with LibraryThing, launched by Tim Spalding in 2005, by funding a social reading platform through Amazon affiliate links.[19] Amazon eventually purchased the start-up in 2008 to form the foundations of the "book extras" function after investing $1 million in the company in 2007.[20] More recent changes in the Kindle platform suggest that this was a forerunner of the consolidation of reading-related activities to Goodreads, an acquisition that was initially positioned as independent from Amazon's core activities but has become more integrated into the platform with each new hardware launch. The six-year period of Shelfari's integration into the Kindle platform helps illuminate how these paratext services survive while Amazon considered them valuable and how the company retains the most useful aspects and deletes the less desirable.

Shelfari data formed the basis of the Kindle's "book extras" feature until the introduction of "About the Book" and integration of Goodreads in 2014. "Book extras" contained a range of trivia related to the title including a synopsis, awards, and brief descriptions of characters. A small disclaimer at the top of the pop-up started: "This content comes from Shelfari, the editable book encyclopedia." The feature is only available in books downloaded before the introduction of "About the Book." Newer titles integrate data from Goodreads, and any extra contextual information in the "X-Ray" sidebar appears directly from Wikipedia, removing any book-specific information. While the switch removed several core features of Shelfari, it also decreased redundancy between features present on both platforms, including outlining characters and awards.

Shelfari was initially kept separate from the main Amazon services before its integration into the Kindle reading system. This follows the example of both the Internet Movie Database (IMDb) and Twitch.tv, which were acquired by Amazon in 1998 and 2014 respectively, with press releases indicating that the services would remain separate from Amazon's primary businesses. While both sites remain independent through mid-2017, there has been an increased level of integration between primary and secondary businesses. In the case of IMDb, the vast cache of actors, trivia, and other film-related data has been used as part of "X-Ray for Movies and TV shows," a service for Amazon Video that replicates the functionality of Kindle X-Ray for visual content. Twitch.tv's independence has already been challenged by the launch of Twitch Prime, linked to Amazon Prime accounts.

Shelfari remained semiautonomous from the Kindle, as directly editing content from the reading system was never possible. Users would need to sign in to the service via a web browser to update any incorrect information. The social network functioned primarily in a similar way to Goodreads, allowing users to create virtual bookshelves and review content in a social network dedicated to book reading. In late 2009, Amazon made a major alteration to the design of Shelfari pages through a beta editable book details page.[21] Users were now directed to produce information on specific topics such as "description," "ridiculously simplified synopsis," brief descriptions of characters, bibliographic information, quotations, themes, interpretation, and other paratext that might be expected in a critical edition.[22] Amazon changed Shelfari from a third-party marketing tool for affiliate sales to a labor force for an optional paratext feature. The user base was not large enough to undertake this work in any uniform fashion, leaving the "Book Extras" page uneven across ebooks.

The integration of user-generated content into the "authorized" space of the book masked the underlying exploitative wiki-based labor practices on sites such as Shelfari. Users were encouraged with frequent references to editing pages or seeing their history. Even though Shelfari offered a direct login from Amazon accounts, no clear information indicated that any edits on the website would be scraped for inclusion in commercial ebooks. New pages were left empty, and users were expected to fill them in with a series of edits. As a consequence, the pages for popular books such as the *Harry Potter* series were replete with relevant information and minutiae, while many pages were left empty. The quality of the final product was variable and based on the free labor of volunteers. This was further complicated by the presence of "Shelfari librarians," who monitored changes and often rejected changes made by Shelfari staff.[23] The community policing and affective labor behind Shelfari librarians ensured a baseline for quality, but without further investment from either publishers or Amazon, the resource was inconsistent and dependent on the whims of a book's fan base.

In 2017, Amazon closed the remaining Kindle Popular Highlights and Shelfari services to consolidate reading social networks. Numbers talk; Goodreads boasts over twenty million active users. After resisting integration, the service's "To Read" lists and a feed of friends' activity appeared on the Kindle home screen for users.[24] This new feature lacked the ability to talk about the book without exiting the primary reading interface or edit the data about a book, as is possible with Shelfari. Users can access the full range of Goodreads services through a link, but this remains at a distance to the Kindle content beyond the home page. The new social infrastructure lacked the granularity of the separate social networks available to readers beforehand. Users could no longer directly influence on the information "About the Book," and Goodreads encourages them to comment on pages rather than specific quotations.

The restructuring also created borders between the distinct parts of Amazon's service paratext. Rather than gravitating around a centripetal force, users needed to leave the main book interface to access new features related to the book. For example, the Kindle for Fire OS 10.29, one of the most feature-rich reading systems, separates the Kindle Store, Goodreads, Audible, Wish Lists, Word Runner, and Flashcards into discrete entities. Readers could access a wealth of extra information about a book or otherwise view or hear the book in a different form, but this needed to be a conscious decision rather than accidentally clicking on the wrong option. The separation of different paratext service indicates Amazon's acknowledgment that the platform's feature creep challenged the unity of a discrete book.

Automation

While its reliance on user labor for paratext services has diminished, Amazon continues to use automation as a remedy for the lack of platform-exclusive content from publishers. Many of these services for the Kindle rely on text processing, which requires high competencies in natural language processing, from the ability to deduce the meaning of a word from context to disambiguation of words and correctly identifying parts of speech.[25] The algorithms and data structures underpinning these efforts remain proprietary, but errors in available tools show that Amazon is unlikely to have invested the resources into refining the automation to avoid incorrect markup for a corpus featuring billions of words, despite investment in these areas to develop the Alexa voice assistant ecosystem. Three major services—the dictionary, X-Ray indexing, and ebook searches—depend heavily on automation to provide users with adequate definitions and navigation.

The dictionary function suffers from both presentational and semantic issues. The feature is emphasized by a pop-up box that appears with a definition if a user highlights a word on all but the Kindle 1. If a definition is too short, multiple words are displayed to fill the space. For example, when searching for the definition of "cofounder" in "EDWIN CATMULL. A cofounder of Pixar and later a Disney Executive,"[26] the two-line definition states:

co·found·er n. a joint founder, co-found v,

co·func·tion n. [MATHEMATICS] the trigonometric[27]

This is followed by a prompt for users to view the definition with the dictionary ebook. Users will likely recognize "cofunction" as a separate definition rather than an extension of the looked-up word. Nonetheless, the presentational quirk could be avoided if Amazon loaded the dictionary as a database rather than pulling content from a regular ebook without checking for overlapping definitions. Since this would require a different content license and more investment, the lack of nuance for this feature demonstrates Amazon's inability to develop features that would benefit the user unless they offer a substantial payoff in data collection or audience development.

In an extensive analysis of the Kindle's dictionary mechanism, two lexicographers, Theo Bothma and D. J. Prinsloo, document a smorgasbord of errors in the automated tagging system as the result of incorrect links between words and definitions.[28] Automated dictionaries require accurate tagging, particularly with identifying lemmas, or the "canonical" form of a word. For example, the word "men" does not have its own dictionary entry but should redirect to the lemma "man" with a note that "men" is the plural form. The researchers found several major parsing errors. For example, "who's" correctly linked to "who," but if the first letter was capitalized, the algorithm rendered the whole word in uppercase, leading to a definition of "World Health Organization" instead. Other errors are more inexplicable, including "but" linking to "and" as well as "lay" changing to "burn."[29] Bothma and Prinsloo could not identify the cause of these errors, but their analysis points toward some significant fissures in the dictionary algorithm. Since 2013, Amazon has invested substantially in voice recognition for Alexa, which requires more nuanced natural language processing to respond correctly to questions. The Kindle's dictionary errors point toward this infrastructure not being integrated into the ebook services, revealing its place in the Amazon hierarchy.

If the dictionary does not contain a definition, which is often the case for proper nouns such as famous people or companies, Wikipedia is the fallback. Users can also search for phrases via Wikipedia where the dictionary only defines a single word. The website mixes Amazon's predilection for both automation and user labor. Kindle integration endorses Wikipedia's quality despite frequent controversies regarding its commitment to "neutral points of view" and uneven coverage of subjects according to users' interests.[30] Where multiple instances of the same name exist, users are presented with the disambiguation page. For example, a search for "Bistritz" in *Dracula* links to a page that lists several locations across Romania and the Czech Republic, where readers unfamiliar with the novel's context may not know that the top result in Transylvania is the likely destination.[31]

Despite these limitations, sideloading Wikipedia and the dictionaries is cheaper for both platforms and publishers, although without careful NLP and human auditing to ensure that the correct reference always appears, the resource can only be as valuable as the "I'm feeling lucky" result for each definition.[32] Paratext services that update can relieve the burden of updating an ebook's metadata, but the system is only as reliable as the data and algorithms underpinning it.[33] The Kindle's service paratexts are often superficial and therefore lead to errant responses.

When a word might have multiple definitions, the algorithm does not flag the word for review to ensure the most accurate definition is returned, but the first result in the chosen dictionary appears by default. For example, on my Kindle 2, when I click on "Lee," the software returns the first biographical result for the surname Lee in the dictionary ("**Lee**[1] Ann [1736–84] U.S. religious leader . . .")[34] rather than noting the word is a popular fore- and surname. Proper nouns can be disambiguated through context, which could be provided by the publisher or otherwise deduced by the text, but Amazon's efforts largely depend on the available external data. Despite the issues with developing sophisticated NLP techniques for dictionary identification, Amazon was confident in its service infrastructure to correctly identify definitions through a combination of machine learning and Mechanical Turk volunteers.[35] Daniel Rausch, a publisher who was hired by Amazon to lead Kindle product management, filed a patent in 2010 that used the dictionary extensively as a service. Rausch detailed Amazon's ability to build vocabulary tests, diachronic analysis of meaning changes, and recommendations for titles using the word in the same sense (figure 6.3). When combined with demographic data including reading level, the service paratext would also alter the text to adjust to the literacy of the reader.[36] This intrusive service exists only in the theoretical realm of patents, not least because editing texts would present challenges with intellectual property. All evidence of language-based automation also demonstrates that attempts to alter the text would likely lead to incorrectly changed material.

Amazon's marketing for X-Ray states that the feature "lets you explore the 'bones of a book.' You can also view more detailed information from Wikipedia and from Shelfari, Amazon's community-powered encyclopaedia for book lovers."[37] X-Ray uses a "term frequency–inverse document frequency (TF-IDF)" algorithm to determine which terms are significant enough to index rather than more nuanced or human-curated mechanisms.[38] As the name suggests, the Kindle's TD-IDF compares how frequently a word appears in a text with other Kindle titles. The algorithm can identify unusual terms but would not necessarily identify common terms

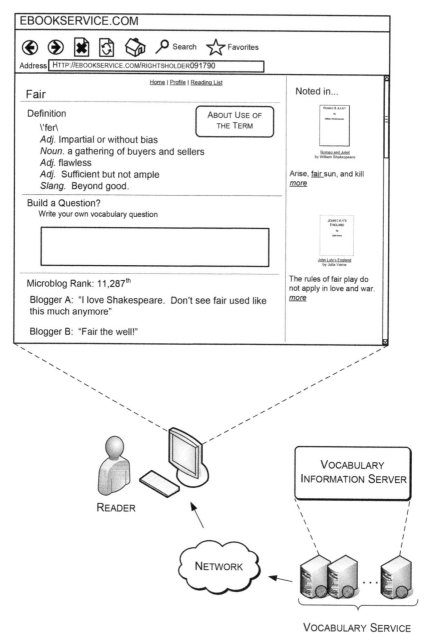

6.3 Amazon's prototype "vocabulary service" (adapted from patent). Source: Killalea and Hamaker, Disambiguation of term meaning.

such as "God" or "books" that might be central to a particular title. Amazon discourages the use of a print index in favor of X-Ray. Jan Wright questions the intellectual property of this arrangement: "Who owns the X-Ray file: the author, Amazon, the publisher?"[39] This question can be extended to multiple elements of the automated Kindle infrastructure. Elsey notes that the licensing mess associated with backlist titles—ensuring ebook edition rights for photographs, illustrations, and quotations—creates an extra burden.[40] Automated paratext exacerbates the challenges of both licensing and updatability, since it takes agency from the publisher, which may no longer control the overall quality of its project despite an association with all the material provided by the platforms.

Wright concludes that X-Ray lacks the finer detail made possible through a carefully curated index.[41] For example, in Richard Wrangham's *Catching Fire*, indexes contain relational information allowing a reader to identify passages on "fat" and more specifically on the relationship between "fat" and "energy."[42] Despite this lack of complexity in mapping relationships, the X-Ray format is technically sophisticated compared to other paratext services after Amazon changed the storage medium from JSON to SQL, a database language that emphasizes relationships between entities. X-Ray files now construct relationships between excerpts, book locations, concepts, and definitions to ensure information is delivered consistently across reading systems. The data are still prepopulated, however, and users need to update the content manually or through an update pushed by Amazon and the publisher. Mistakes are common, as descriptions frequently come from Wikipedia, leading to awkward references to apple trees in place of Apple Inc., or Muhammad the Prophet rather than a character called Muhammad. Human intervention could catch these errors, although it would require understanding the context, and this would be an additional cost for publishers or Amazon.

Of the 210 titles available for the Kindle that appeared on Amazon Charts lists between May and September 2017, around 70 percent use X-Ray. Fiction is more likely (80 percent) to feature the function than nonfiction (64 percent). Print versions of nonfiction titles often include an index, which is easier to convert to an ebook, while fiction may benefit from this conceptual map if automated even when the print edition does not require an index. No correlation exists between the publisher's investment in a book and the appearance of an X-Ray index, as prominent publications such as Hillary Clinton's *What Happened* launched without the feature. X-Ray is not universal; since it requires publishers to create a dedicated index for the Kindle, this is unsurprising. Amazon's rejection of broader cross compatibility reduces the number of features available compared to competitor platforms, which do not have the same user base, ensuring development is limited. This limits the potential of ebooks over-all, as there is no one platform where innovation is profitable for publisher or platform.

Amazon promoted X-Ray's ability to visualize the book on a one-dimensional plane, showing where characters, places, and themes appear across the novel.[43] Readers can use this information to ascertain how important a character or theme is to the book, although in fiction this led to spoilers if a character reappears after a lengthy absence from the narra-tive.[44] Since the process is automated, clustering can occur in interesting ways. For example, in Donna Tartt's *The Goldfinch*, the relational database entries from excerpts can be 3,835 bytes long and contain as many as ten entities (three locations and seven characters).[45] If an entity is referenced multiple times in a single passage, the data are amalgamated into a single reference. For instance, Hobie appears in the excerpt but is continuously highlighted for a much larger region of the text. Likewise, the indexing catches the variations between "Andy," "Andy's," and "Andy Barbour." The index algorithm is greedy, matching the garbled phrase "Andy's death, Death in general) if I thought a familiar person came to meet us at the door, because—writing this now, I'm close to tears—I think of poor Andy" as a single instance because of how Amazon's search tool splits the blocks of text into the discrete chunks of text as locations.[46] The index therefore returns entries in proximity rather than revealing multiple instances in short passages. Since the algorithm iterates the overlap detection mecha-nism, results can encapsulate lengthy passages unintentionally.

The in-text search feature reveals the limitations of Amazon's natural language processing facilities.[47] A search for "man" in Milton's *Paradise Lost* returns all words in the text containing "man," including "manner," "commander," "mans," and "Adamantine," even when punctuation or white space is included at the beginning or end of the word.[48] The only exception comes from "man!" which only matches exact results, includ-ing punctuation. While the patterns appear to suggest that the search results favor "man" as a prefix, returning "Adamantine" demonstrates that the pattern also matches the term in the middle of a word. If white space is added to both sides of the word to indicate searching for the word in isolation, the results are greedier, returning "command" and other words not present in the original search. "Man." and "man?" follow the same patterns respectively. This comes at a cost, as any other search for "man" will not catch this in the results because the exclamation mark is inextricably bound to the word. Likewise, any instances of "man" at the end of a sentence are not included owing to the proximity of a punctuation mark. Due to this awkward mix of part-of-speech tagging without associated documentation to explain discrepancies, the search function is highly volatile and cannot return reliable results. Automation has become a crutch for Amazon in the harsh reality of publishers' hesitance to create content optimized for the Kindle. These extra features are useful marketing tools, but without further investment and quality control, the invisible biases and limitations of the tools hinder reader interpretation, thus running counter to their designed use.

The natural language struggles are matched by further challenges in constructing new navigation idioms with the flat screen. In one instance, Amazon considered extending the X-Ray/spine metaphor of the book further through a new navigation tool described in the patent "Edge navigation user interface."[49] Scott Dixon, a Kindle Software Development Kit (SDK) engineer, conceptualized X-Ray as the literal spine of three-dimensional book interface (figure 6.4). The metaphorical use of three-dimensional space to navigate the book was just one of several experiments, although it was the most grounded in physical metaphors. The patent contains several images of more complex navigational tropes that rely on users' knowledge of multitouch interfaces. Augmenting the book is a central element of the patent's background. Dixon suggests that "as electronic devices continue to evolve, there remains a need for improving a reader's ability to interact with these devices."[50] The X-Ray metaphor requires further visual elements to enhance the reader's understanding of the ebook's representation of a two-dimensional object. This intervention sought to use the visualizations as a direct navigational tool. Unfortunately, this was never integrated and was superseded by the later addition of Page Flip as a two-dimensional version of the same trope. Alongside other new navigation elements and counter to improving the automation of X-Ray, search, and other features, these new paratext features emphasize feature creep and innovation. The reading space of the Kindle has remained consistent over its first decade, but new paratext services serve to justify yearly updates on the marketing copy for the product page. Hardware innovations have been glacial, so minor software adjustments and new services represent the best opportunity for marketing.

Synchronizing Media

While automation is used primarily for metadata production, it has been most successful in linking media. This refashioning of the text as a malleable object to be reused in various contexts was one of the strengths of the

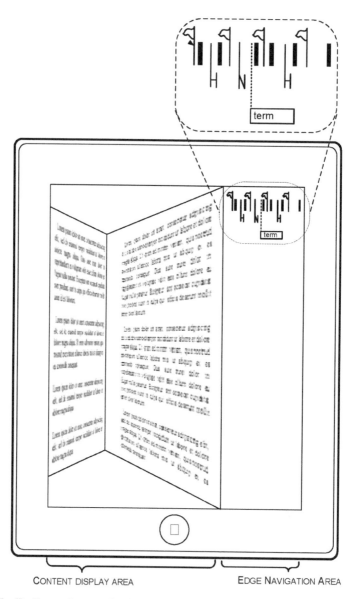

6.4 The Kindle team's vision for three-dimensional navigation using a multitouch interface (adapted from patent). Source: Dixon, Edge navigation user interface, figure 3.

ebook's promise. Platform developers were early to explore this promise. For example, in 2009 Intel launched its own e-reader, which specialized in text-to-speech conversion for users with visual impairments.[51] The Intel Reader scanned text provided by readers with optical character recognition. The Digital Accessible Information System (DAISY) standard provided its framework, but data could also be formatted in EPUB to store any relevant paratext. A high-quality marked-up file improves the quality of text-to-speech conversion, and EPUB or the Kindle file formats represented a robust commercial format rather than using a more open-source format such as TEI (Text Encoding Initiative), which prioritizes semantics over representation. Ebooks with full tagging offer untapped potential, with humans and machines equally able to read the text. While the semantic potential of natural language processing has not been fulfilled on the Kindle, Amazon has invested more substantially in linking audio and ebook implementations of the same book.

The company experimented with using paratext services to enhance the reading experience with the launch of Word Runner exclusively on Android-based Kindle apps including the Fire. Amazon describes Word Runner as "a fun new way to read faster. It keeps your eyes focused on the center of the page and brings each word right to where your eyes already are."[52] This speed-reading concept harks back to Bob Brown's *The Readies* but attempts to use an algorithm to improve on the concept by slowing down for difficult words.[53] Amazon employs gamification to encourage readers to use the feature. Readers are encouraged to share their speed-reading results on Twitter and Facebook, and each chapter is segmented according to how long it would take the reader to complete it on the basis of their average reading speed and the time-saving potential of using Word Runner to speed-read the book. The feature emphasizes speed over comprehension, which goes without mention in the marketing for Word Runner. The research into similar applications suggests that there "is probably no quick fix for circumventing the temporal demands of reading without a cost to some aspect of comprehension."[54] The feature therefore exists as another paratext service designed for fun rather than function. The emphasis of such features is often to separate the Kindle platform from others for marketing purposes.

The link between audio and text was more productive. The Kindle 2 courted controversy with its built-in text-to-speech capabilities when the Authors Guild immediately responded to the feature by arguing that it breached copyright law, since Amazon did not own audio rights.[55] In a press release responding to the claims, Amazon rebutted: "Kindle 2's experimental text-to-speech feature is legal: no copy is made, no derivative work is created, and no performance is being given"[56] Amazon continued to affirm that it sells audiobooks through Audible and the decision to compete against itself was counterintuitive.[57] The response indicates a distinction between the automated and curated, as the press release emphasizes the benefits of human intervention over algorithmic creation. Despite this and the company's framing as a customer-centric business, algorithms dominate many paratext services. The text-to-speech feature complements rather than replaces the Audible version of the text, as users who wish to have a fuller experience will choose to purchase the audiobook. In 2019 the introduction of Audible Captions reignited the same controversy, but in reverse, when users could view the written text of an audiobook.

The flagship tenth-anniversary release of the luxury Kindle Oasis introduced the first e-reader to offer Audible integration despite earlier use of audio ports on dedicated hardware. The decision was a core separator between the basic and luxury devices. The text-to-speech controversy led to a shift in Amazon's approach to audio with dedicated devices. All Kindles launched before the Paperwhite in 2012 featured 3.5 mm audio ports. The first-generation device offered an "experimental" MP3 player, and subsequent iterations used the feature for text-to-speech. Amazon phased out the software and hardware capability with the Paperwhite, and this only returned with the Oasis through integration with Bluetooth headphones or speakers, a requirement because of the device's waterproofing.

The second revelation from the announcement—the integration of Audible with the Kindle Oasis—highlights the increased fragmentation of the Kindle ecosystem. Mobile device implementations of the Kindle app have offered a "read and listen" function that allows users to access Audible content from within the Kindle app. The Kindle for Android app has further advantages over the iOS implementation, as it borrows from the Fire software, which currently offers the greatest variety in paratext services. Kindle in Motion, the integration of animated GIFs into Kindle titles, is available only for Android and iOS, not on the dedicated hardware or the desktop software packages available for PC or Mac. The Mac version went two years without an update from June 2015 to September 2017. We can rank the prioritization of hardware and software as follows:

1. Kindle for Fire OS (and Android derivatives)
2. Kindle for iOS58
3. Flagship Kindle device
4. Other dedicated hardware (descending according to age of device)
5. Kindle for Mac/PC

This hierarchy establishes Amazon's strategic priorities according to what hardware it updates most frequently. As ebook reading has expanded from dedicated hardware to multifunctional devices including the

Amazon Fire, e-readers have been left behind in the rollout of new para-text services, although users can still access the same range of titles across hardware configurations. The limitations of electronic paper screens and requirements for low battery consumption determine this separation. The lack of interest in Kindle for Mac/PC reveals a dilemma: why do the most powerful computers have the worst versions of the reading system? Simple: a lack of users. Ebooks are designed to read on a smaller screen.

Beyond the tiered provision of services, the Audible-Kindle integra-tion completes the feedback loop of paratext services and text. Amazon largely runs Audible and the Kindle as two discrete business lines.[58] By offering users the opportunity to connect the two, the Kindle book becomes an additional paratext service of the Audible content, and vice versa. The Whispersync for Voice scheme codifies the link between the two even outside their respective software packages. The feature extends the Whis-persync functionality to different media by allowing a user to read part of an ebook and then sync up to the exact location with the audiobook.[59] This mechanism only functions if the two media work together through curated metadata. In this instance, Amazon has invested in ensuring that Whispersync effectively traces the relative position of the reader in both Audible and the Kindle. Amazon's scale and dominance in both ebook and audiobook platforms allow the company to build cross-media links, while rivals do not have the same infrastructure. The company can afford to pro-vide poor-quality automated services at the periphery if it offers unique features that are more important to customers' concerns, and the links between Audible and Kindle certainly offer a good incentive.

The decline of large publishers' interest in ebooks since 2011 with the introduction of agency pricing has created a dilemma in marketing ebooks. The rhetoric of "outbooking the book" is difficult to actualize if ebooks are perceived as second-class citizens compared to print. Automa-tion of paratext services has become a cornerstone of Amazon's strategy for enhancing ebooks while occasionally using the vast consumption data set the company has captured. While not always successful, the practice demonstrates how platforms can create a baseline for paratext where authors and publishers might not have the resources. The more substantial recastings of the ebook-as-text have led to greater success in turning the container into the paratext in the form of the links between Word Runner, Audible, and the base Kindle reading application. The three media work in tandem to create different visual or auditory experiences that build on one another. The value of augmentation thus comes from how Amazon can build an infrastructure around the text that allows readers to create the most appropriate method of consumption for their needs.

The constant addition of new paratext services has become a bugbear for many users. This has led some to maintain support for their older devices, which have not been updated to add these new features. Others latched on to a proposed India-only version of the Android app called "Kindle Lite." The app was advertised as taking up just two megabytes of space and facilitating data transfer on 2G networks.[60] As a compromise, Amazon stripped features such as Goodreads and Word Runner to enhance performance, acknowledging that the features were not a core part of the platform. Amazon's cross-media integration of Audible and Kindle runs counter to the weaker attempts at automation of services including indexing and searching. The two core innovations of digital publishing platforms have been the introduction of manipulable text and the ability to use it to link different media into a coherent book unit. Not all of Amazon's paratext service experiments have been successful, but as the platform matured, a range of tools has been whittled down to the elements users are most interested in. Nonetheless, the broader method of paratext services, drawn from both user and automated labor, enabled Amazon to attempt to "outbook the book" while working in an environment where publishers are unlikely to invest extra resource in producing customized Kindle titles.

Dog-eared pages, highlights, marginal notes, ripped-out pages, physically copied-and-pasted remixes: we have endless ways to interact with a book that will influence how future readers interpret the same text. Beyond the object, readers arrange discussion clubs; attend talks, festivals, and communal readings; and queue for hours to briefly chat with an author and receive a signed copy of a prized edition. While we no longer read aloud by default, we rarely consume books in isolation. The rise of social media allows readers to find a community dedicated to discussing their favorite publications, whether on a platform such as the Kindle or off-site on Twitter.

Amazon used social reading to build its data on consumption by tracking the actions of fifty million registered Kindle users. Whispersync collects data about individuals' Kindle reading habits, both passively through recording reading patterns and actively through storing private or shared highlights and notes. The Reading, Mining and Analytics team formed in 2011 to explore how data might be used for internal consumer profiling and its potential as a marketing tool for demonstrating reader engagement, mirroring an earlier shift from professional to customer-submitted reviews.[1] Between 2009 and 2017, the company made a sliver of these data publicly available via the Kindle Popular Highlights website. The service featured a historical list of the million most popular highlights from 2014, but Amazon also released more granular data about readers' consumption of individual titles. The publicly available data did not reveal broader trends in contemporary literary culture but rather showed how Amazon has formed shared reading on the platform by algorithmically filtering the billions of highlights stored on its servers. The scale of social reading on the Kindle invites closer scrutiny of how the service might shape our understanding of contemporary publishing.

Users receive frequent prompts to share on the platform. The Kindle 1 featured "My Clippings," a function "to capture your favorite quotes and share with others."[2] The Reading Experience team experimented with other forms of user interaction, including prototyping in-app book clubs according to region, age, education level, or profession.[3] The idea was never implemented, but traces remain in the Kindle's social infrastructure, such as the Popular Highlights website, where users were encouraged to follow readers with similar tastes to track what they read and highlighted. The most direct implementation of the book club came in the form of supplementary PDFs with questions for book clubs in 2012.[4]

Amazon's social reading strategy was solidified with the Kindle 2. The Reading Experience team listened to feedback about web access to personal "clippings" and was tasked with creating a website for organizing users' highlights and notes. Deanna Glaze designed several prototypes for the platform to emphasize three main activities: "Read. Review. Remember."[5] The home page featured a prominent "Daily Review" flash card to encourage users to review their previous highlights when entering the site. The website offered tools for exporting clippings and tracking reading progress by noting completion of books or desire to pick up new titles. The prototype downplayed sharing through adopting a broadcast model in early iterations. Users were encouraged to "publish" highlights while noting the number of their "subscribers" and only prompting subscriptions to books. Reciprocity was prioritized at launch, with users following one another with the ability to comment on highlights from other users.

Shared highlights were opt-in, and users could individually select what would remain private or be seen by a wider audience. The Kindle Popular Highlights website offered private access to users' personal clippings and displayed shared quotations from both individuals and in aggregate. The most frequently shared passages were prominently displayed on the home page, with the ability to click through to a dedicated highlights page linked to an ebook's ASIN, leading to multiple individual pages for each digital edition of a title. The dedicated pages featured a selection of five popular highlights in aggregate and a live feed of recently shared quotations and notes. Access through the reading system would offer more granular data in the form of the ten most popular highlights for a title. Readers who follow others can see their shared annotations when reading the same book.

Pride and Prejudice

by Jane Austen

Chapter 1

It is a truth universally
acknowledged, that a single
man in possession of a good
fortune, must be in want of a
wife.

7.1 An example of a popular highlight from Jane Austen's *Pride and Prejudice* (2007). Screenshot from Kindle for PC 1.23.1.

Kindle Popular Highlights hints at the scale of Amazon's data surveillance practices. Titles such as Victor Hugo's *Les Misérables* and the English Standard Version Bible feature over a million highlights. The eight hundred ebooks discussed in this chapter have received a cumulative twenty-five million annotations. Many titles are not as popular as those discussed here, but overall, Amazon has a data set containing billions of shared highlights, with an even larger cache of saved "clippings" that users elected to keep private but store via Whispersync. The data asymmetry between Amazon and the public grew in mid-2014, when the list of most shared passages was removed from the Kindle Popular Highlights website.[6] The list had been static since the last update in 2012, but it had become a "spine" for navigating the website and discovering popular Kindle titles. Searching via the site or using exact ASINs allowed users to find individual product pages, but this required preexisting knowledge of the book's existence.

The closure of Kindle Popular Highlights in 2017 marked a turning point in Amazon's public-facing services. While the company has blocked public access to the website, it continues to develop new methods for analyzing and using its large data sets to model consumption, including personalizing advertisements in print-on-demand books according to a user's metadata profile to defray costs.[7] Understanding what readers are interested in and how far through a book they will get, data only available through profiling digital consumption, creates more accurate profiles for personalization. Zuboff argues that the term "personalization" under surveillance capitalism is contradictory, as "it defiles, ignores, overrides, and displaces everything about you and me that is personal."[8] Since the data are aggregated, they do not reflect individual habits as much as a homogeneous "audience." Publishers have the same level of access as the general public due to Amazon's self-interest in surveillance practices when completion rates and most highlighted passages might inform editorial and marketing developments. But what value do these data have? Can shared highlights provide insight into social reading?

Previous answers to these questions avoid the issues of scale and the limitations within the Popular Highlights data set with smaller case studies of shared annotation patterns in *Sherlock Holmes*, public domain works, or the most popular titles.[9] These projects have largely ignored the integrity of the public data sources by focusing on manageable subsets to rein in the potential for chaos. The aggregated and individual highlights show Amazon's mediation of shared reading and how this might influence users' understanding of a book, just as with an annotated copy of a library book. With access to the reading patterns of individuals and the aggregated list of ten popular highlights, we can see the influence of previous readers' interests in shaping new interpretations. Kindle Popular Highlights and associated metrics offer a form of virality akin to retweeting, where resharing amplifies the visibility of a particular passage's sentiment. The algorithmically mediated selection of specific individual and aggregated highlights reflects Amazon's marketing agenda. Authors can use the public slice of Kindle Popular Highlights to assess what material readers engage with and write more on that subject. The market-led focus is reflected in Bezos's boast in a letter to shareholders that "over a thousand independent authors surpassed $100,000 in royalties in 2017 through Kindle Direct Publishing."[10]

The Reading Experience team collaborated with the Reading, Mining and Analytics team to explore how to integrate other social reading elements into the platform. The development of the @author scheme in 2011 allowed readers to post questions to twelve authors through their ebooks or an interface on the Amazon website.[11] A beta version launched in 2011, and the service was live for five years, despite never expanding beyond the initial twelve beta testers.[12] @author used Twitter's @-mentioning system, notifying the author on Twitter whenever a user asked a question via the reading system. Responses were posted on the @author_posts Twitter account, with 1,256 recorded responses between August 2011 and November 2012. Traces of the project were removed in January 2016, although remnants still appear in the Kindle Touch's system files, which launched alongside @author. The Touch's firmware (5.0.0) handled sideloaded content through XML, and several templates were bundled with the device to render the metadata. A file called "stock-authorpage" contains the template for the "About the Book" sidebar and includes an "answersList" with templates for questions, answers, and tracking responses. @author's failure came from replicating Twitter's functionality without adding any benefits. Users flocked to the social media platform to interact with celebrities, including authors, and Amazon's service increased the number of steps required to post to Twitter, dooming the scheme.

Looking at social reading platforms offers a healthy corrective to critics who dismiss digital publishing as inferior to print.[13] Matt Hayler notes that the relationship between print and digital media cannot be reduced to a simplistic binary, since the two media forms are deeply intertwined.[14] Studies of the relative merits of print and digital reading focus on the attention economy, pitting the constant push alerts of mobile devices against an idealized form of distraction-free reading. Environmental factors are necessarily more complicated, and sociality is an important part of the experience. Amazon controls the relationship between readers, ebooks, and other users through its interface and consequently shifts many copy-specific elements of reading—annotations, bookmarks, and so forth—into algorithmically mediated networked experiences. Such mechanisms are essential, since social reading requires annotations to appear across multiple copies of a publication rather than existing in one physical volume.

The shared highlights infrastructure was designed to present different content according to the audience. Figure 7.2 distinguishes between users who have purchased a copy of the text and "prospective customers" who may be browsing Kindle Popular Highlights to identify a title of interest. Users could browse popular titles and discover what passages other readers were highlighting. Each page also featured a link to purchase the title on the Kindle Store. The Public Highlights website was only an important resource for as long as it was a useful marketing tool for the company. Once its marketing potential diminished, it was inevitable that Amazon's desire for secrecy would kick in once more. This attitude toward potentially valuable data sets demonstrates the precarious nature of researching trends in contemporary digital reading.

The extent of the data gap became apparent in 2015, when Amazon introduced "About the Book" as a pop-up that appears when a reader opens an ebook for the first time. The sidebar publicly revealed the scale of highlighting activity alongside information replicating the role of a print book's cover, including a publisher-provided blurb, links to reviews and related titles, and an estimate of reading time. Amazon supplemented this pop-up menu with statistics about shared highlights. For example, an edition of *Dracula* featured "4,673 passages [which] have been highlighted 451,791 times."[15] "About the Book" compiles at point of download and remains static until the user requests a new copy of the book. Its statistics reveal a lower bound of Amazon's extensive surveillance practices, since it

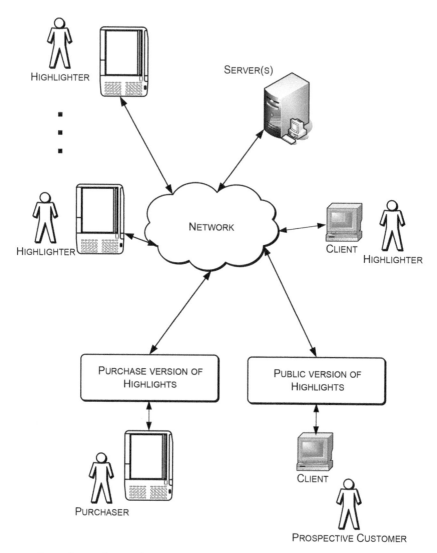

7.2 Patent figure showing Amazon's model for shared annotations (adapted from patent). Source: Tom Killalea et al., Aggregation of highlights, US Patent 9,087,032, filed January 26, 2009, and issued July 21, 2015, sheet 1.

is out of date once the reader receives the data. In figure 7.3, I compare the percentage of shared passages accessible through the Popular Highlights feature with the total reported number of annotations in "About the Book" in eight hundred titles. Readers can only see ten unique shared passages for each title. If an ebook features fewer than ten public annotations, nothing is displayed, ensuring no title features comprehensive information.

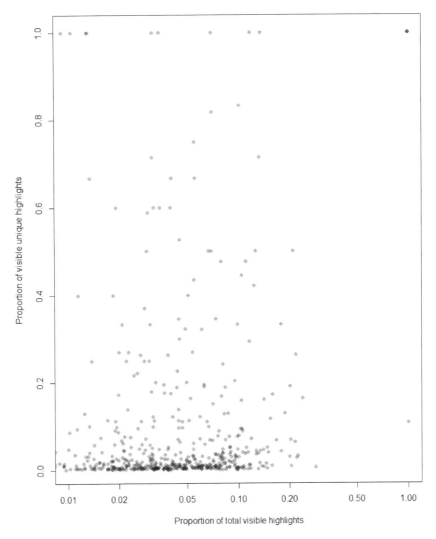

Proportion of visible unique highlights

Proportion of total visible highlights

7.3 Proportion of visible unique and total highlights

Displaying ten popular highlights encourages readers to use the sharing features. Joseph Reagle Jr. argues that a stub, a near-empty page on Wikipedia, encourages users to add new content more effectively than a nonexistent page.[16] Likewise, Kindle users share prehighlighted passages as the interface reminds them that this is an option. Despite the influence of the visible annotations, even large samples from popular books can only account for, on average, 10 percent of highlighting activity. Public highlights reveal a hive mind shaped by corporate interests and algorithms rather than demonstrating the breadth of reading on the Kindle. In more popular books, these annotations perpetuate interest, as it is unlikely that new passages will be highlighted thousands of times without the support of appearing as a shared quotation by default. Amazon's algorithmic mediation of the process further shapes the perception of the text, as the company can elect to remove the most frequently highlighted passages if they are deemed offensive or otherwise unsuitable from a marketing perspective. In fact, the size of the highlight is one of several factors determining the chance of an annotation appearing, hence the use of "popular" over "top" highlights.[17]

The Kindle hardware encourages "always-on" connectivity, but the Popular Highlights files, an XML document with a PHL extension, download asynchronously. Social reading services encourage users to connect to the internet, but the choice to sideload the PHL postdownload dissuades users from remaining connected if they see past the facade of the Kindle's networked connectivity. Users who choose the "download and transfer via USB" option will receive just the main ebook without any sideloaded documents, which must be downloaded on the device itself.[18] Despite the static nature of PHL files, users can only access this content by synchronizing their ebook with Whispersync. Customers must trade their data to receive the service. Even if the data are not shared with other users, the highlights form yet another data point for Amazon's extensive surveillance of contemporary reading.

The Kindle for Mac version of Robin Sloan's *Mr. Penumbra's 24-Hour Bookstore* PHL file shows how Amazon mediates the popular highlights process. The first shared annotation of the novel ("This is Mat's secret weapon, his passport, his get-out-of-jail-free card: Mat makes things that are beautiful")[19] is represented as "<annotation type='popular_highlight' num_users='27' end_pos='54499' start_pos='54383'/>." Annotations are mapped to byte registers rather than the more user-friendly page numbers (288 pages per the US Farrar, Straus and Giroux hardback edition, which forms the basis of the ebook in both the United Kingdom and United States) or the location register, which finishes at 4,158.[20] Byte registers (116) are not identical to character counts (110) owing to Amazon's UTF-8 compression techniques (discussed in chapter 4). Since the schema depends on a granular approach to identifying location, this introduces an additional challenge for Amazon's engineers when updating books with even a single correction. A commitment to diversity and updatability leads to precarity in the case of ensuring consistent highlights.

To illustrate these challenges, the *Penumbra* PHL file contains metadata about its creation, including a time stamp of September 2015 and an update identification number: 105. When revisited in November 2017, the time stamp read October 31, 2017, but the version number had reverted to 14. The updated file introduced several new highlights with fewer shares than more popular sections from the previous copy of the file. Byte registers vary substantially, although some highlights remain persistent, indicating that the update number relates to a change in Amazon's algorithm or a new edition of the text. Other PHL files further call into question the reliability of the figures. The copy of *Pride and Prejudice* that came bundled with the Kindle 3 in Britain received almost 600,000 highlights despite being "out of print" since 2011, but the PHL notes just fourteen updates, with the latest change arriving in January 2016. Asynchronous downloads and new versions of the text might account for the low number. The design of the popular highlights system challenges the marketing of the Kindle as an always-on device. Instead we can see the Kindle as an *always-upload* device that does not necessarily benefit users. Users were offered updates at irregular intervals with the illusion of constant refresh. Lauren Cameron's investigation of patterns in highlighting of *The Adventures of Sherlock Holmes* over the summer of 2011 captures the periodic refresh twice: first in the week commencing June 15, and later in the final week of August.[21] Cameron's analysis is unfortunately based on a coincidence of data rather than mapping the chronological development of shared reading habits. Researchers are not the only casualties of the lack of transparency: Amazon does not offer reliable data for publishers, since the publicly available data are ephemeral and instable.

Highlighting Patterns

Regardless of the limitations of the public data, Kindle Popular Highlights shows clear patterns in Amazon's processing and the substantial variation between individual and aggregated practices. As an illustration, Donna Tartt's *The Goldfinch* has received substantial user interest with more than a quarter million shared highlights. The novel's final paragraph, which begins "It is a glory and a privilege to love what Death doesn't touch," is the book's most shared annotation and appeared on its Kindle Popular Highlights page 103 times out of 2,027 publicly available passages in eleven variations. While the version in the popular highlights stops at "it is a glory and a privilege to love what Death doesn't touch,"[22] in the more extended varieties, readers continue highlighting through to the end of the paragraph and novel. Most users have shared less text than the original highlight, indicating the importance of the popular highlights' framing in the reading system.

The discrepancies between the individual and popular highlights data result from the aggregation process detailed in figure 7.4.[23] Users A, B, C, and D all share similar but unique sections of a title. The aggregation algorithm establishes overlap between annotations before removing any duplicates and combining the discrete passages into a single visible highlight that does not necessarily resemble the intention of any one user. The algorithm corrects perceived errors (for example, where the first word of a sentence has been chopped off), which removes creative elements of interpretation, such as clipping sentences to alter the meaning. Readers lose their agency as Amazon controls the types of highlights that remain in the system. The Kindle Popular Highlights displayed in reading systems show further evidence of truncation, as shared content is substantially shorter in reading applications than on the website, where the limit was determined by the maximum amount of text displayed on a single page. For example, on the Kindle Touch with the Caecilia Condensed font in the smallest available size, it is possible to display locations 385 to 399 of Isaacson's *Steve Jobs* on a single screen, which could then be converted into a single highlight.[24]

Journalists were quick to pick up on the potential of the Popular Highlights data set.[25] Jordan Ellenberg's "The Summer's Most Unread Book" playfully suggests that the average location of the popular highlights is an indicator of the likelihood of a reader finishing the book.[26] He coined the "Hawking Index" as a reference to Steven Hawking's *A Brief History of Time*: a book that sells but is rarely finished. Ellenberg analyzed the popular highlight locations of nine titles including Sheryl Sandberg's *Lean In* and Steven Hawking's *A Brief History of Time* and found a stark contrast between the highlights from Thomas Piketty's *Capital in the Twenty-First Century* with a mean location of 2.4 percent, and Donna Tartt's *The Goldfinch*'s 98.5

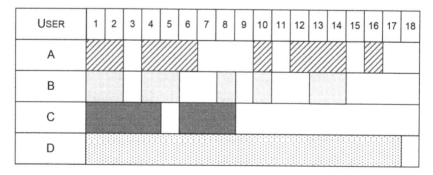

7.4 Collating highlights. Source: Killalea et al., Aggregation of highlights.

percent average. From this, Ellenberg argues that readers were more likely to finish reading *The Goldfinch* than *A Brief History of Time*.

Ellenberg's small-scale experiment was largely supported by a report by Kobo on big data and publishing that revealed that only half of readers would ever finish a book, although Kobo noted a clear correlation between the brand recognition of the author and completion.[27] Overall, nonfiction, including *A Brief History of Time*, had lower competition rates that fiction because nonfiction titles include additional end matter and readers are less likely to complete a reference guide. If a book has a 50 percent attrition rate, it follows that most highlights will be shared closer to the beginning before most readers stop. In figure 7.5, I expand on Ellenberg's method

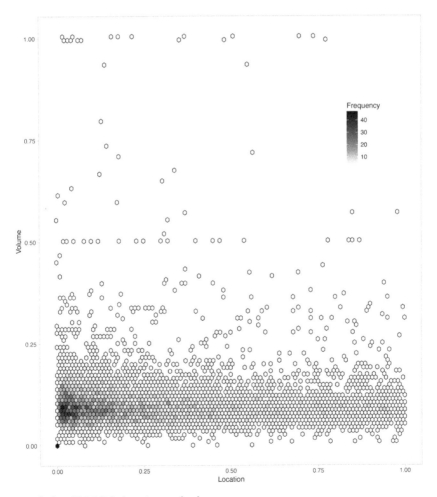

7.5 Indexed highlight locations and volumes

to eight hundred Kindle titles for a range of fiction and nonfiction genres (see appendix A for further details). Highlights appear most frequently in the first quarter of the text, especially within the first 10 percent. A slight peak occurs at the end of texts, but otherwise, the volume of highlights dissipates in the second half of the book.

What factors affect the distribution of shared highlights? Algorithmic fissures play an important role. For example, in the "About the Book" for Joseph M. Reagle Jr.'s *Good Faith Collaboration* from October 2014, my file's last update notes 2,514 overall annotations across 241 unique passages. Conversely, the publicly visible popular highlights display between four and seven shares each. "About the Book" features a ratio of unique to total annotations as 10.4:1, while the underlined passages in the text only average four shared highlights each. Clear discrepancies exist between the in-text reporting of popular annotations and the "About the Book" figures, demonstrating a technical or algorithmic adjustment. All ten of the highlights appear in the first 40 percent of the ebook. The large unseen corpus of more popular highlights, along with the sharp shift in emphasis in the *Mr. Penumbra* example detailed earlier, suggests that Amazon uses algorithms or humans to curate the popular highlights with a specification beyond frequency.

The algorithmic distortion of shared annotations does not preclude social influences such as users not finishing titles, although no clear correlation exists between reading progress and annotation patterns.[28] While users may continue to read beyond their last highlight, it is unlikely that a user will share a section beyond their final reading location, although consulting an index in an abandoned book may distort any collected data. Clustered shared passages in an ebook's first quarter might reflect editorial practices: a lively introduction is more likely to attract readers and improve retention. A highlight reflects an exceptional part of the text rather than a marker of progress. The location of annotations reveals how books are distributed and authored more than how they are read. For example, many of the books I analyzed were available through Kindle Unlimited, a subscription service that pays creators per page read, encouraging authors to create engaging openings to improve retention. Equally, many ebooks on Amazon are marketed by offering the first chapter for free, creating a further incentive for making the beginning of the book interesting.

The Goldfinch is an exception to the rule, as its ten most popular highlights all appear in the final 10 percent. While not designed for the Kindle, the novel's denouement encourages closer engagement. *The Goldfinch*'s exceptionalism is clear from an Ellenberg-inspired analysis of the average highlight location of eight hundred Kindle ebooks.[29] Figure 7.6 shows

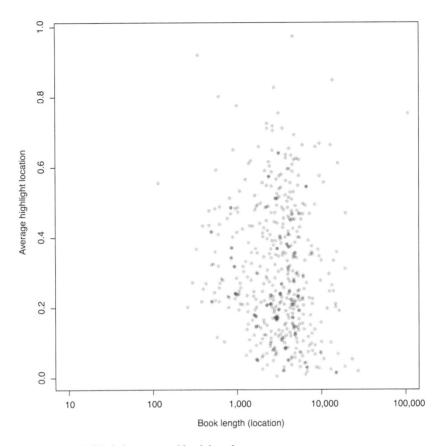

7.6 Average highlight location and book length

the distribution of average highlight location in comparison to the length of a title measured by "location." These data show no correlation between the length of a book and the mean highlight location. Only twelve titles have average highlight locations above 75 percent. Four ebooks feature fewer than five shared annotations, increasing the level of variation. The remaining eight ebooks are dominated by Bella Forrest's *A Shade of Vampire* series. In sum, outside a few exceptions, users are more likely to highlight the first and last quartile of a book than the middle. A book such as Piketty's *Capital* was an unfortunate target for Ellenberg, as it is unremarkable in its completion compared to books where the highlights focus on the last 40 percent of the novel. Any title that subverts this usual pattern is of greater interest than those that display lower average annotation locations. In fact, books such as *The Goldfinch* and the Bible demonstrate that length presents no obstacle to readers remaining interested toward the end of the text.

Triangulating different publicly available sources provides a clearer picture of social reading habits. If an algorithm focuses on the same segment across texts, it is possible to look at variation between books in a series according to discrepancies between titles. For example, shared highlights in the main seven *Harry Potter* titles appear in consistent places across the series. On average, the highlights come at around 60 percent through the novel, although most appear in the second half of the book. Figure 7.7 shows the spread of highlights in all seven *Harry Potter* books. The lengthier titles in the series do not deter highlights toward the end of the novel, which becomes the norm as the series progresses. Highlight patterns in *The Philosopher's Stone* reveal the general trend. Several highlights

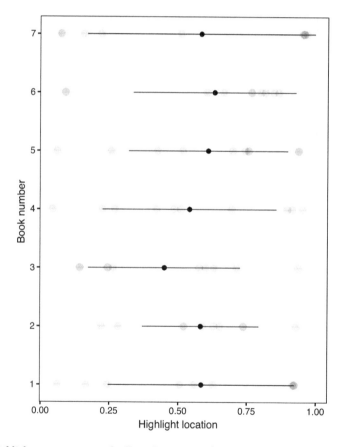

7.7 Highlight patterns across the *Harry Potter* series (bars indicate mean and standard deviation)

at the beginning of the novel typically start with Harry's hijinks with his uncle and aunt. Readers show relatively little interest during the Hogwarts school year, but the final chapters feature the bulk of the annotations. Three quotations come from a two-page (or five-location) spread, and all contain direct speech from Dumbledore to Harry, including "After all, to the well-organised mind, death is but the next great adventure,"[30] and "Always use the proper name for things. Fear of a name increases fear of the thing itself."[31] The focus on Dumbledore's speech emphasizes pivotal narrative moments and Dumbledore's aphorisms. Readers wish to signal their fandom of specific characters while also sharing wisdom to a wider community.

Dumbledore's death in *Harry Potter and the Half-Blood Prince*, the sixth book, breaks this trend. After a couple of early aphoristic interactions between Harry and Dumbledore, seven of the ten highlights appear in the last quarter of the novel and focus on two pivotal moments in the series. The first is the discovery of "Horcruxes," or the objects the primary antagonist, Voldemort, uses to be immortal. For a book that has had a rigid episodic recurring structure, this represented the first major shift in the plot toward a conclusion and therefore prompted excitement for many fans. The remaining highlights focus on Harry's burgeoning relationship with Ginny Weasley, and their first kiss. This romantic moment is pertinent for the fandom who wished to see this coupling and demonstrate their appreciation through sharing highlights of this passage. It is telling that given this interest in book 6, there are no highlights from the much-maligned epilogue to *Deathly Hallows*, which confirms the romance between Harry and Ginny. The convergent highlights demonstrate fan approval on a large scale but did not shape how Rowling wrote the final books.

The *Harry Potter* series is exceptional due to the long-term commitment of fans and its publication life cycle as one of the last major non-digital book series, but what about a series conceived and written entirely for a born-digital audience? The main *Potter* series finished before the launch of the Kindle, as the novel was published in July 2007, just months before the device's launch in November. On the other hand, Bella Forrest's *A Shade of Vampire* was first published in 2012. Within the eight hundred Kindle books, the series was noteworthy, as many of the books feature average highlight locations in the final quartile. This pattern is the result of each book's position within a series, as readers need to have an incentive to continue reading at the end of each novel. Serialization requires commitment, and authors can encourage readers to continue by ensuring that the ending is sufficiently interesting to ensure the conversion of readers to fans. Writers can employ cliff-hangers to avoid the common threat of a reader losing interest between books.[32] The series reached a landmark fiftieth volume in 2017, averaging a new release once a month. The theme and genre both indicate that the series was inspired by the boom in vampire fiction following the success of Stephenie Meyer's *Twilight* tetralogy. The books are born digital and are only available through Amazon as either a Kindle ebook or print on demand through CreateSpace, registering occasional sales through non-Amazon outlets on Nielsen BookScan. Forrest's digital-facing and rapid publishing strategy allows her to react to the shifting interests of fans.

A longitudinal study of the Popular Highlights for the first two *A Shade of Vampire* series reveals how fan service and other factors help form a reading community on the Kindle. The patterns in figure 7.8 show how

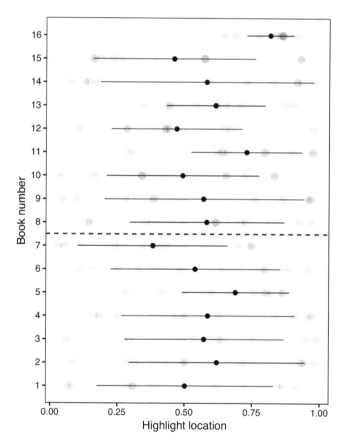

7.8 Highlighting patterns in the first sixteen titles of Bella Forrest's *A Shade of Vampire* series (dashed lines represent the start of a new series; bars indicate mean and standard deviation)

technological innovations and the reactions of fans are leading to a shift in writing. Forrest refreshes the narrative with new series according to shifting reader engagement. The first seven books document Derek and Sofia's story; books 8 to 16 change focus to Rose and Caleb. The switch of protagonists led to more highlights averaging in the final half of the books after a dip in interest from books 5 to 7. Refreshing the narrative's focal point regenerated the series until interest began to wane. The conclusion to a story line the second time around aroused greater interest, as indicated by the high proportion of shared annotations in the final quarter of book 16. If reader engagement moves from the end of the book, Forrest can take this information to either review the plot or begin another series. As a prominent Kindle Unlimited author, if Forrest produces an engaging book once a month, she will continue to maintain her best-seller status. Timothy Laquintano argues that authors such as Forrest are beholden to Amazon's algorithms and must "feed the beast" by republishing "their books as box sets or anthologies" or expanding narrative worlds "in ways that let them release their writing often in order to appease the algorithms."[33] Readers' highlights for the *A Shade of Vampire* series show that Forrest can use feedback to know when to shift focus to ensure the brand's longevity in spite of Amazon's algorithmic forces and dwindling reader engagement. Through the ability to track the success of a narrative arc, combined with an agile writing style, it is possible to ensure that a series does not outlast its welcome.

Highlights as Text

The text of highlights reveals universal themes shared across diverse genres. Table 7.1 lists select words that appear frequently on Kindle Popular Highlights. Given the diverse range of reading interests present on the Kindle, it is unsurprising that the most frequently highlighted words would converge toward universals such as "god," "world," and "love." The relative frequency of each term's appearance reveals more about the values emphasized through highlighting. For example, "you" appears almost twice as often as "I," indicating a preference toward highlighting passages that reference the reader (excluding reported speech) rather than emphasizing the authority of the narrator. Likewise, "god" appears with greater frequency than "people" or "man," despite the latter two terms having a wider field of reference. Words of this nature tend to be aphoristic rather than literal, demonstrating users' interest in reviewing the material when visiting their clippings and often sharing this with a broader audience.

Highlights become more meaningful in context. For example, readers focus on the affective narrative climaxes in works such as *Pride and*

Table 7.1 Select word frequencies from the 2014 Kindle Popular Highlights data set

Rank	Frequency	Term
9	408,051	you
14	220,605	I
37	107,016	our
42	98,658	god
49	84,605	life
50	79,514	people
65	55,346	time
69	52,353	love
70	52,100	world
82	43,750	things
84	42,673	man
85	41,907	good
89	40,285	being
112	30,950	work
124	28,238	power

Prejudice. Shared highlights include "In vain I have struggled. It will not do. My feelings will not be repressed. You must allow me to tell you how ardently I admire and love you."[34] While this quotation needs further context, it provides other readers with a teaser that reveals key narrative information without being a spoiler, as it does not name any characters. This form of in medias res highlighting, or the selection of text that takes place in the middle of the action, is replete with unidentifiable actors and decontextualized dialogue. These annotations can only be understood by the community of readers who have completed the book or otherwise have some prior knowledge of the narrative. The intention for the highlights to be used as a marketing tool might be more difficult, as new readers will not be able to engage with the content fully. The early technical infrastructure of the Kindle Popular Highlights website encouraged in medias res highlighting, as the web page for each title contained each quotation in its context. Figure 7.9 shows an example of *Pride and Prejudice* and how readers who did not have access to the full text gained some context for the highlight. The feature was removed from subsequent iterations of the website in favor of decontextualized chunks of text.

7.9 In medias res highlighting in the early Kindle Popular Highlights

The opening of *Pride and Prejudice*—"It is a truth universally acknowledged, that a single man in possession of a good fortune, must be in want of a wife"[35]—was the second most shared highlight on the Kindle Popular Highlights website. The data set includes forty-one editions of *Pride and Prejudice* in total, ignoring the three instances of Seth Grahame-Smith's infamous remix, *Pride and Prejudice and Zombies*. Outside the most popular edition, which has received 40,000 highlights, the remaining books have only received 750 altogether. The value of these other titles instead comes from looking at patterns and repetition. "It is a truth universally acknowledged . . ." appears as the most popular annotation for sixteen of the titles. Since various editions often share similar highlight locations, it is possible to search for patterns and differences in sharing practices. Where highlight data from multiple editions remain, it is possible to assess the most popular highlights where readers have not been influenced by inflated sharing statistics.

The algorithmic aggregation of different quotations into a single homogeneous response does not affect different editions of the same text. The forty-one copies of *Pride and Prejudice* therefore reveal more granular data about how readers use the same text in different ways. The book's opening sentence remains intact, except on two occasions, when the latter half of the aphorism ("single man in possession of a good fortune, must be in want of a wife") is all that remains. Partially, this may reflect a technological problem: users may not necessarily know exactly how to highlight the section they want, but equally, without direct influence of other readers, they still converge toward similar quotations without being mediated by the aggregation algorithm. Figure 7.10 shows a more complex example

1		4		
imaginary.	Vanity and pride are different things, though the words are often used			
4	13	15	16	18
synonymously.	A person may	be proud without being	vain.	Pride relates more to
18				
our opinion of ourselves, vanity to what we would have others think of us.				

7.10 Heat map of a single quotation (produced by author through examining variants of quotation)

of variable highlighting, as users have altered the quotation's length. The final sentence receives the most overall highlights (8,437), while the others all receive fewer than 100, except for *Pride and Prejudice and Zombies*, which features the exact same quotation without added zombies.[36] The most telling sign of the commonplace is subtle: the full sentence "A person may be proud without being vain" is not direct enough, so the first four words are removed to transform the aphorism into an imperative ("be proud without being vain") to share with fellow users. Up to four thousand readers have shared this clipped imperative across fifteen editions of the work, reforming the common aphorism as a command.

The Street Finds Its Own Uses for Things

Individual books' Popular Highlights pages reveal further nuances of how users appropriated the social reading services. For example, several readers added shared notes in *The Goldfinch* with definitions of "frivolity," a note to remember "chthonic," and the disappointment of not finding "agoramaniac" in the dictionary. These highlights demonstrate readers using the system as an aide-mémoire, but it is unclear if they intended to share these annotations. Elsewhere, in Isaacson's *Steve Jobs*, a user highlighted every piece of classical music or book mentioned, including *Diet for a Small Planet*, by Frances Moore Lappé, to create a list to return to later. The gap between the individual's intent and the likely audience is best summarized by the user who scoured *Fifty Shades of Grey* to share every instance of Pinot Grigio in context with the Kindle Popular Highlights user base (figure 7.11).

A group of users elected to turn the Kindle Popular Highlight website into a chat room by using the ability to enter comments via both the Kindle application and website. This had surprising ancillary effects with the

▇▇▇▇▇ shared from Fifty Shades of Grey by E L James
❝ I take a large slug of Pinot Grigio—he's right, of course, it's delicious. ❞

▇▇▇▇▇ shared from Fifty Shades of Grey by E L James
❝ "The Pinot Grigio here is a decent wine. It will go well with the meal, whatever we get," he says patiently. ❞

▇▇▇▇▇ shared from Fifty Shades of Grey by E L James
❝ "Two glasses of the Pinot Grigio," ❞

7.11 Every instance of Pinot Grigio in *Fifty Shades of Grey* (usernames redacted)

embedded dictionaries that were integrated into the Kindle as ordinary ebooks rather than a separate database: users could highlight and note share using the dictionary, which became a subversive chat room for younger users of the Kindle whose internet access was limited to the Kindle as a "safe space." Since the Kindle offered free access to 3G and Wi-Fi, parents would provide their child with a Kindle expecting them to engage with the reading practices, unaware that it was possible to transform ebooks into ad hoc chat rooms. As Tully Barnett argues, "Notes like 'Hey anyone on?' [in the *New Oxford American Dictionary*] strengthen the case that the page is used as an online social forum demanding immediate communication and reply from an existing social network rather than considered slow reading."[37] Even the most innocuous of books on the Kindle can be transformed into a full social network because of the following function. Since the dictionary was installed by default on all Kindle devices, shared notes could reach the widest audience if based on the dictionary.

The user's default dictionary plays an important role in discovering this community. For example, a user stated "lmao this is dead" on the third edition of the *New Oxford American Dictionary*, while activity—although primarily spam—continued in the second edition, the default dictionary for older devices. Some users found the ad hoc chat room, which had little support for notifications, and difficult logging, nearly impossible to navigate, leading to messages such as "Sigh I might have to x this app off because I can't see you comets. :=[." While the dictionary has been used as a chat room for teenagers and young adults, this is often a starting point for further interaction elsewhere, and thus a form of discovery rather than a sustainable location due to both the ephemerality of the publicly available record and the desire for more standardized practices of online communication. Users would often refer to other social media in their messages to other users: "I saw your tweet and I've been coming on everyday to cheek . . . to check if you know." The discussion by these readers transitioned to other young adult titles, as well as Twitter and Facebook.

The End of Kindle Popular Highlights

Amazon's acquisition of Goodreads in 2013 marked the beginning of the end for Kindle Popular Highlights. The acquisition was accompanied by reassurances that Goodreads would remain independent from the Kindle reading experience, which largely remained true until 2016 with the integration of Goodreads. Amazon had made several attempts at social reading. Kindle Popular Highlights was the only real success story in a wave of failures including @author, Kindle book clubs, and Shelfari. These failures highlight the core tension behind the "track everything, monetize later" mentality, as it is unclear if many of these data have a meaningful use. Amazon slowly shut down the Kindle Popular Highlights website. Initially, the data for the Kindle Popular Highlights were frozen, and then the site was removed in 2017, taking the largest body of shared highlights down with it. After the early collaborations between the Reading Experience and Reading, Mining and Analytics teams to form the front and back ends of the website, the latter team's approach has proved to be more sustainable. The Kindle Popular Highlights website no longer displays users' highlights but rather redirects users to Kindle Cloud Reader to view their notes or visit Goodreads to interact with other readers, and the domain is now a back-end API used to transfer reading data to Whispersync.

Despite the limitations of the publicly available data and the clear evidence of algorithmic manipulation, the Kindle Popular Highlights website, and the platform's broader social reading services, helped shape readers' understanding of popular and niche titles. The limited data can still be useful to authors looking to refresh their series based on the feedback of keen fans and otherwise shows general themes users are interested in. The closure of the site is a net loss for both publishers and researchers interested in the history of reading, as the equivalent of a large library of used books has now been removed from the web. Even this limited slice of Amazon's complete data set allowed users to explore the interests of fellow readers and tailor their reading. The complexities and limitations of the publicly available data reveal the problems of algorithmically mediating the complexities of social reading, but this trend extends the company's aims to develop technology and infrastructure at the expense of a more focused platform.

In July 2009, Justin Gawronski, a high school student from Detroit, sued Amazon after the removal of unlicensed, yet officially purchased, copies of George Orwell's *1984* and *Animal Farm* from Gawronski's Kindle.[1] The backlash caused Bezos to post an apology directly to the Kindle forums, stating: "Our 'solution' to the problem was stupid, thoughtless, and painfully out of line with our principles. It is wholly self-inflicted, and we deserve the criticism we've received."[2] Amazon settled the lawsuit out of court and updated its policy to clarify that ebooks would only be removed in the future to comply with a court order, if the title contained malicious code, or if the user failed to pay for a copy.[3] The incident raised important questions about the ownership of ebooks and Amazon's control of the Kindle: What exactly do customers own when they purchase Kindle hardware and ebooks? If Amazon decides to no longer support the Kindle, what will remain? I conducted research for *Four Shades* between 2013 and 2020, and during those eight years, many services were shut down. The historical record of contemporary publishing is at risk, dependent on the whims of a corporation uninterested in institutional and cultural memory. Indeed, as with instances such as Weathervane Press and Kindle Popular Highlights, Amazon obscures its own history to prioritize new initiatives. While the Kindle ecosystem has many important parts, three areas—hardware, content, and services—present the greatest challenges for the long-term preservation of the ebook's history.

Hardware

The Kindle 1's product page made bold claims about the device's hardiness, including a video of a drop test. Early users found this durability illusory. Electronic paper screens are notoriously delicate, with the electrophoretic capsules susceptible to bursting if excessive pressure is applied to the screen. The screen of a Kindle 3 I owned broke from the pressure of an airplane seat-back pocket. In response to the fragile screens, Silvio Lorusso and Sebastian Schmieg published *56 Broken Kindle Screens*, emphasizing the aesthetic value of ruptured Kindle screens.[4] The reader may still be able to use the device in a zombie form, as unaffected capsules continue to display new content when the reader turns a page. The resulting images in *56 Broken Kindle Screens* feature remixed screen savers with chunks of text from the last book the reader opened or reminders to update the device. Since electronic paper displays an image indefinitely, the final screen is recorded for posterity rather than a blank screen with a crack.

Despite the devices' fragility, users developed sentimental attachments to older Kindle hardware, procuring spare parts to maintain e-readers initially purchased a decade ago. Alongside the electronic paper screen, batteries are the most likely component to fail.[5] Because manufacturers have stopped producing components for the Kindle 1 and DX, two popular devices, Frankenstein ebook readers cannibalize other broken hardware to extend the life of a treasured device. Garnet Hertz and Jussi Parikka, two media archaeologists, coined the term "zombie media" to describe the use of media beyond their planned obsolescence through innovative projects, "resurrecting" the hardware.[6] Hertz and Parikka offer the example of Reed Ghazala's *The Incantor*, which circuit bends devices such as Texas Instruments' Speak & Spell, an educational toy designed to help children's verbal development, "to spew out a noisy, glitchy tangle of sound that stutters, loops, screams and beats."[7] Zombie media build on the Gartner Group's Hype Cycle and Cumulative Consumer Adoption Curve diagram, which maps early adopters through to laggards by introducing a "DIY/Archaeology phase" for technology that has faced "mainstream obsolescence."[8] Kindle hardware is currently in the late stage of consumer technology, as dedicated e-readers have largely been replaced by multifunctional mobile computers except in niche demographics. E-readers sit on the precipice of mainstream obsolescence, which encourages users still interested in the format to experiment with the hardware.

Amazon's resistance to planned obsolescence cycles for the Kindle is a boon for preservation, as older devices are still supported. Budget versions of the e-reader are sufficient for most consumers and are unlikely to be replaced by newer versions. Amazon attempted to encourage readers to follow more traditional upgrade cycles with the release of Kindle Voyage in 2014, but as the reading system is available on a broad range of operating systems, this is unlikely to encourage users to return to dedicated hardware. The aesthetic of e-readers remains central to Amazon's cross-hardware cloud-based platform development. Reading ebooks on e-readers provides the most authentic experience, but dedicated hardware continues to become less important. The legacy of e-readers will rely on their influence on content rather than hardware design.

Hardware Hacking

While the hardware did not have a major influence on mainstream computational culture, hobbyists worked on creating a vibrant DIY culture of hardware modification. The MobileRead community exploited Lab126's choice of Linux to create a range of alternate hardware projects based on the Kindle's unique features. With the knowledge of this operating system, it is possible to "root" the software (gain administrator access to the firmware) and reuse the device for other purposes. Hardware hackers often turn to id Software's classic first-person shooter *Doom* to demonstrate the scope of subversive creativity for a device,[9] but the Kindle's hardware is limited, and fighting hellspawn with a "Big Fucking Gun" is beyond the limitations of the fastest-refreshing electronic paper. Any creative reuse of the Kindle must instead work within the boundaries of electronic paper rather than pushing the frame rate. For example, the Kindle Weather Station replaces the generic screen savers of classic texts and bookish images with the local weather in the user's area. The platform's early years were a hotbed for innovation, as the Kindle was one of the first devices to feature a cheap electronic paper display. The hardware experimentation was the result of Amazon's decision to run its reading system in Linux, which enables users to quickly manipulate the software. Given the limited specifications of even contemporary versions of the Kindle—the Voyage has 512 megabytes of RAM and a 1 GHz dual core processor, which is optimized for low power consumption rather than as a computational powerhouse—it would be difficult to convert the dedicated hardware into a full computer. The Kindle as a piece of hackable hardware mirrors the rise of the Raspberry Pi and maker culture. Despite the device's extensibility because of the use of open platforms such as Linux, it has limitations. As David Given warns: "The Kindle is a *very fragile device*. It's incredibly easy to crash; there's no isolation between user applications and the system user interface."[10] The system was designed with a specific purpose and was not tested for more general computational purposes.

Geoffroy Tremblay created the KindleBerry Pi, a device that uses the electronic paper display from the Kindle as a makeshift monitor for the Raspberry Pi.[11] The use of electronic paper in a general personal computer recalls Nick Sheridon's vision of the display technology for desktop computers at Xerox PARC in the 1970s.[12] Tremblay used USBNetwork, one of the Linux files included with the device, to turn the electronic paper screen into a monitor, which unfortunately tied the user to the on-device keyboard. The software only offered command line accessibility, which suited the low refresh rate and fidelity of E Ink's technology.

Other hobbyists built new uses within the Kindle hardware. MobileRead users collaborated on "Kindlets," or Kindle-based Java applets, to enable the development of a hobbyist software ecosystem that included readily compiled bootloaders and shortcuts.[13] The architecture was used to create diverse applications, including Kindle voice control and Kinamp. Kindle voice control exploited Launchpad's ability to change interfaces to allow users to control the keypad via voice commands using the Kindle's integration into local Wi-Fi.[14] The work was largely proof of concept and was never developed beyond a prototype. Kinamp extended the functionality of the "experimental" MP3 player available on the first four Kindle generations by embedding MPlayer, an audiovisual media player for Linux, in the Kindle.[15] Not only did this offer greater control and optionality, but it allowed users to stream audio, a possibility embedded within the Kindle hardware but never natively available owing to the rise in data costs with audio streaming. Users were willing to experiment with the Kindle hardware, as it offered a unique setup without requiring a high start-up cost. The results reveal some of the untaken pathways for computing outside the monolithic smartphone paradigm.

Beyond these changes to the Kindle software, users have also tried to integrate the wider history of digital publishing into the device. Authors have created several text-only digital genres that update slowly enough for the electronic paper screen to keep up. Choose Your Own Adventure style books, including a popular range of "Choose Your Own Erotica," have developed a niche on the Kindle Store through using the Kindle's native support for linking. Other users saw the slow refresh of the Kindle screen as harking back to the terminal-based printer conditions of early interactive fiction (IF).[16] Interactive fiction advances at a perfect pace for the refresh rate of the Kindle, as new content is only displayed once a user responds to a prompt. Electronic paper offered a more authentic experience for early works of IF that had been developed as printed responses.[17]

These early attempts to create interactive content on the Kindle unofficially through both jailbreaking and pushing the limits of the file formats were acknowledged by Amazon when the company launched Kindle Active Content and the Kindle Developer Kit in 2010. In a press release, Amazon announced with bombast that the company would be working with Zagat, Sonic Boom, and EA Mobile to develop interactive guides and word-based games.[18] The scheme led to the development of several board game ports optimized for the Kindle's electronic paper screen, including *The Settlers of Catan*.[19] Kindle Active Content allowed select developers to fulfill the platform's potential beyond ebooks, a potential initially promised by the inclusion of *Minesweeper* as an Easter egg with the original Kindle's launch. The bookish/board game genre, which functions without the requirement for constant screen refresh, offered users interactive content optimized for dedicated hardware. Amazon dropped support for Active Content in 2014.[20] The Fire's success overshadowed a more interesting experiment in developing software within the constraints of electronic paper, leaving this work to Kindlet developers. The potential of electronic paper as a display medium has never extended beyond replicating paper, compared to the dynamism of the Atari VCS 2600's Television Interface Adapter, which contributed to the unique aesthetic of the console.[21] Beyond *56 Broken Kindle Screens*, the aesthetic dimensions of dedicated hardware were never allowed to mature. The lack of new, native born-digital Kindle genres contrasts starkly with Audible's growth in the late 2010s, which was accompanied by extensive and sustained investment in Audible Original podcasts and acquiring rights to produce audiobooks internally. As a result, Audible has developed beyond the initial business model of offering audiobooks of print titles. Unfortunately, this market-driven approach (money begets investment and development) creates a more conservative approach to platforms like the Kindle, where less excitement leads to less interest.

Content

While hardware has become less central to the platform, what about content? Jesse England responded to the removal of *1984* by creating a physical backup of Orwell's novel with photographs of every "page" of his Kindle 3 edition with the hardware remaining in frame. England scanned the book to create a digital facsimile, which he published as a print-on-demand book and a Kindle-readable PDF. The provocation emphasized the ephemerality of a single edition of a book available in other print and digital forms, but more pressing questions surround the preservation of titles only available via the Kindle Store, including digital-only and self-published works. Peter Purgathofer, a human-computer interaction professor, elaborated on the thought experiment with his DIY Kindle book scanner built with Lego Mindstorms, a lightweight robotics platform.[22] The project replicates the two-part process of print digitization as the scanner automatically turns the page—in this case by pressing a button—followed by taking a photograph. Purgathofer's Rube Goldberg machine was not designed to be scalable and is more cumbersome than making a copy of the book in a digital environment. Nonetheless, the project highlighted the precarity of titles on the platform. Even within professional preservation settings, proprietary formats are at risk of secondary documentation, as national libraries prefer open standards to preserve material.

Amazon has a track record of removing ebooks. While it elected not to acquire NuvoMedia and the Rocket eBook in 1998, selling ebooks directly through the web store could provide additional revenue with low risks. During the early 2000s, Microsoft Reader and Adobe Reader were the most commonly used reading systems, so Amazon offered ebooks in these formats, including popular titles such as Dan Brown novels. It is no longer possible to download these ebooks, as the "E-book and E-Doc" store was removed at the Kindle's launch. The willful erasure of institutional memory is encapsulated in the company's rhetoric of "Day One" emphasized in Bezos's letter to shareholders, which includes reprints of the 1997 letter in full each year and opens with "This is Day 1 for the Internet and, if we execute well, for Amazon.com."[23] If two decades are condensed into an opening day, there is less incentive to preserve the longer history.

Luckily for the historical study of the Amazon infrastructure, ASINs are persistent, making it possible to trace titles and their disappearance. Many public domain titles published between 2007 and 2011 are now no longer available to purchase, but their ASINs are persistent to ensure the titles can be integrated with services such as shared highlights and reviewing. For example, the version of Jane Austen's *Pride and Prejudice* that came bundled with the international Kindle 3 is unavailable in the US store, but the product page remains in the British store with a publication date of "1 Jun. 1998," its publication date on Project Gutenberg. The edition exists in a state of limbo: readers can access the original version via third parties, and this historically important title remains in the catalog; but if one cannot access a user's downloaded version of the ebook, it remains unavailable. Other "out-of-print" ebooks have been less lucky. If users attempt to access an "out-of-print" Microsoft Reader title published before the Kindle's launch, they are redirected to a 404 page. The Internet Archive only holds records of 40,000 ASINs across all product types, which is fewer than the 50,000 Mobipocket titles available via Amazon before the Kindle's launch, let alone the one million Microsoft and Adobe Reader titles available via Amazon in 2006. This period of ebook history has largely been forgotten owing to the erasure of a core central repository. Given the divergence between the print and ebook markets since the early 2010s, especially with the rise of Kindle Direct Publishing, this not only affects the availability of digital surrogates of print material. The self-publishing boom, fueled in part by the early success stories of John Locke and Amanda Hocking discussed in chapter 5, encouraged authors to cut out print-oriented publishers in return for a greater share of the royalties. While this choice had immediate benefits for the authors, the longer-term durability and sustainability of publications rely on a currently nonexistent working relationship between Amazon and large deposit libraries.

Despite improving discoverability of some out-of-print titles, the prominence of ASINs presents further challenges for preservation in an era beyond Amazon, as the company does not provide contextual information for the standard and does not distinguish between deleted and nonexistent product pages. ASINs are nonsequential and human illegible, so it is impossible to determine the scope of deleted ebooks outside the company's own records, and Amazon denies access to Kindle product pages to third parties such as CamelCamelCamel. Unless Amazon aids preservation, its catalog will become a digital Library of Alexandria. An archive of Kindle titles would depend on the decentralized assembly of readers' copies of individual ebooks, but since these copies would be compiled for specific devices, this would only provide a slice of the actual format and content. Ebook preservation is an urgent concern in a time when publishers are distancing themselves from the medium. Without a stronger collaboration between publishers, archives, and libraries, Amazon's monopoly on ebook sales places the medium in a precarious position.

The company's ability to update ebooks automatically is a more widespread issue for preservation. The service is opt-in, so users are unlikely to select the option unless they are aware of the feature. It is not uncommon for books to receive updates. For example, 54 of the 560 books in my Kindle library have "updates available." Publishers do not issue change logs, making it difficult to know what has changed, and unless an older version is backed up, it is erased, making comparisons difficult. The 10 percent of ebooks requiring updates in my collection will include the occasional update to content, but most will introduce new format specifications to keep up with contemporary style developments. With a print run, by contrast, there is no requirement to update the format to account for new paper requirements. When Amazon introduces new features such as Word Wise, Enhanced Typesetting, and X-Ray, publishers may choose to use these new features, which require a manual update from readers. The older editions are not officially recorded via Amazon, and unless a publisher has fastidiously kept archives of each update, they likely exist nowhere. Files are processed remotely on Amazon's servers, so publishers cannot archive updates internally. In fact, due to the discrepancies discussed in chapter 4, an authoritative version of a Kindle edition no longer exists.

Legal deposit libraries play a vital role in preserving a nation's cultural record. Publishers are legally obliged to submit copies of print books to national libraries such as the Library of Congress and National Library of Scotland, as well as institutions with historic arrangements such as Oxford University's Bodleian Library or the University of Sydney Library. Legislators revised legal deposit mandates in recent years to account for digital publications including national web archives and ebooks, which can be filed as a surrogate for a print copy. In the the United Kingdom, the Legal Deposit Libraries (Non-print Works) Regulations 2013 outline the requirements for preserving ebooks and other born-digital publications.[24] The legislation covers the legal deposit of future material and does not apply to any ebooks published before 2013. The bill also declares that the legal deposit is not required if "substantially the same work is published in the United Kingdom in print."[25] Despite evidence that platforms are internally variable, the policy follows a "one size fits all" rule for ebooks without considering the difference between a Kindle or Kobo file. While a reprint or new edition is well understood in traditional publishing, should updates be preserved? What constitutes a new edition rather than a constantly iterated update? Ebooks are second-class entities in the framework. No provision exists to ensure the capture of ebooks that do not feature an ISBN—in other words, all self-published books and many digital-only publications. Given the fall in digital sales for books by legacy publishers in comparison to new digital-only and self-published titles, a significant proportion of the current cultural record will remain absent from legal deposit libraries. For example, Bella Forrest's substantial back catalog is unavailable through the British Library or Library of Congress, and if Amazon closes the Kindle Store, these titles will be lost cultural memory. Nonetheless, if an ebook is considered worth cataloging, legal deposit libraries are required to provide hardware access, a practice that is easier for an open format than a platform that requires special software or hardware.[26]

The National Library of Scotland is one of the seven legal deposit libraries in the United Kingdom and has an ancillary role to the British Library for ebook legal deposit. Its catalog boasts at least ten thousand legal deposit ebooks, and many new titles, such as Dean Koontz's *The Silent Corner*, exist only in digital form, as companies such as HarperCollins and Ingram just provide ebook access.[27] For the national library of a vibrant literary culture, ebook access through EPUB rather than a Kindle format is acceptable except in cases of cultural significance. Publishers including Canongate and Edinburgh University Press must submit print copies regardless of their intent to preserve the cultural record of Scotland to ensure continued preservation if ebook platforms fail.

Amazon's use of digital rights management and encryption with Kindle files presents an obstacle for preservation, since libraries prefer to receive ebooks in a more open format such as EPUB. Even without encryption, the Library of Congress recommends using EPUB instead of other "acceptable" "XML-based formats that use proprietary DTDs or schemas."[28] Library-based preservation of Kindle titles would therefore depend on Amazon releasing the specifications for proprietary standards such as AZW and KFX. Users could then understand exactly how these files were created and interpreted by KindleGen and other cloud-based format parsers. Even if the final documents were not presented in a Kindle reading system, the documentation would allow for a more accurate re-creation of the idiosyncrasies of the Kindle's rendering of ebooks. All these challenges around hardware and content coalesce into a major bottleneck for preserving the history of the ebook in the early twenty-first century. It is still possible to look at copies of the Gutenberg Bible, but how many Kindle titles will still be accessible fifty years after their publication, let alone five hundred? Given the sheer volume of self-published works in the Kindle Store, and the fluidity with which they are released and taken down, we are unlikely ever to have accurate documentation of this significant moment in publishing history.

Services

As discussed in chapter 6, Amazon frequently changes or removes the Kindle's paratext services. While services are often disrupted for users, space also exists for users to exploit the systems. For example, Kunsthal Aarhus commissioned the Kindle Forkbomb (now known as Ubermorgen) to explore the potential for exploiting the Kindle's infrastructure artistically. Ubermorgen published "robot-generated ebooks" consisting of text "from millions of YouTube comments" with the aim of revealing "a compressed written view of our contemporary world, a frozen moment of collective expression sent back into the next recycling loop."[29] Ubermorgen does not identify examples, which would quickly be removed if discovered, but the documents on the website are less impressive than the blurb, with some titles as brief as twenty-seven pages. The project instead focuses on a self-publishing equivalent to a denial-of-service (DoS) attack, whereby it becomes impossible to find relevant titles in searches, since the store is flooded by automatically generated titles. Ubermorgen weaponized Amazon's infrastructure in the project by using AWS's Elastic Compute Cloud (EC2) and Mechanical Turk to automate the content extraction process to reveal ruptures in the Kindle Direct Publishing process. While it is not unusual for Amazon's cheap computational power to be used for spam,[30] the project demonstrated how this vast infrastructure could be used against Amazon itself. Since the art project wound down in 2013, the expansion of Kindle Direct Publishing and CreateSpace, Amazon's print-on-demand service, has led to further attempts to weaponize the self-publishing platforms for profit and money laundering. In response, Amazon has further altered the algorithms and calculations, creating an indeterminate platform that may shift multiple times daily.

Ubermorgen's experiment revealed one of Amazon's inherent infrastructural tensions: it is easier to input than export material from the company's services. We have encountered these issues throughout this book: from creating new product pages if metadata have been incorrectly entered to the closure of Kindle Popular Highlights while maintaining data collection processes. Retaining content within the Kindle ecosystem clearly benefits Amazon. Exclusive ebooks can encourage readers to use the platform. The accumulation of data that are then difficult for both individuals and publishers to export, even when doing so would be beneficial and potentially profitable, points to a larger shift in Amazon's business model. Shoshana Zuboff coined the phrase "behavioral futures markets" to describe the accumulation of data with the hopes of monetizing it later through predictive marketing.[31] Even if the reading data Amazon collects have no current value for marketing, which they clearly do, the possibilities for future monetization are only enhanced by retaining control of the data.

The rise of the cloud as the dominant computational metaphor has seen a shift from products to services. If the book is a service, then what does it mean to preserve a service? Is it sufficient to preserve examples of the hardware and copy-specific editions? Book historians often have rich archives, such as Robert Darnton's sustained use of the Société typographique de Neuchâtel's archive, to reconstruct the book trade of their chosen period. No such equivalent exists yet for Amazon, and reverse engineering algorithms or mining the patent filings can only provide a partial overview of the platform's development. Even Amazon is unlikely to have a complete archive, since algorithms assemble Kindle files remotely rather than existing as a coherent set of assets on a corporate server. Because the Kindle depends on its innovations, including subscription-free EV-DO, network capabilities are just as important as ebooks in documenting the platform. Dummy servers could replicate some of the functionality of Amazon Web Services, such as synchronizing across devices and a public record of highlighting practices.[32] My experience of documenting the Kindle platform has led to several of these challenges around reverse engineering, especially in collecting data for chapter 7. These personal struggles reflect the greater challenges in making good use of the Kindle as a platform. If services can be revoked or overhauled at short or no notice, what incentive do publishers have to encourage readers to use personal highlights, integration to external platforms, or born-digital indexes? The inherent instability of the platform only further reinforces a mutual conservatism on the part of both Amazon and publishers.

Amazon's reliance on service paratext marks the greatest weakness of the Kindle platform. Users can still access ebooks on the Kindle 1, but the obsolescence cycle of service paratext reveals further issues in the long-term sustainability of a stable platform. The first-generation device only shares a single service with the Oasis: Whispernet. While other services have been introduced (and removed), Whispersync has been an anchor for the platform by emphasizing "always-on" reading habits despite the relatively static nature of popular highlights and X-Ray indexes. The inconsistent delivery of these features across reading systems makes it difficult to conceptualize a "complete" edition of a Kindle book.

Non-book-related services also define the platform and can be difficult to re-create for posterity. For example, take Ask NowNow, one of the Kindle 1's "experimental" features, which did not even appear on the second device and was slowly eradicated through successive changes to the Amazon platform and Mechanical Turk offerings more generally. Ask NowNow predicted the emergence of Siri, Cortana, Amazon's Alexa service, and other "personal assistants," as it offered a service for asking questions directly from the device. Mechanical Turkers searched for answers, and the three best answers were displayed to the user, who could then select the most helpful response. Although the Mechanical Turk business model was scalable, the costs of the services outweighed the benefits, encouraging Amazon to shut down the service. This ideology pervades technology companies' decision-making, as free services only remain viable if they bring some extra value to the platform. Closing experimental features such as Ask NowNow and removing headphone jacks were part of a wider distinction between products in Amazon's hardware range. The launch of the Fire tablets offered multifunctional devices, which allowed the Kindle to focus on delivering book-related content rather than a range of unrelated ancillary features.

Re-creating the infrastructure requires archiving material before it is taken down. Often this happens too late. For example, Amazon shut down the dedicated forums for discussing the Kindle, directing users to a specific help forum or Goodreads to replace this void.[33] The Kindle Popular Highlights website, discussed in the previous chapter, was closed in September 2017 without an announcement. Visitors to the site get the message "Looking for something? We can help," while directing users to a notebook on the web-based Kindle app.[34] Readers who wish to discuss books with other users are directed to Goodreads as the sole remaining social network for the platform. The consolidation allows personal access through an official client while removing data about other users. The website's marketing potential was no longer viable, and the data were too revealing. This extended the removal of most popular highlights in 2014. Unfortunately what remains is only limited preservation of every single note and highlight on the platform, as well as the profiles of fifty million registered Kindle users. The Internet Archive captured almost sixty thousand pages, but the majority of user- and book-related data is now invisible.

The challenges around hardware, content, and services all highlight the highly contested relationship between Amazon control and publisher and reader autonomy within the Kindle platform. Users can either break out of the Amazon platform by rooting their devices and exploring the alternative possibilities of a low-power, slow-refreshing display or choose to face the potential loss of data and content when Amazon changes policy. These tensions also challenge the stable concept of an ebook, which may not exist as a fixed unit or have any form of permanence. The ebook depends on the Kindle, but how much support it will continue to receive from the company is unclear. Every aspect of the Kindle platform must be considered as contingent, and the publishing industry would strongly benefit from considering alternatives to relying on Amazon for ebookish infrastructure.

The golden age of the Kindle is over unless we see substantial innovations in color electronic paper, but Amazon and Lab126's impact on digital publishing has been substantial. While Amazon's development of the Kindle has slowed since the initial enthusiasm from 2007 to 2011, the platform remains synonymous with "ebooks" in Anglophone markets. Its consistent approach to hardware has been instrumental in defining ebooks. Except for occasional major hardware specification upgrades between generations, the Kindle evolved incrementally without substantially affecting the older generations. As a result, the underlying computational architecture and format standards remain an unwieldy mix of contemporary technology and 1990s anachronisms. This mix has not hindered the platform, however, as the competing demands of backward compatibility and innovation have limited the Kindle to replicating the affordances of print rather than attempting to compete with other media. To succeed, the ebook needed to excel in comparison to print while also conforming to a strict set of expectations. Every new format change has attempted to push beyond the initial formula, but the constraints of electronic paper, and the larger unwillingness of legacy publishers, have led to a technological plateau where ebooks are good enough to supplement print.

While the Kindle platform has remained relatively consistent over the last decade, more substantial change has occurred since the late 2010s. In late 2016, the International Digital Publishing Forum (IDPF), custodians of the EPUB specification, merged with the World Wide Web Consortium to form the Publishing@W3C group. When the group initially formed, it produced a flurry of activity around creating a successor to EPUB: the Packaged Web Publication (PWP), a document that sits between a website available off-line and an ebook. The new format would take a step closer to the "interactive electronic book" promised by hypertext scholars in the 1990s that challenged the dominant paradigm of scarcity in the ebook trade. Unfortunately, this excitement never materialized into a coherent specification, as early progress fizzled into a conceptual cul-de-sac when attempting to define the boundaries between books, publications, and websites. This stasis has reinforced Amazon's tight grip on the ebook market, as the Kindle's competitors have not created a feasible alternative that completely revises the current paradigm. Without such an intervention, neither side is likely to invest in improving infrastructure.

Amazon has resisted the constant challenges of the publishing industry on either side of the Atlantic over the last two decades. The Kindle remains the de facto ebook reader as rivals including Kobo and Nook flounder. Despite solidifying this position, Amazon's interest in hardware lies elsewhere with the launch of Alexa and the Fire range. Books are no longer central to Amazon's media interests, and this is reflected in its hardware. Movies and audiobooks now drive hardware decisions rather than attempting to re-create the fidelity of print. Within publishing, Amazon has been demonized for the Kindle, but the recent rise of Audible has been more broadly welcomed despite forming a similar threat. In fact, since Audible often acquires audio rights, the service is arguably more monopolistic than the Kindle. Audible's success comes from a mutual understanding that both Amazon and publishers benefit from investment. Print and its digital surrogates remain legacy publishers' strengths, though they are more willing to collaborate on new media. The arrival of Alexa and devices such as the Echo Show emphasize the "talking book" over ebooks, which merit only a minimal reference on the help pages for the Echo Show.

Prophecies of the electronic book were more radical than the Kindle. The rhetoric of hypertext fiction in the early 1990s embodied by titles such as J. Yellowlees Douglas's *The End of Books—or Books without End?* primed users for a revolutionized form of reading that would extend beyond the book to take full advantage of the affordances of digital media.[1] Ted Nelson predicted a digital revolution through microtransactions, reusable content, and interconnected books, but legacy publishing has resisted change to replicate a print model digitally. A pragmatic model triumphed over the mythical digital revolution, with new workflows taking precedence over changing the reading experience. Ebooks are stuck in the rut of technological conservatism that ensures there will always be a market for e-readers and ebooks, but this is unlikely to challenge the dominance of print within genres that have not yet moved online.

It is too early to tell whether the longer-term aims of Publishing@W3C will represent a significant challenge to Amazon's dominance of the ebook marketplace, but the merger of the IDPF and W3C represents an opportunity to reconsider the scope of digital publications. The Publishing@W3C working group's mission statement is as ambitious as Lab126's aims for digitization: "to enable all publications—with all their specificities and traditions—to become first-class entities on the Web."[2] The mission statement does not explicitly mention books as privileged, but the ideology suggests a move toward a uniform body of "first-class entities on the Web" that would render books identical to magazines or other forms of publications within the boundaries of web-based standards. While the first push to implement these aims through the Packaged Web Publication specification resulted in failure, the group's ambitions demonstrate the challenges faced by any rivals to the current Kindle paradigm.

A rival specification will only pose a significant challenge to Amazon's dominance with the Kindle if the new specification also accounts for the infrastructural demands of an ebook platform. Amazon managed these challenges through a complex, vertically integrated infrastructure: users can buy dedicated hardware that allows them to purchase, consume, and discuss the books entirely within the confines of the software. Other reading systems are derivative of dedicated e-readers and offer similar options to varying degrees. The web has the infrastructure to compete with Amazon on equal terms, but this comes with challenges for accessibility and discoverability: how will users find ebooks if access is decentralized? Not all of Amazon's infrastructural experiments are successful, but Amazon has invested where other technology companies and publishers were wary. Despite a near-continuous battle with the publishing industry—initially with regard to physical books, but more recently with digital editions—Amazon's investment in the Kindle developed ebooks from a niche product to a requirement for any new title.

The Kindle's lasting influence will be on publishing and social reading rather than on shaping broader media technological trends, a fate ensured by the dominance of smartphones and tablets in the 2010s. The Kindle 1 was a landmark device in the replication of print on-screen, but the emergence of smartphones and tablets ensured a larger shift in mobile computing beyond e-readers. Even the novelty of the Kindle 1 is contentious. The first-generation launch popularized electronic paper after the Sony PRS-500, the first device launched outside Japan to feature electronic paper, failed to meet sales expectations. Beyond bringing this technology to a wider audience, the hardware has remained relatively consistent; any upgrade has been iterative rather than a true innovation. Nonetheless, Amazon developed ebooks from a product to a service to finally become part of the publishing infrastructure. Initially this took the form of "Look Inside" and other services that used a manipulable digital text as its foundations. An early focus on hardware to encourage adoption beyond technologically savvy ebook readers ensured the sustainability of the format once Amazon's hardware ambitions expanded. Once a market developed, Amazon could maintain the infrastructure and remain the dominant ebook brand. Amazon was not interested in what device readers were using to consume on, just as long as their primary ebook platform was Kindle rather than the competition. Nonetheless, the original Kindle hardware configurations continue to shape what is possible to read on any software.

The endless skirmishes between Amazon and the book trade will continue as long as the company sells books. Despite this pushback, the Kindle was instrumental in generating a wider acceptance of the use of digital publications and workflows. Since Amazon understood the importance of scale and was able to use its substantial preexisting infrastructure, the company overcame both publishers' and consumers' hesitance to engage with the Kindle to make ebooks a success story. Early predictions of ebooks replacing print have faded away, to be replaced with more nuanced distinctions between the two media. Readers choose to consume different genres in print and digital form, leading to a divergent marketplace. Genres such as romance, erotica, and YA have flourished in this new market, while print-oriented publishers have doubled down on the materiality of "bookishness" by creating luxury and high-cost editions.[3] As a result, the average sale price of books has increased by 11 percent between 2007 and 2017 in the United Kingdom, while the total volume has decreased by 20 percent, leading to an overall contraction of the print book market of 11 percent. Conversely, digital publications have failed to overcome the perception of disposability, hence the rise of genre fiction and the relative lack of literary fiction published successfully through the Kindle platform. The new market dynamics of the Kindle and the associated growth of genres often ignored by print-oriented publishers reflect the divergence seen in Netflix, which has witnessed the rise of feature-length documentaries.[4]

The publishing industry remains resilient due to the addition of digital and audio sales, ensuring growth in recent years, but despite the supposed resurgence in print sales for sectors of the market, Angus Phillips argues that in Great Britain, despite year-on-year growth in the book trade, this has been uncoupled from economic growth as measured by gross domestic product, demonstrating an underperformance of the industry.[5] The quandary is mirrored by struggles in other traditional creative industries, including print journalism, film, and music, as they face the new challenges of digital consumption. The Kindle and similar ebook platforms remain a space for experimentation, and schemes such as subscriptions will continue to reshape industry business models. Digital publishing start-ups have attempted to reshape various aspects of the publishing industry, but up to a third fail within a decade of launching, and more are acquired by larger businesses for the staff rather than the product, as happened in the case of Readmill when it was acquired by Dropbox.[6]

The Kindle has transformed from hardware to a diffuse network of reading systems. This shift in strategy hid the technological obsolescence of the dedicated e-reading devices that were only of interest to a subset of the potential audience for ebooks. As the Publishing@W3C working group and Amazon's Kindle Cloud Reader continue to erode the distinction between ebooks and the web, digital publishing will lose its position as a discrete form. The Kindle will thus represent a transitional moment when the publishing industry was able to continue working in the older model of production and reception. While Amazon continues to invest in the platform as a pseudomonopoly, the digital book will remain similar to print; but with the challenge of more diverse formats, and of funding such production, publishers' symbiotic relationship with Amazon is likely to continue.

Amazon is removing the Kindle name from various parts of its infrastructure. The Kindle Fire became the Fire in 2014, and the Kindle app was changed to "Books" in the 5.6 update to Fire OS. Adoption of "Kindling" as a verb never took off, and mobile reading takes many different forms rather than focusing on dedicated e-readers. Nonetheless, ebooks are now a viable medium, albeit with a different market from traditional print publications. A decade after its launch, the Kindle is established as a medium less derivative of print, with its own trends and audience, but nonetheless tied to the successes and failures of its predecessor. Amazon's continual diversification to become an essential part of technological infrastructure in emerging markets will pull the company farther from its origins as an online book retailer, but it remains the custodian for the future of the ebook. The Kindle may well be extinguished, but it fired up both legacy publishers and technology companies to consider the place of the book within the complex media ecology of the early twenty-first century.

Glossary

Italics indicate a cross-reference.

Agency pricing. Publishers fix the price of a publication with the retailer receiving a predetermined percentage of sales.

Alexa. The name assigned to both Amazon's web metrics website and the voice-activated service equivalent to Siri or Cortana.

Amazon Standard Identification Number (ASIN). Amazon's proprietary cataloging system that incorporates *ISBN-10* while accounting for nonbook products.

Amazon Web Services (AWS). Amazon's suite of "cloud computing" services, where users can rent parts of Amazon's large data centers to avoid large start-up costs.

Android. An open-source mobile phone operating system maintained by Google and based on Linux.

ASCII. A *character map* developed for the telegraph with a focus on the Latin alphabet and common punctuation.

Audible. Audiobook company acquired by Amazon in 2008.

AZW. Amazon's original file format for Kindle ebooks.

Backlist. Books in the publisher's back catalog that can be reprinted or converted into ebooks if they continue to be profitable.

Book Industry Standards and Communications (BISAC). Categories relating to the genres of books, maintained by the Book Industry Study Group (BISG).

Cascading Style Sheets (CSS). A markup language for the presentation of *HTML*.

Character map. A standard for converting binary or hexadecimal numbers into text through conversion tables. Examples include *ASCII*, *Unicode*, and *Latin-1*.

DAISY (Digital Accessible Information System). A consortium founded in 1996 to create standards for accessible digital publications, primarily through *text-to-speech*.

Digital rights management (DRM). Software installed alongside media content to protect the material from being shared.

Digitization. The process of converting analog material to a digital format.

Electronic paper. A screen that attempts to replicate the affordances of print without backlighting or high-power consumption. Electronic paper is the generic name; E Ink is the name of the most prominent company, although the terms are often used interchangeably.

EPUB. An open-source ebook format maintained by the *World Wide Web Consortium* and a rival to the Kindle's file format. EPUB is an industry standard for all major ebook platforms except the Kindle.

Fiona. The code name for the first-generation Kindle, released in 2007.

Format. The guidelines for presenting and interpreting files, codified in format names such as *AZW*, *EPUB*, and *PDF*.

Frontlist. A publisher's new titles that receive promotion. A book may only be considered frontlist for a couple of months before entering the backlist.

Functional Requirements for Bibliographic Records (FRBR). A library-developed standard for identifying conceptual links between different editions or adaptations of the same book.

Goodreads. A social network for sharing reading habits acquired by Amazon in 2014.

HyperText Markup Language (HTML). The presentational markup language for the World Wide Web.

International Digital Publishing Forum (IDPF). The industry network for digital publishing and custodians of the *EPUB* specification until a merger with the *W3C* in early 2017.

International Standard Book Number (ISBN). A standard for identifying editions of a book according to where it was published and the publisher.

ION. Amazon's proprietary *JSON* standard, used as the basis of the *KFX* file *format*.

iOS. Apple's operating system for the iPhone and iPad.

JavaScript. A lightweight scripting language for web-based interactive content.

JSON (JavaScript Object Notation). A markup language for storing data in an interchangeable format, often used to store metadata.

KFX. The cutting-edge Kindle file format as of early 2018, designed for the release of the "luxury" line of Kindle hardware beginning with the Oasis in 2014.

Kindle Create. A software package designed by Amazon to allow authors to convert Microsoft Word documents into files suitable to upload to *Kindle Direct Publishing*.

Kindle Direct Publishing (KDP). Amazon's *self-publishing* platform.

Kindle in Motion. A series of ebook publications featuring enhanced typographic layouts and animated GIFs.

Kindle Popular Highlights. A website formerly dedicated to aggregated data about reading habits on the Kindle.

Kindle Unlimited. An ebook subscription service primarily featuring titles from *Kindle Direct Publishing.*

Kobo. The Kindle's main e-reader competition, maintained by Rakuten.

Lab126. The Amazon subsidiary set up to develop hardware starting with early work on the Kindle in 2004.

Latin-1. A *character map* for letters used in European languages, which reduces file size but restricts internationalization efforts.

Location. Amazon's alternative measure for identifying extracts in the text according to a relative location rather than page number or byte location.

"Look Inside the Book." Amazon's first digitization scheme that allowed users to look inside books before purchasing them.

Machine-readable cataloging (MARC). A *metadata* standard developed and used by libraries for cataloging.

Mechanical Turk. Amazon's website for paid crowdsourced transactions.

Metadata. Data about data. For example, a book's *ISBN*, title, and cataloging information.

Mobipocket. The French company that developed the ebook format (MOBI) and store that formed the basis of the Kindle. Acquired by Amazon in 2004.

Online Information Exchange (ONIX). An *XML* specification for book trade related metadata.

Open eBook Publication Structure (OEBPS). Early name for *EPUB*, changed with the release of EPUB2 in 2009.

Optical character recognition (OCR). The process of extracting text from a photographed page.

Paratext. Parts of the book that supplement the book but are not part of the main body, e.g., page numbers, indexes, table of contents, and running headers.

Personal digital assistant (PDA). Small mobile computers similar to contemporary smartphones but without roaming data access.

PHL. The *XML* file containing an ebook's top ten most popular highlights.

Portable Document Format (PDF). A facsimile archival file format developed by Adobe (now an open standard). A popular file format for digital publishing.

PRC. The precursor to MOBI and AZW, developed for reading on the Palm series of personal digital assistants.

Prime Reading. An ebook subscription library available to users of Amazon Prime, the company's main subscription service.

Print on demand. Technology designed to enable publishers to move from cost-effective print runs to printing once a customer has ordered a copy.

Project Gutenberg. A website dedicated to digitizing and hosting *public domain* texts.

Public domain. Books no longer protected by copyright, often due to expiration.

Reading system. The generic term for software, website, or app used to access and read ebooks.

Reflowable text. A design principle for ebooks where formatting is nonspecific to allow readers to change the font size and layout to suit their needs.

Scalable Vector Graphics (SVG). An *XML* markup language listing the vectors of shapes to display instead of bitmaps (pixel-by-pixel representations of images).

"Search Inside the Book." An extension of *"Look Inside the Book"* featuring *optical character recognition* that extracted the text to be used for Kindle titles.

Self-publishing. A slight misnomer. Historically referred to authors undertaking the labor of producing books but now refers to process of publishing material outside the power of gatekeepers via large publishers including Wattpad and *Kindle Direct Publishing*.

Shelfari. A reading social network developed to annotate information about characters and books' accolades. Acquired by Amazon in 2008.

SQL (Structured Query Language). A popular open programming language for database structure and queries.

Text-to-speech. Software that converts marked-up text into a synthesized human voice.

Trade publishers. Companies that publish books aimed at the widest possible audience.

Unicode. A consortium with the mission to ensure cross-compatible *character maps* for global languages. Unicode also maintains emoji.

UTF-8. The 8-bit character map designed by *Unicode* with the potential to store over a million unique characters.

Virtualization. The process of re-creating a computer environment virtually.

Whispernet. The name for Amazon's wireless network designed for users who purchased 3G devices.

Whispersync. A subsection of *Whispernet* that facilitates the synchronization of user data between devices and Amazon's cloud computing services with the dual purpose of data collection for Amazon and cloud-based bookmarking for users.

Word Runner. Amazon's speed-reading software.

Word Wise. A paratext service designed by Amazon to improve readers' vocabulary by including in-text definitions between lines.

World Wide Web Consortium (W3C). The organization responsible for maintaining various web-based specifications including *XML*, *HTML*, *CSS*, *EPUB*, and *SVG*.

XML (Extensible Markup Language). Markup language developed to allow cross-platform compatibility and user-generated data standards.

X-Ray. Amazon's indexing service.

Appendix A: Methodology

This appendix provides a more comprehensive overview of the data collection and analysis process. I used freely available packages including Gephi for network analysis, AntConc's corpus linguistics functions, and R for statistical analysis. Since Amazon's data are proprietary and several important sources are no longer publicly available, I can only share overviews of the data, but where possible I have indicated where the data can be accessed for replication purposes.

The research for *Four Shades* was conducted between 2013 and 2018. Over the five years, several of my e-readers and computers stopped functioning or were replaced, allowing for a variety of devices to be studied, including the following:

- Kindle Keyboard (3rd generation)
- MacBook Pro (2010)
- Kindle Touch
- Kindle 7
- iPad 3
- Sony Xperia E1
- MacBook Air (2015)
- Kindle Fire 5 (2016)
- HP 8300 Elite (Windows 2010; released in 2016)
- Kindle Cloud Reader (various devices)

Where possible, I noted the software versions used, but automated software upgrades on Apple and Android devices made it difficult to track exact versions, and change logs are not archived.

A Note on Archives and Sources

Working on a proprietary, commercially sensitive platform still in operation poses challenges for access. This is exacerbated in a case such as Amazon, which thrives on secrecy. In response to an interview question about not releasing sales figures for the Kindle, despite outselling predictions, Bezos stated, "It's tradition, mostly."[1] In place of institutional archives and interviews, one of the most reliable sources of information was the US Patent and Trademark Office's (USPTO) archives, which feature over seven thousand patents from Amazon employees. While the patents feature obsolete or theoretical technologies, they provide a conceptual framework for understanding the company's ideology when developing the Kindle. These are not a substitute for company archives and elite interviews, but patents can identify the company's strategic priorities more than documenting innovation. For example, Amazon's infamous patent filing for its "one-click" technology, discussed in further detail in chapter 2, reveals the aspects of Amazon's shopping technology that were considered important enough to protect.[2]

Capturing historical snapshots of Amazon's website, the Internet Archive was an invaluable source for *Four Shades*. Alexa, a company subsidiary, provided the Internet Archive with data about Amazon's web pages. The data set therefore represents the closest to an official open company archive, although the complexity of Amazon's website infrastructure ensures this is a limited snapshot, and coverage may be as patchy as less than 1 percent of all of Amazon's web pages. I supplement this evidence with data collated from MobileRead, a popular web-based forum for discussing the technical elements of ebooks, and a community that has tirelessly documented changes to software, hardware differences, and other otherwise ignored elements of the Kindle infrastructure. Finally, I used "View Source" on pertinent Amazon web pages to reveal the underlying data structures. I use this variety of sources to corroborate claims.

Chapter 2

Corpus Analysis (Table 2.1)
I used Brigham Young University's News on the Web (NOW) corpus—a cross section of online news articles published between 2010 and 2017—to assess

patterns in news organizations' portrayal of Amazon.[3] *Collocation* is the linguistic measure of how frequently two words appear in "proximity" to each other and how these words "subsist in the characteristic associations that the word participates in, alongside other words or structures with which [they] frequently co-[occur]."[4] For example, the meaning of "Apple" can be determined through its proximity to the word "iPad," "tree," or "Beatles." I conducted a collocate search of "Amazon" for any words appearing five words to either side. I removed words pertaining to the Amazon rain forest and clustered words into categories according to emergent themes.

Patent Analysis (Figures 2.1–2.2 and Table 2.2)

I discovered patents through the USPTO Patent Full-Text and Image Database (PatFT) search function. While a range of employees are named inventors for Amazon's patents, the parent company remains the "assignee." The exact name of the research and development company has shifted from "Amazon.com Inc" to "Amazon Technology," but a search for "(AN/"Amazon.com" OR AN/"Amazon Technologies")" catches all variations of the company's patent output. I classified the patents according to the filing date, which might be years before the patent was accepted. The analysis accounted for all granted patents as of February 5, 2018, the first batch of patents released for the month. The filing date is a more accurate marker of the company's position at the time of development than the eventual filing. For example, a subgroup at Amazon led by Janna Hamaker and Tom Killalea filed a series of patents related to book versioning and authority in 2010, but "Book version mapping" was not granted until December 2017, years after Amazon had moved on from developing new ebook technologies to focus on drones, other media, and cloud computing.[5]

Figure 2.1 was calculated directly from within the USPTO search by limiting the search to a year. Due to the lag in the USPTO granting applications and the ongoing review process, the data from 2013 onward indicate not a decline but rather that numerous patents filed since 2013 are still under review. Given the upward tick in filings, this is likely to exceed the output before 2013. Figure 2.2 was compiled by extracting the USPTO classifications for the patent applications and creating pairs where classifications collocated. I imported the data to Gephi to create a network. I manually identified the denser clusters and labeled them with the most common classification term and its relationship to the Amazon ecosystem.

I compiled table 2.2 through a keyword analysis of the abstract and claims of the textual corpus of Amazon's granted patents. The linguistic analysis of "keyness" focuses on words that appear more frequently in a corpus compared to a reference corpus. This technique is used to identify the words that are more pertinent in one set of text compared to another. While "the" might appear more frequently in one body of texts than another, this does not translate to salience: the use of modal verbs is more common in instructional text than in poetry. Modal verbs should rank higher in terms of keyness, even if they appear less often than "the," "a," and other commonly used words. I downloaded the text directly from the USPTO PatFT full-text database and sorted patents into three-year intervals according to filing date. I calculated the keywords using three-year moving averages, so each set of keywords reveals the terms that appeared more frequently in a period compared to the preceding past years other than 1995–1997, which I compared to the 1998–2000 data sets. This highlights emergent trends in three-year periods, although it cannot be generalized to show that the terms in each list were a greater focus in that period than any other.

Chapter 3

Recommendations Network Analysis (Table 3.1)

The recommendation data were produced by a team led by Julian McAuley in 2014 in a project that required a large body of data from Amazon.[6] I used the subset of Kindle recommendations that contains a variety of metadata for 900,000 ebooks. Since Amazon limits recommendations to categories, it was possible to extract the "purchased with" and "also looked at" data for just the Kindle items without verifying that all books came from the Kindle Store. The size of the data set made a network visualization prohibitive and unlikely to yield interesting results. I instead gauged the scale and density of the network by calculating the volume of inbound and outbound links. After sorting them, I looked up the ASINs of the ten titles with the most inbound links.

Chapter 4

Since the Kindle creates different files according to the reading system configuration, the analysis of formats made full use of the diverse range of hardware I had at my disposal, including supplementary evidence from friends' and family's older devices. I collected a unique copy of my own ebooks through Amazon's "Download and Transfer via USB" option to access versions of files designed for my broken Kindles, including the first two Kindle Keyboards. Where possible, I loaded files onto the devices to capture any ancillary files included once the book is opened for the first time. The iOS devices remained inaccessible owing to the obfuscation of folders without jailbreaking devices. Documentary evidence for the iPad file format therefore comes from secondary sources. I used a suite of tools including Hex Fiend (a so-called hex editor designed to read binary files) and Calibre, an ebook conversion tool, to analyze the files as both raw binary text and as they would appear if converted to EPUB. Due to the complexity of Amazon's format ecosystem, my analysis contains traces of Hex Fiend and Calibre. This comes with its own limitations, as Kirschenbaum warns that "both the emulator *and* the hex editor are programmatic computational environments applying some particular logic—a certain formal materiality—to the string of bits in question."[7] My approach in chapter 4 therefore mixes what Kirschenbaum has called "formal materiality," or "the relational attitudes by which [digital objects] are naturalized as a result of the procedural friction," and "forensic materiality," "the idea that no two things in the physical world are ever exactly alike."[8]

Chapter 5

Digitization of Titles from 1989 (Table 5.1)

The British National Bibliography (BNB), maintained by the British Library, offers records of every book published in the United Kingdom since 1950. I downloaded all records with a publication date of 1989. After cleaning the data, I had 30,940 titles published in 1989, including books reissued with a new ISBN. The resulting snapshot is arbitrary, but the sample size is sufficiently large to identify pertinent trends across genres and publishers. Since 1989 was a half decade before Amazon launched, all entries were intentionally uploaded as stock in its warehouses or via a third party, and therefore any evidence would demonstrate the company's commitment to maintaining a complete record of ISBNs rather than a direct import from Bowker's *Books in Print*. The main product page for each ISBN was manually examined and categorized according to each title's availability on the site during July 2017.

Amazon Charts

I collected data from the *New York Times* Best Sellers list and Amazon Charts between May and September 2017. The "Combined Print & E-Book" fiction and nonfiction lists were the closest equivalents to Amazon's "Most Sold." Since both lists are created using proprietary methodologies (including, for example, excluding certain genres), the data are not representative but instead reveal the ideological leanings of both data providers.

Chapter 6

Searching

All search results came from the Kindle for Mac 1.20.2 edition of John Milton's *Paradise Lost*. The latest version of Kindle for Mac (1.21) refactored the indexing system to discard all punctuation and spacing to consistently return 174 results regardless, removing some of idiosyncratic nuances visible in earlier versions of the indexing algorithm. This is not consistent with the indexing of Kindle for iPhone 6.3, however, which lists 420 results for "man." The inconsistency between reading systems is indicative of the discrepancies across the automated service paratext.

Chapter 7

"Social Reading" contains the largest data set, comprising over a million popular highlights and a selection of highlights from a further eight hundred titles. The volatility of the Kindle infrastructure during the five-year research period underpinning this book led to a degradation in the data's availability, including the removal of several titles in the eight hundred ebooks data set, and the slow erosion of the Kindle Popular Highlights website from the removal of the most popular list in 2016 to its closure in 2017.

The Kindle Popular Highlights Website

The primary website for viewing public highlights was started to allow users to access their highlights from an external location but grew into a valuable source of a slice of the data around the Kindle. I used two main sources to compile the data: (1) a list of the million most popular highlights based on static data from 2014, and (2) pages for each ebook title that contained a random selection of highlights pertaining to the book.

Eight Hundred Titles

The location data for the top ten most popular highlights are publicly available only through ebooks the user has either purchased or borrowed through Kindle Unlimited or Prime Reading. There is also no guarantee that a title, however popular, features a popular highlights list. I assembled the titles by sifting through the library of titles I had purchased for leisure or research in combination with free titles downloaded or borrowed through the Kindle Unlimited scheme during June 2017. The top ten popular highlights were extracted manually through a Kindle for Mac application. No API exists for downloading popular highlights, as the data are available directly only through dedicated software.

I had initially hoped to equally represent the twenty-seven top-level categories Amazon offers for the Kindle Store, but categories such as "art and photography" are less likely to feature shared highlights than "fiction." Several issues emerged when attempting to find titles:

1. *Audience size:* Public domain books were the most likely to contain highlights, given their visibility as free books in comparison to the slurry of Kindle Unlimited. Smaller titles may occasionally contain single popular highlights or highlights that contradict information offered elsewhere. Since Kindle Unlimited offers limited access to best sellers, many of the books would be classified as midlist and not feature enough highlights.

2. *Genre expectations:* After sifting through more than one thousand titles to compile the corpus, I found clear differences between genres. For example, self-help guides marketed at women are more likely to be highlighted than books designed for pickup artists. Books that blur the lines between romance and erotica were more likely to contain highlights than those that had been classified as "adult." Since a substantial proportion of books did not feature highlights in an initial audit, I elected to focus on building a corpus from genres with a high probability of containing highlights.

3. *Comparability:* Amazon does not frequently update the publicly available public domain files, and as no data show how representative the highlights are, it is impossible to compare books based on their life span or publication. Every aspect had to be aggregated and indexed to allow for comparisons.

Due to these limitations, the collection overrepresents classic public domain titles and genres associated with the Kindle Direct Publishing boom, including self-help, romance and erotica, young adult, and fitness guides.

A collated list of the eight hundred titles and their ASINs (with a few exceptions) can be found online at sprowberry.com/800.xlsx.

Visible Highlights (Figure 7.3)

When Amazon introduced the "About the Book" sidebar, the feature introduced data about the total volume of highlights alongside the number of unique selections. I compared these data with the sum of the top ten most popular highlights to calibrate how much material was unavailable through the ebook. The "About the Book" data do not feature dates when they were updated and, as with many aspects of Kindle Popular Highlights, can only offer an indication of the total volume. The analysis also reveals discrepancies between the data, as any result that moves closer to showing the complete set of highlights indicates an inconsistency in the numbers.

Highlighting Patterns

I created the heat map of a single quotation from Jane Austen's *Pride and Prejudice* (figure 7.10) by comparing highlights from the quotation from a range of editions that appeared in the 2015 list of most popular highlights. The data from Donna Tartt's *The Goldfinch* were extracted from the available data on the page dedicated to the title. I manually compiled a corpus of 2,239 publicly available highlights from *The Goldfinch* to assess variation between micro- and macro-level sampling. This represents only 1 percent of the total volume of highlights, but the sample is large enough to identify patterns that corroborate the data Amazon has aggregated about the most popular highlights. The sample was randomly generated by Amazon and therefore not representative but begins to identify patterns in the company's algorithmic curation of the popular highlights both within the reading system as indicated by patents and externally on the website.

Aggregate Reading Location (Figures 7.7–7.8)

I generated the boxplots in R from the internal highlight data from *Harry Potter* and *A Shade of Vampire* books published up until 2016. The boxplots show the distribution of the ten visible highlights in each book, showing the full distribution, median, and standard deviation.

Highlights as Text (Table 7.1)

I ran a word-frequency analysis of the 1.1 million highlights in the Kindle Popular Highlights database through AntConc, removing common articles and conjunctions to focus on nouns, adjectives, and verbs. The relative ranking was included to contextualize the position of the words within the wider corpus. I chose frequencies over a more sophisticated analysis such as keyness as an indication of words of interest, since a reference corpus would need to be representative of the books under discussion, many of which are still protected by copyright and remain unavailable for analysis.

Dictionary as Social Network

I scraped a set of comments on the Kindle Popular Highlights page for the *New Oxford Dictionary of American English*, second edition, in July 2016. The algorithmic mediation of the available comments only revealed data from the preceding week and year-old comments.

Appendix B: Ebook Bibliography

Kindle files are compiled at point of download on Amazon's servers and cannot be treated as consistent beyond individual files. Ebook bibliography requires a new vocabulary to distinguish between unique editions and account for the variability between dedicated e-readers and their simulation via Kindle for PC. Academic style guides have been slow to react to the changing demands of ebooks. The eighth edition of the *MLA Handbook*, published in 2016, largely ignores ebook platforms within a broad conceptual framework of media in the early twenty-first century. The revised *MLA Handbook* introduced the media metaphor of "containers" and "content" to its citation system, where a citation can simply note that the version consulted was an "e-book" and specify the copy as a "Kindle ed." As I demonstrated in chapter 4, this approach cannot provide sufficient detail of the item in a cloud-generated format specification. The in-text reference section mentions only citing a "part number" if it is "explicit (visible in the document) and fixed (the same for all users of the document)" but does not offer an example of this in principle.[1] The seventeenth edition of *The Chicago Manual of Style*, published in 2017, offers a more nuanced breakdown of ebook citations, although the information is contradictory, wavering between adding the broadest possible title of a platform (such as "Kindle edition") to the end of an otherwise regular reference and including location information.[2] As variations exist within platforms, let alone between them, scholars need a more robust framework for identifying and citing ebooks as unique digital objects.

In the appendix to *I AM ERROR*, Nathan Altice demonstrates the need for closer attention to medium-specific bibliography for digital objects, noting that "platform studies owes much to the discipline of bibliography."[3] Altice further argues that even though the fidelity of these objects and surrogates, such as cartridges and their ROMs, may appear to be identical, "we know that they often carry along unseen textual artifacts of their history, circulation, and distribution. None of these aspects should be ignored when we take bibliographic account of our digital objects."[4] The work of platform studies helps to illuminate the material conditions of creation and circulation, but this needs to be supplemented by traditional bibliographical rigor to encourage appropriate documentation in nonspecialist works.

Digital bibliography often focuses on the exceptional—video games,[5] electronic literature,[6] digital-physical hybrids[7]—but mundane digital objects such as web pages, facsimiles, Instagram feeds, and Word documents have not received the same level of attention. Ebooks appear familiar on the surface, drawing on the rich bibliographical and logistical traditions of print, but despite this supposed dull exterior, the objects present new challenges for bibliography, as evidenced throughout *Four Shades*. It is possible to see the EPUB source files created by a publisher or self-publishing author and compare them to a local copy of the final publication, but Amazon's black-box cloud processing and delivery of ebook content ensure that the Kindle format remains a distant object. The descriptive bibliography of Kindle ebooks requires an understanding of cloud computing bibliography and the book-as-continuous-object. I offer some suggestions for referencing ebooks in this appendix, but conventions and standards evolve on the basis of further knowledge and developments.

Mechanisms remains a foundational text in both platform studies and digital bibliography due to Kirschenbaum's introduction of digital forensic analysis into both media and literary studies. Kirschenbaum provided case studies for a range of static digital objects including Michael Joyce's *afternoon* and Roberta and Ken Williams's *Mystery House*, which provide the foundations for understanding less-fixed artifacts.[8] The dynamic generation of ebooks ensures that every copy is unique. The typical Kindle ebook does not have sufficiently complete and verified metadata on Amazon product pages, prompting the need for further forensic analysis. Amazon maintains control over publicly available metadata on product pages, but this information can be unreliable. For example, the product page for Christopher Rice's *Bone Music* features a file size in the "product details" of 1,960 KB, but when the book is downloaded, the size ranged from 786 KB to 812 KB depending on the file format.[9] An opened copy of the title on

Kindle for Mac OS 1.20.2 clocked in at 1,772 KB with ancillary documents. Similarly, the product page does not list the "location" size but references the "Print Length" accompanied by "Page Numbers Source ISBN," a useful measure for comparison, but not accurate enough to ensure that page numbers transfer between media.

As with forensic evidence, it also important to note the difference between tampered and untampered files. An unopened Kindle file is substantially different from a loaded ebook, since the ancillary files are only downloaded once a user begins to read. This creates a significant difference for the user experience beyond any bibliographical variation. Amazon facilitates the collection of "new" ebooks through the "Download and transfer via USB" option when managing Kindle content associated with a device. It is possible to collate a full bibliographical record from this file alone other than the location length, which requires an open app. Since metadata around ancillary files and the location length are necessary to create accurate bibliography records, one should assume that files have been opened in generating bibliographies.

From Collation to Location

Ebook bibliography has more in common with the pre-nineteenth-century print book than with mass-produced twenty-first-century books. Early modern books featured unreliable pagination with a mixture of unnumbered pages and signatures that might mix letters, roman numerals, and other elements primarily intended to aid the book binder in ensuring correct order. Pagination for Kindle titles is equally unreliable, and page numbers are algorithmically generated according to nonstandard rules. The book trade typically identifies the title page as the first page with Arabic numerals, ensuring the first page of the main body rarely begins with page 1. Conversely, the Kindle's algorithmic generation assumes the main body marks page 1, ensuring any additional accuracy is at least a couple of pages out of synchronization.

The early modern bibliographical practice suggested that books should be handled according to each unique copy. The formula includes the binding of the book (folio, quarto, octavo) followed by a method of identifying an edition. In *Principles of Descriptive Bibliography*, Fredson Bowers provides an example issue formula of "4°: $A^2B\text{-}C^4D^2$" to represent "a quarto [consisting] of the following gatherings: 2 leaves signed A, 4 leaves signed B, 4 leaves signed C, and 2 leaves signed D."[10] The alphabetical signatures were used to allow binders to collate the book effectively rather than to aid navigation, but this was a useful tool for checking if two versions of the same book were printed in the same run. Just as early modern bibliographers adapted to the material conditions of letterpress printing, ebook bibliography must develop conventions suitable for formats rather than algorithmic page numbers. The solution is platform dependent, as iBooks, for example, removes all traces of static pages, rendering in-text citations impossible. For the Kindle, we have two prebuilt solutions. First we can use the underlying byte register location used in the internal files for marking the position of highlights, index entries, and reading locations. The byte-level location is difficult to access and requires use of ancillary files such as an ebook's PHL. Second, the location information is available for all titles, even if it is obfuscated by an attempt to render "real page numbers," and is the most appropriate in-text citation mechanism.

Kindle Bibliography

The following principles assume that it is sufficient to identify a publication at the higher level rather than individual copies of digital objects. All extra details should be available to compile from various sources without recourse to subverting DRM.

Format
Creator(s) (Release date). *Title* [Hardware and firmware or Software and version].
  Format. Catalog ID. Publisher. Version. Location.

The first three elements—creators, date, and title—follow standard bibliographical conventions and can be adapted according to the referencing template of a specific editing style.

The middle section, comprising the software through the catalog ID, represents the most valuable medium-specific information for identifying differences in the same ebook. The platform is usually noted after the title, but this should be supplemented by further information about the method of access. The required information depends on whether the text has been accessed via a dedicated ebook reader or through software. E-readers should feature information about the device generation and firmware; software should indicate the software and version. For the Kindle Cloud Reader, version and build date appear in the website's source code.

The format should be the default when the file is downloaded. The same file may be rendered differently according to its format on the same hardware-software combination. This can be obfuscated through reuse of the same file extension despite rendering different content. The main cutoff occurs with the launch of KF8 and KFX, where newer devices download content in this format. Older AZW files can also be opened with a PRC extension. TPZ most often refers to Apple desktop and mobile implementations.

The catalog ID for Kindle titles is the ASIN, which can be found through the file name of the ebook or through the URL of the Kindle title's product page. This is best recorded at time of download, as new editions of the same text can occasionally generate new ASINs for the same ebook. An ASIN is a persistent identifier even after an ebook has been removed from the Kindle Store, and therefore is a useful tool for distinguishing between editions of a text when not clearly marked, as has happened with Amazon-issued public domain texts.

Information about the publisher should be restricted to name, as the location of publication is difficult to ascertain and irrelevant in the case of Kindle Direct Publishing titles. Where a book has been published via Kindle Direct Publishing without an imprint, the "sold by" field should be included. For example, in the British market, this is typically "Amazon Media EU S.à r.l." Occasionally the publisher will include version information, which should be included, although this might not be updated with successive updates. The copyright page of Ben Goldacre's *Bad Science* not only distinguishes between print and ebook ("Ebook Edition © December 2008 ISBN: 9780007283194") but continues to note that the current ebook is "Version: 2013-09-03."[11] The versioning depends on good publisher workflows and will not apply to updates from Amazon, but once again, this offers a rough guide of the book's provenance.

The location should be the total location count for the entire book in lieu of a page count. This information can be important for identifying minute differences between editions, as the unit of a location is lesser than the equivalent page.

Examples

Albanese, Andrew Richard (2013). *The Battle of $9.99: How Apple, Amazon, and the "Big Six" Publishers Changed the E-book Business Overnight* [Kindle Cloud Reader 011201999]. B00DH8JCOC. PWxyz. Loc. 979.

Goldacre, Ben (2008). *Bad Science* [Kindle for Android 8.0.0.68]. AZW3. B002RI-9ORI. HarperCollins. Version 2013-09-03. Loc. 5474.

Isaacson, Walter (2011). *Steve Jobs: The Exclusive Biography* [Kindle 8, 5.9.4]. KFX. B005J3IEZQ. Little, Brown. Loc. 12321.

Pitzer, Andrea (2017). *One Long Night: A Global History of Concentration Camps* [Kindle 2, 2.5.8]. AZW. B01N5XNWEP. Loc. 7442.

Sterne, Laurence (2012). *The Life and Opinions of Tristram Shandy* [Kindle for Mac 1.20.2]. AZW. B008NZGMVo. HarperCollins. Loc. 9863.

Sterne, Laurence (2012). *The Life and Opinions of Tristram Shandy* [Kindle for PC 1.21]. KFX. B0082RZPWG. Amazon Media EU S.à r.l. Loc. 7773.

Copy Specific

If the citation should identify a specific copy for provenance purposes, the EXTH headers provide additional copy-specific data. For example, figure 12.1 shows two copies of the same file downloaded within a minute of each other. As these material differences occur between different copies of the same file, copy-specific reference may also rely on checksums such as MD5 to demonstrate the unique aspects of a copy.[12] In the example shown in the figure, an MD5 calculation performed through the Mac OS command line demonstrated material differences:

1: ad93a79acfb043ed2e7dfe033ea92627

2: a89114eddob084d6ocoof9c8c66a7doc

This level of copy specificity is not necessary in most cases and has not been applied to the bibliographical specification of digital objects in this book. If such specificity is necessary for analysis, I suggest referring to the MD5 hash for the title.

I have documented best practice for Kindle-based bibliographies based on the sociotechnical conditions of Amazon's platform. Some of the principles here will not transfer to other ebook platforms, while others can easily be adapted. For example, iBooks stores relevant metadata in "Books.plist," a file contained in the same folder as the raw EPUB files. The document lists important information including the unique iBooks "itemID" and "publication-version." From these metadata, it is possible to compile a comparable reference for J. J. Abrams and Doug Dorst's S. for iBooks:

J. J. Abrams and Doug Dorst (2013). S. [iBooks 1.5 (Mac OS X 10.11.6)]. EPUB. 726968790. Canongate. Version 3612477.

12.1 Ebook signatures for two otherwise identical copies of Christopher Rice's *Bone Music* [Kindle 3, 3.4.2], AZW, B07354S1K7 (Thomas & Mercer, 2018), loc. 6395. Detail from Hex Fiend. Screenshot by the author.

I have purposefully omitted the page number information, despite internal consistency with *S.*, since the text is presented in a fixed layout, because by design iBooks pages are dynamic. This is a common problem for EPUB, as the format has no normative specification for in-text locations beyond attempts by the IDPF to create EPUB Canonical Fragment Identifiers (CFI), which remained recommended in the EPUB 3.1 specifications. The specification provides an example of CFI implementation:

book.epub#epubcfi(/6/4[chap01ref]!/4[body01]/10[para05]/3:10)[13]

The system used XPath, an XML-based navigation syntax, to identify a precise location based on the "spine" of an EPUB file. The technique would be more difficult to implement in encrypted Kindle files and can only identify a passage for a machine. Therefore, while the specification offers an additional level of technical specificity, the trade-off between machine- and human-legible forms of citation is important in identifying citations for the broadest possible audience. While granular citation remains an open issue, I recommend using locations for Kindle ebooks and the proprietary standards for other platforms with direct quotations where possible to ensure text can be identified.

Notes

Introduction

1. Rupert Neate, "Amazon's Jeff Bezos Pays Out $38bn in Divorce Settlement," *The Guardian*, June 30, 2019, Technology, https://www.theguardian.com/technology /2019/jun/30/amazon-jeff-bezos-ex-wife-mackenzie-handed-38bn-in -divorce-settlement.

2. Amazon.com Inc., "2006 Annual Report" (Seattle: Amazon.com, 2007), http:// media.corporate-ir.net/media_files/irol/97/97664/2006AnnualReport.pdf.

3. Andrew Richard Albanese, *The Battle of $9.99: How Apple, Amazon, and the Big Six Publishers Changed the E-book Business Overnight* [Kindle for PC 1.21.0], KFX, B00DH8JCOC (PWxyz, 2013).

4. Harsimran Gill, "'The Ebook Is a Stupid Product: No Creativity, No Enhancement,' Says the Hachette Group CEO," Scroll.in, 2018, https://scroll.in/article /868871/the-ebook-is-a-stupid-product-no-creativity-no-enhancement-says -the-hachette-group-ceo.

5. Beth Driscoll and Claire Squires, "'Oh Look, a Ferry'; or The Smell of Paper Books," *Lifted Brow*, October 24, 2018, https://www.theliftedbrow.com/lifted brow/2018/10/24/oh-look-a-ferry-or-the-smell-of-paper-books-by-beth -driscoll-and-claire-squires.

6. Steven Heller, "Who Named the Kindle (and Why)?" *Print Magazine* (blog), accessed July 27, 2015, http://www.printmag.com/article/who-named-the-kin dle-and-why/.

7. Heller, "Who Named the Kindle" (italics mine).

8. Brad Stone, *The Everything Store: Jeff Bezos and the Age of Amazon* (London: Bantam, 2013), 231.

9. Nick Montfort and Ian Bogost, *Racing the Beam: The Atari Video Computer System* (Cambridge, MA: MIT Press, 2009), 2.

10. Montfort and Bogost, *Racing the Beam*, 2 (italics mine).

11. Amaranth Borsuk and Brad Bouse, *Between Page and Screen* (Los Angeles: Siglio, 2012).

12. Tom Boellstorff and Braxton Soderman, "Transplatform: Culture, Context, and the Intellivision/Atari VCS Rivalry," *Games and Culture* 14, no. 6 (2019): 680–703.

13. Nathan Altice, *I AM ERROR: The Nintendo Family Computer / Entertainment System Platform* (Cambridge, MA: MIT Press, 2015), 5.

14. Thomas Apperley and Jussi Parikka, "Platform Studies' Epistemic Threshold," *Games and Culture* 13, no. 4 (2018): 5.

15. Esther Weltevrede and Erik Borra, "Platform Affordances and Data Practices: The Value of Dispute on Wikipedia," *Big Data and Society* 3, no. 1 (June 1, 2016), https://doi.org/10.1177/2053951716653418.

16. Tarleton Gillespie, "The Politics of 'Platforms,'" *New Media and Society* 12, no. 3 (2010): 347–364.

17. Steven Levy, "The Future of Reading," *Newsweek*, November 26, 2007, 57.

18. Sven Birkerts, *The Gutenberg Elegies: The Fate of Reading in an Electronic Age* (New York: Fawcett Columbine, 1994).

19. Naomi S. Baron, *Words Onscreen: The Fate of Reading in a Digital World* (Oxford: Oxford University Press, 2015).

20. For two recent review essays on developments in contemporary publishing, see Rachel Noorda and Stevie Marsden, "Twenty-First Century Book Studies: The State of the Discipline," *Book History* 22, no. 1 (2019): 370–397; and Matthew Kirschenbaum and Sarah Werner, "Digital Scholarship and Digital Studies: The State of the Discipline," *Book History* 17 (2014): 406–458.

21. Matthew Kirschenbaum, "Book.Files: Preservation of Digital Assets in the Contemporary Publishing Industry; A Report" (College Park, MD, and New York: University of Maryland and Book Industry Study Group, April 2020), https://drum.lib.umd.edu/handle/1903/25605.

22. Lisa Nakamura, "'Words with Friends': Socially Networked Reading on Goodreads," *PMLA* 128, no. 1 (2013): 243.

23. Amazon.com Inc., "Critical Software Update for Kindle E-Readers," Amazon.com Help, 2016, http://www.amazon.com/gp/help/customer/display.html?nodeId=201994710&tag=mr060-20.

24. Frederick Kilgour, *The Evolution of the Book* (New York: Oxford University Press, 1998), 5.

Chapter 1

1. Richard Brandt, *One Click: Jeff Bezos and the Rise of Amazon.com* (London: Portfolio Penguin, 2011), 139.

2. Steven Levy, "The Future of Reading," *Newsweek*, November 26, 2007, 57–64.

3. Matt Hayler, *Challenging the Phenomena of Technology: Embodiment, Expertise, and Evolved Knowledge* (Basingstoke: Palgrave Macmillan, 2015), 121.

4. IKEA riffed on the debate in a 2014 advertising campaign. IKEA Singapore, "Experience the Power of a Bookbook™," YouTube, September 3, 2014, https://www.youtube.com/watch?v=MOXQo7nURso.

5. This last claim is particularly interesting, since paper formats are variable, and paperbacks have no standard page limits. This rhetoric was later reinforced by

the introduction of the Paperwhite range and the marketing of the luxury Kindle range. Amazon.com Inc., "Kindle: Amazon's Original Wireless Reading Device," Amazon.com, 2011, http://www.amazon.com/dp/B000FI73MA.

6. Amazon.com Inc., "Kindle: Amazon's Original Wireless Reading Device."

7. Charlie Rose, "Interview with Jeff Bezos," November 19, 2007, https://charlie rose.com/videos/11791

8. Foundational studies in book history include Lucien Febvre and Henri-Jean Martin, *The Coming of the Book: The Impact of Printing, 1450–1800*, ed. Geoffrey Nowell-Smith and David Wootton, trans. David Gerard (London: Verso, 2010); Elizabeth L. Eisenstein, *The Printing Press as an Agent of Change* (Cambridge: Cambridge University Press, 1980); Adrian Johns, *The Nature of the Book: Print and Knowledge in the Making* (Chicago: University of Chicago Press, 1998); Robert Darnton, "What Is the History of Books?" in *The Book History Reader*, ed. David Finkelstein and Alistair McCleery, 2nd ed. (Oxford: Routledge, 2006), 9–26.

9. M. B. Parkes, *Pause and Effect: An Introduction to the History of Punctuation in the West* (Aldershot: Scolar Press, 1992), 23.

10. Gérard Genette and Marie Maclean, "Introduction to the Paratext," *New Literary History* 22, no. 2 (Spring 1991): 261–272; Thomas N. Corns, "The Early Modern Search Engine: Indices, Title Pages, Marginalia and Contents," in *The Renaissance Computer: Knowledge Technology in the First Age of Print*, ed. Neil Rhodes and Jonathan Sawday (London: Routledge, 2000), 95–105.

11. David McKitterick, *Print, Manuscript and the Search for Order, 1450–1830* (Cambridge: Cambridge University Press, 2003), 22.

12. Jeffrey Todd Knight, *Bound to Read: Compilations, Collections, and the Making of Renaissance Literature* (Philadelphia: University of Pennsylvania Press, 2013); H. J. Jackson, *Marginalia: Readers Writing in Books* (New Haven, CT: Yale University Press, 2002); William H. Sherman, *Used Books: Marking Readers in Renaissance England* (Philadelphia: University of Pennsylvania Press, 2008).

13. Levy, "The Future of Reading."

14. Joshua Cuneo, "'Hello, Computer': The Interplay of *Star Trek* and Modern Computing," in *Science Fiction and Computing: Essays on Interlinked Domains*, ed. David L. Ferro and Eric G. Swedin (Jefferson, NC: McFarland, 2011), 131–147.

15. John Maxwell makes the connection between ebooks and PADDs in "E-Book Logic: We Can Do Better," *Papers of the Bibliographical Society of Canada* 51, no. 1 (2013): 32, http://jps.library.utoronto.ca/index.php/bsc/article/view/20761/16996.

16. David Livingstone, "Homefront," *Star Trek: Deep Space Nine* (CBS, January 1, 1996), 24:19.

17. Michael Hart, "Re: 3.301 e-Texts (65)," *Humanist*, July 29, 1989, https://human ist.kdl.kcl.ac.uk/Archives/Virginia/v03/0305.html.

18. The King James Bible's publication date of 1989 makes it one of the first ebooks, but other initiatives, including the Oxford Text Archive, had already been established in the late 1970s.

19. Thomas J. Hennen, "OCLC Invitational Conference: Public Librarians Take Cool View of Future," *American Libraries* 19, no. 5 (1988): 391.

20. Bob Brown and Craig Saper, *The Readies* (Roving Eye Press, 2014); Vannevar Bush, "As We May Think," *The Atlantic* 176 (July 1945): 101–108.

21. Alex Preda, "Socio-technical Agency in Financial Markets: The Case of the Stock Ticker," *Social Studies of Science* 36, no. 5 (2006): 767.

22. A. Kay and A. Goldberg, "Personal Dynamic Media," *Computer* 10, no. 3 (March 1977): 31–41.

23. See, e.g., Seiichi Ooba et al., Dictionary reading device, US Patent 3,612,676, filed November 22, 1968, and issued October 12, 1971; Gerald C. Fowler and Terence D. Hughey, Reading machine, US Patent 4,160,242, filed June 28, 1977, and issued July 3, 1979; David P. Rubincam, Electronic book, US Patent 4,159,417, filed October 28, 1977, and issued June 26, 1979; Shunpei Yamazaki and Toshiji Hamatani, Paperless portable book, US Patent 5,339,091, filed October 14, 1992, and issued August 16, 1994; Emilio A. Fernandez, Microprocessor based simulated book, US Patent 4,855,725, filed December 28, 1988, and issued August 8, 1989.

24. Robert A. Wisher and J. Peter Kincaid, "Personal Electronic Aid for Maintenance: Final Summary Report" (Alexandria, VA: US Army Research Institute for the Behavioral and Social Sciences, March 1989).

25. Jacob M. Schlesinger, "Walkman of Words: Sony's Data Discman Can Squeeze an Encyclopedia into a Portable Electronic Book," *Wall Street Journal*, October 21, 1991, r12.

26. Bob Johnstone, "Electronic Paperbacks," *Wired*, March 1, 1994, https://www.wired.com/1994/03/electronic-paperbacks/.

27. Andersen Consulting, "Reading in the New Millennium, a Bright Future for Ebook Publishing: Facilitating Open Standards" (Washington, DC: AAP Annual Meeting, March 22, 2000), http://web.archive.org/web/20021227113121/http://www.publishers.org/digital/dec2000anderson.ppt.

28. New York Times Editorial Desk, "King Closure," *New York Times*, December 1, 2000, A36; Stephen King, "Messages from Stephen," StephenKing.com, 2000, http://web.archive.org/web/20081007114133/http://stephenking.com/stephens_messages.html.

29. Rose, "Interview with Jeff Bezos."

30. Rose, "Interview with Jeff Bezos."

31. Gregg Zehr and John Hollar, "Zehr, Gregg, Oral History," May 14, 2014, 35, http://www.computerhistory.org/collections/catalog/102739920.

32. Brad Stone, *The Everything Store: Jeff Bezos and the Age of Amazon* (London: Bantam, 2013), 225.

33. Paul Hilts, "Book Tech Looks at E-Publishing," *Publishers Weekly* 248, no. 10 (March 5, 2001): 46.

34. Gemstar TV Guide International, "Another Important EBook Announcement," Gemstar eBook, February 9, 2006, http://web.archive.org/web/20060209023520/http://www.gemstar-ebook.com:80/cgi-bin/WebObjects/eBookstore.woa/wa/.

35. Calvin Reid and Karen Holt, "Barnes & Noble.com Exits E-book Market," *Publishers Weekly* 250, no. 37 (September 15, 2003): 9.

36. This precedes the Google Book project by three years, although Google's project is often lauded as the more disruptive force. Brandt, *One Click*, 12.

37. James Somers, "Torching the Modern-Day Library of Alexandria," *The Atlantic*, April 20, 2017, https://www.theatlantic.com/technology/archive/2017/04/the-tragedy-of-google-books/523320/.

38. For a summary of Google Books as a mass digitization project, see Nanna Bonde Thylstrup, *The Politics of Mass Digitization* (Cambridge, MA: MIT Press, 2019), chap. 3.

39. Gary Wolf, "The Great Library of Amazonia," *Wired*, December 2003, http://www.wired.com/wired/archive/11.12/amazon.html.

40. Pearson, "Penguin Signs Up to 'Search Inside!' Programme with Amazon.co.uk," Pearson, 2006, https://www.pearson.com/corporate/news/media/news-announcements/2006/10/penguin-signs-up-to-search-inside!-programme-with-amazoncouk.html.

41. Amazon.com Inc., "Search Inside!" Amazon.co.uk Help, 2017, https://www.amazon.co.uk/gp/help/customer/display.html/?nodeId=200182580.

42. Jim Milliot, "Amazon Upgrade Tops 100,000 Titles," *Publishers Weekly*, December 24, 2007, 5.

43. Amazon.com Inc., "Read Your Books Online," September 27, 2014, http://web.archive.org/web/20140927045348/https://www.amazon.com/gp/digital/sitb/help/learn.html/ref=si3_learn_dtls?ie=UTF8&details=1&navbar=0; Amazon.com Inc., "Amazon Upgrade," Amazon Device Support, 2016, https://www.amazon.com/gp/help/customer/display.html?ie=UTF8&nodeId=110744011; Rebecca Greenfield, "Amazon's Kindle MatchBook: Good Idea, Not Such a Great Deal," *The Atlantic*, September 3, 2013, https://www.theatlantic.com/technology/archive/2013/09/amazons-kindle-matchbook-program-isnt-good-deal-most-time/311521/.

44. Hilts, "Book Tech Looks at E-Publishing."

45. According to Dan Rose, a member of the early Kindle team, Bezos aimed to have 100,000 titles available for $9.99 at launch. Dan Rose, "In 2004 I got the opportunity . . ." Twitter, 2020, https://twitter.com/drose_999/status/1287944667414196225.

46. Bill Rosenblatt, "Amazon.com Acquires Mobipocket," *Ebooklyn* (blog), 2005, http://web.archive.org/web/20160324100829/http://www.ebooklyn.net/p/amazoncom-acquires-mobipocket.html.

47. Calvin Reid and Steven Zeitchik, "Gemstar E-books Shutdown," *Publishers Weekly* 250, no. 25 (June 23, 2003): 10; Reid and Holt, "Barnes & Noble.com Exits E-book Market."

48. Neal Stephenson, *The Diamond Age* [Kindle Cloud Reader 011201999], B002RI9DQ0 (Penguin Random House, 1998), loc. 1047.

49. Robin Sloan, "The Kindle Wink," *The Message* (blog), 2014, https://medium.com/message/the-kindle-wink-4f61cd5c845.

50. Zehr and Hollar, "Zehr, Gregg, Oral History."

51. Bezos, quoted in Levy, "The Future of Reading," 57.

52. Levy, "The Future of Reading," 57.

53. Amazon.com Inc., "Lab126," Lab126, 2005, 126, http://web.archive.org/web/20051124085428/http://www.lab126.com:80/. The "About" page clearly identifies Lab126 as an Amazon division, as it mentions that Lab126 is located next to A9.com, Amazon's search division.

54. Amazon.com Inc., "Kindle Source Code 1.0.0.292," Kindle Amazon Web Services, 2007, https://s3.amazonaws.com/kindle/Kindle_src.1.0.0.292.tar.

55. Neal Karlinsky, "The Inside Story of How the Kindle Was Born," US Day One Blog, November 15, 2017, https://blog.aboutamazon.com/devices/the-inside-story-of-how-the-kindle-was-born.

56. Amazon.com Inc., "Kindle Source Code 2.2," Kindle Amazon Web Services, 2009, https://kindle.s3.amazonaws.com/Kindle_src_2.0_291330095.tar.gz.

57. Ryan Block, "Amazon Kindle: Meet Amazon's E-book Reader," *En Gadget*, September 11, 2006, https://www.engadget.com/2006/09/11/amazon-kindle-meet-amazons-e-book-reader/.

58. The FCC website has since become an important source for leaks about Amazon hardware.

59. Stephanie Burns, "FCC ID No. UUU-L7E20070323 Short Term Confidentiality Request," October 19, 2007, http://web.archive.org/web/20210623100724/https://fccid.io/UUU-L7E20070323/Letter/Short-Term-Confidentiality-Request-862773.pdf; Amazon.com Inc., "About Your Kindle [2006 Version for FCC]," 2006, https://apps.fcc.gov/eas/GetApplicationAttachment.html?id=862803.

60. Amazon.com Inc., "Amazon Kindle Project Fiona Prototype Unit [X7198.2014]," 2005, Computer History Museum, http://www.computerhistory.org/collections/catalog/102747839.

61. Amazon.com Inc., "Amazon Fiona Reading Light [X7198.2014]," Computer History Museum, 2006, http://www.computerhistory.org/collections/catalog/102747856.

62. Amazon.com Inc., "Amazon Fiona Rear Cover [102747848]," Computer History Museum, 2006, http://www.computerhistory.org/collections/catalog/102747848; Amazon.com Inc., "Amazon Fiona Rear Cover [102747850]," Computer History Museum, 2006, http://www.computerhistory.org/collections/catalog/102747850.

63. For an overview of open-source culture, see Gabriella Coleman, *Coding Freedom: The Ethics and Aesthetics of Hacking* (Princeton, NJ: Princeton University Press, 2013).

64. Amazon.com Inc., "Kindle Source Code 1.0.0.292."

65. Stone, *Everything Store*, 239.

66. Intel, "Marvell to Purchase Intel's Communications and Application Processor Business for $600 Million," Intel Press Room, 2006, https://www.intel.com/pressroom/archive/releases/2006/20060627corp.htm.

67. Broadcom Corp. v. Qualcomm Inc., 501 F. 3d 297 (Court of Appeals, 3rd Circuit 2007).

68. Stone, *Everything Store*, 239.

69. Devin Coldewey, "How the Kindle Was Designed through 10 Years and 15 Generations," *TechCrunch* (blog), 2017, http://social.techcrunch.com/2017/11/20/how-the-kindle-was-designed-through-10-years-and-15-generations/.

70. "Kindle Ready on UK Launchpad," *The Bookseller*, October 2, 2009, 3.

71. Catherine Neilan, "Amazon Urges Indies to Digitise," *The Bookseller*, March 13, 2009, 10.

72. Graeme Neill and Catherine Neilan, "Amazon Launches Kindle Worldwide," *The Bookseller*, October 12, 2009, 3; Neill Denny, "The Kindle Has Landed," *The Bookseller*, October 9, 2009, https://www.thebookseller.com/blogs/kindle-has-landed.

73. Jim Milliot, "The Nook Arrives," *Publishers Weekly*, October 26, 2009, 6.

74. Amazon.com Inc., "Kindle DX Wireless Reading Device," Amazon.com, 2010, http://web.archive.org/web/20100131052954/http://www.amazon.com:80 /Kindle-Wireless-Reading-Device-Display/dp/B0015TCMLo.

75. "Kindle DX Marks Gear Shift for Amazon," *The Bookseller*, May 22, 2009, 8.

76. Trina Marmarelli and Martin Ringle, "The Reed College Kindle Study" (Reed College, 2010).

77. Thomas E. Perez et al., "Letter of Resolution between the United States and Reed College," Information and Technical Assistance on the Americans with Disabilities Act, 2009, http://www.ada.gov/reed_college.htm.

78. A search for completed sales in January 2018 identified a working "as new" DX that sold for $300. "Search: Kindle DX," eBay, 2018, http://web.archive .org/web/20180122115624/https://www.ebay.com/sch/i.html?_from=R40& _sacat=0&LH_Complete=1&LH_Sold=1&_nkw=kindle+dx&_sop=16.

79. Tripp Mickle, "Among the iPhone's Biggest Transformations: Apple Itself," *Wall Street Journal*, June 20, 2017, Tech, https://www.wsj.com/articles/among-the -iphones-biggest-transformations-apple-itself-1497951003.

80. Maxwell, "E-Book Logic," 40.

81. All technical information in the following section comes from the EPUB 3 specifications. IDPF, "EPUB 3 Overview," EPUB 3, 2014, http://www.idpf.org /epub/301/spec/epub-overview.html; IDPF, "EPUB 3 Publications 3.0.1," EPUB 3, 2014, http://www.idpf.org/epub/301/spec/epub-publications.html; IDPF, "EPUB 3 Open Container Format (OCF) 3.0.1," EPUB 3, 2014, http://www.idpf .org/epub/301/spec/epub-ocf.html.

82. Adriaan van der Weel, *Changing Our Textual Minds: Towards a Digital Order of Knowledge* (Manchester: Manchester University Press, 2011), 1.

83. Stone, *Everything Store*, 219.

84. Stone, *Everything Store*, 219.

85. Tom Standage, *The Turk: The Life and Times of the Famous Eighteenth-Century Chess-Playing Machine* (New York: Berkley Trade, 2003).

86. Jeffrey P. Bezos, *Opening Keynote—MIT World* (MIT, 2006).

87. Jeremy Antley, "From Data Self to Data Serf," *Peasant Muse* (blog), 2012, http:// www.peasantmuse.com/2012/06/from-data-self-to-data-serf.html.

88. Lilly Irani, "Difference and Dependence among Digital Workers: The Case of Amazon Mechanical Turk," *South Atlantic Quarterly* 114, no. 1 (January 1, 2015): 231.

89. Stone, *Everything Store*, 219.

90. Bookeen, "Bookeen Cybook," Bookeen, 2007, http://web.archive.org/web/2007 1002212414/http://www.bookeen.com:80/specs/ebook-specs.aspx.

91. R. M. Schaffert and C. D. Oughton, "Xerography: A New Principle of Photography and Graphic Reproduction," *Journal of the Optical Society of America* 38, no. 12 (December 1948): 991–998.

92. I. Ota, J. Ohnishi, and M. Yoshiyama, "Electrophoretic Image Display (EPID) Panel," *Proceedings of the IEEE* 61, no. 7 (July 1973): 832–836; Isao Ota, Electrophoretic display device, US Patent 3,668,106, filed April 9, 1970, and issued June 6, 1972; N. K. Sheridon and M. A. Berkovitz, "The Gyricon—a Twisting Ball Display," *Proceedings of the Society for Information Display* 18, no. 34 (1977): 289–293.

93. John Seely Brown, "1997 Objectives" (1997), Mark Weiser papers, ca. 1975–1999, series 5, box 41, folder 10; Mark Stefik, "The Digital Document Company" (Palo Alto: Xerox PARC, July 29, 1995), Mark Weiser papers, ca. 1975–1999, series 2, box 8, folder 12.

94. Charles Platt, "Digital Ink," *Wired*, May 1, 1997, https://www.wired.com/1997/05/ff-digitalink/.

95. Megan Costello, "'Radio Paper' from E Ink," *Publishers Weekly* 248, no. 12 (March 19, 2001).

96. "Prime View International Reaches Agreement to Acquire E Ink," Business Wire, June 1, 2009, http://web.archive.org/web/20100920185513/https://www.busi nesswire.com/news/home/20090601005656/en/Prime-View-International -Reaches-Agreement-Acquire-Ink.

97. Peng Fei Bai et al., "Review of Paper-Like Display Technologies," *Progress in Electromagnetics Research* 147 (2014): 97.

98. E Ink, "E Ink Pearl Imaging Film," 2017, http://www.eink.com/sell_sheets/pearl _spec_sheet.pdf.

99. Brian X. Chen, "iPhone 4's 'Retina' Display Claims Are False Marketing," *Wired*, June 9, 2010, https://www.wired.com/2010/06/iphone-4-retina/.

100. Robert A. Hayes and B. J. Feenstra, "Video-Speed Electronic Paper Based on Electrowetting," *Nature* 425, no. 6956 (September 2003): 383–385.

101. Stephen J. Telfer and Michael D. McCreary, "A Full-Color Electrophoretic Display," *SID Symposium Digest of Technical Papers* 47, no. 1 (2016): 574–577.

102. Zehr and Hollar, "Zehr, Gregg, Oral History," 40.

103. Amazon.com Inc., "Kindle Source Code 1.0.0.292."

104. John E. Johnston and Gregg E. Zehr, Configurable keypad for an electronic device, US Patent 8,692,736, filed June 14, 2007, and issued April 8, 2014.

105. Stone, *Everything Store*, 237.

106. Stone, *Everything Store*, 237.

107. Stone, *Everything Store*, 238.

108. The web is also built to be reflowable, but its dependence on CSS for aesthetics means that in practice, web pages tend to be less reconfigurable without distorting formatting elements.

109. Derek T. Jones and Oleksandr Berezhnyy, Electronic book pagination, US Patent 9,892,094, filed June 19, 2014, and issued February 13, 2018. MobileRead forum member "rodrigoccurvo" discovered the calculation in a now unavailable version of Kindle Cloud Reader. rodrigoccurvo, "Correct Mobi Location Formula (Maybe)," MobileRead Forums, 2011, https://www.mobileread.com /forums/showthread.php?t=159357.

110. Gregg E. Zehr et al., Page turner for handheld electronic book reader device, US Patent 8,018,431, issued September 13, 2011.

111. Amazon.com Inc., "Page Flip," Amazon.com, 2016, https://www.amazon.com /b?ie=UTF8&node=13632018011.

112. David Usbourne, "Amazon's Electronic Book Turns a New Page in the History of the Written Word," *The Independent*, November 20, 2007, 2, 3.

113. Amazon.com Inc., "Kindle."

114. Amazon.com Inc., "Critical Software Update for Kindle E-Readers," Amazon. com Help, 2016, http://www.amazon.com/gp/help/customer/display.html?nod eId=201994710&tag=mr060-20; knc1, "K5 Notice from Amazon," MobileRead

Forums, March 4, 2016, 1, https://www.mobileread.com/forums/showpost
.php?p=3274121&postcount=8.

115. Amazon.com Inc., "Kindle Keyboard 3G, Free 3G + Wi-Fi, 6" E Ink Display,"
Amazon.com, 2010, https://www.amazon.com/Kindle-Wireless-Reading-Dis
play-Globally/dp/B002LVUX1W/.

116. An up-to-date map of Amazon's coverage can be found at Amazon.com Inc.,
"Amazon Kindle 3G Coverage," 2017, http://cliento.cellmaps.com/viewer.html
?view=intl&cov=3.

117. Amazon.com Inc., "Kindle Wireless Reading Device (6" Display, Global Wireless, Latest Generation)," Kindle Store, November 27, 2009, http://web.archive
.org/web/20091127191626/http://www.amazon.com:80/Kindle-Wireless-Reading
-Display-Generation/dp/B0015T963C.

118. Kay and Goldberg, "Personal Dynamic Media."

Chapter 2

1. Werner Vogels, "Amazon and the Lean Cloud," HackFwd Build 0.7, posted to
Vimeo, September 2011, https://vimeo.com/29719577.

2. Danny Forston and Simon Duke, "Alexa, What Shall We Do Next? Take Over the
World, Jeff," *Sunday Times*, June 18, 2017; In an Op-Ed for *The Guardian*, the
former Silicon Valley programmer turned author Wendy Liu argued that Amazon
had turned into a public utility in the wake of the COVID-19 pandemic. Wendy
Liu, "Coronavirus Has Made Amazon a Public Utility—So We Should Treat It
like One," *The Guardian*, April 17, 2020, Opinion, https://www.theguardian.com
/commentisfree/2020/apr/17/amazon-coronavirus-public-utility-workers.

3. Adam Satariano et al., "How the Internet Travels across Oceans," *New York Times*,
March 10, 2019, Technology, https://www.nytimes.com/interactive/2019/03/10
/technology/internet-cables-oceans.html; for an introduction to the Internet's
physical infrastructure, see Andrew Blum, *Tubes: Behind the Scenes at the Internet* (London: Viking, 2012); Nicole Starosielski, *The Undersea Network* (Durham,
NC: Duke University Press, 2015).

4. Susan Leigh Star and Martha Lampland, "Reckoning with Standards," in *Stan-
dards and Their Stories: How Quantifying, Classifying, and Formalizing Practices
Shape Everyday Life*, ed. Martha Lampland and Susan Leigh Star (Ithaca, NY:
Cornell University Press, 2009), 17.

5. Paul N. Edwards et al., "Understanding Infrastructure: Dynamics, Tensions, and
Design," 2007, http://hdl.handle.net/2027.42/49353.

6. Jeffrey P. Bezos, "2015 Letter to Shareholders." Investor Relations, 2016. https://
amazonir.gcs-web.com/annual-reports.

7. Jean-Christophe Plantin et al., "Infrastructure Studies Meet Platform Studies in
the Age of Google and Facebook," *New Media and Society* 20, no. 1 (2018): 303.

8. Geoffrey A. Fowler, "E-Readers: They're Hot Now, but the Story Isn't Over," *Wall
Street Journal*, December 1, 2009, Tech, http://www.wsj.com/articles/SB1000142
405274870432810457451985155784862.

9. Brad Stone, *The Everything Store: Jeff Bezos and the Age of Amazon* (London: Bantam,
2013); Richard Brandt, *One Click: Jeff Bezos and the Rise of Amazon.com* (London:
Portfolio Penguin, 2011).

10. Stone, *Everything Store*, 223.

11. Amazon.com Inc., "Form 10-Q: Q2 2020," June 2020, http://d18rnop25nwr6d
.cloudfront.net/CIK-0001018724/a77b5839-99b8-4851-8f37-0b012f9292b9
.pdf.

12. Farhad Manjoo, "Which Tech Giant Would You Drop?" *New York Times*, May 10,
2017, https://www.nytimes.com/interactive/2017/05/10/technology/Ranking
-Apple-Amazon-Facebook-Microsoft-Google.html.

13. Several book-length treatments have covered the rise of Amazon, including
Stone, *Everything Store*; Brandt, *One Click*; James Marcus, *Amazonia: Five Years at
the Epicenter of the Dot.com Juggernaut* (New York: New Press, 2004). Ted Striphas,
The Late Age of Print: Everyday Book Culture from Consumerism to Control (New York:
Columbia University Press, 2011), chap. 3, also provides a comprehensive schol-
arly overview of the development of Amazon.

14. Carole Cadwalladr, "My Week as an Amazon Insider," *The Guardian*, December 1,
2013, Technology, http://www.theguardian.com/technology/2013/dec/01/week
-amazon-insider-feature-treatment-employees-work; Jodi Kantor and David
Streitfeld, "Inside Amazon: Wrestling Big Ideas in a Bruising Workplace," *New
York Times*, August 15, 2015, http://www.nytimes.com/2015/08/16/technology
/inside-amazon-wrestling-big-ideas-in-a-bruising-workplace.html; Gethin
Chamberlain, "Underpaid and Exhausted: The Human Cost of Your Kindle,"
The Guardian, June 9, 2018, Technology, http://www.theguardian.com/technol
ogy/2018/jun/09/human-cost-kindle-amazon-china-foxconn-jeff-bezos.

15. Brian Merchant, "How Google, Microsoft, and Big Tech Are Automating the
Climate Crisis," Gizmodo, February 21, 2019, https://gizmodo.com/how-google
-microsoft-and-big-tech-are-automating-the-1832790799.

16. Caroline O'Donovan and Ken Bensinger, "The Cost of Next-Day Delivery: How
Amazon Escapes the Blame for Its Deadly Last Mile," BuzzFeed News, September 6, 2019, https://www.buzzfeednews.com/article/carolineodonovan/amazon
-next-day-delivery-deaths.

17. Mark Sweney, "Amazon Breaks Premier League Hold of Sky and BT with Prime
Streaming Deal," *The Guardian*, June 7, 2018, Media, http://www.theguardian
.com/media/2018/jun/07/amazon-breaks-premier-league-hold-of-sky-and
-bt-with-streaming-deal.

18. See, e.g., Hayley Tsukayama, "Why Amazon Is Paying Nearly $1 Billion to Acquire
Twitch," *Washington Post*, August 25, 2014, The Switch, https://www.washing
tonpost.com/news/the-switch/wp/2014/08/25/amazon-said-to-be-close-to
-acquiring-twitch/.

19. Stone, *Everything Store*, 109.

20. Striphas, *Late Age*, 83.

21. See chapter 5 of Janet Abbate, *Inventing the Internet* (Cambridge, MA: MIT Press,
2000).

22. Striphas, *Late Age*, 102.

23. G. Bruce Knecht, "Wall Street Whiz Finds Niche Selling Books on the Internet," *Wall Street Journal*, May 16, 1996, http://www.wsj.com/articles/SB8322044
37381952500.

24. Stone, *Everything Store*, 211.

25. Jeffrey P. Bezos, *Opening Keynote—MIT World* (MIT, 2006).

26. Amazon.com Inc., "Form 10-K," 1999, 8, http://web.archive.org/web/20210623 093958/https://d18rnop25nwr6d.cloudfront.net/CIK-0001018724/07ab23e8 -be7f-44ba-9765-44979c4516a1.pdf.

27. Stone, *Everything Store*, 223.

28. Werner Vogels, "How and Why Did Amazon Get into the Cloud Computing Business?" January 14, 2011, https://www.quora.com/How-and-why-did-Amazon -get-into-the-cloud-computing-business.

29. Ingrid Burrington, "Why Amazon's Data Centers Are Hidden in Spy Country," *The Atlantic*, January 8, 2016, http://www.theatlantic.com/technology/archive /2016/01/amazon-web-services-data-center/423147/.

30. Amazon.com Inc., "2019 Annual Report" (Seattle: Amazon.com, 2020), 24–25, https://s2.q4cdn.com/299287126/files/doc_financials/2020/ar/2019-Annual -Report.pdf.

31. IBM, "Virtualization in Education," 2007, 3, http://www-07.ibm.com/solutions /in/education/download/Virtualization%20in%20Education.pdf.

32. Amazon.com Inc., "Amazon Prime Air," Amazon.com, 2013, http://www.amazon .com/b?node=8037720011.

33. Alessandro Delfanti and Bronwyn Frey, "Humanly Extended Automation or the Future of Work Seen through Amazon Patents," *Science, Technology, and Human Values*, July 29, 2020, https://doi.org/10.1177/0162243920943665.

34. Amazon only produced 240 research outputs in the ACM and IEEE databases by June 2017. In the same time, Microsoft had produced 1,500 outputs. Facebook and Apple were the closest to Amazon with 500 each.

35. Allen School, "Carlos Guestrin and Emily Fox Join the University of Washington," *Allen School News* (blog), April 27, 2012, https://news.cs.washington .edu/2012/04/27/carlos-guestrin-and-emily-fox-join-the-university-of-wash ington/; Amazon.com Inc., "Amazon Catalyst," 2017, https://catalyst.amazon .com/uw/.

36. Amazon Web Services, "AWS Programs for Research and Education," 2017, http:// aws.amazon.com/grants/.

37. Amazon.com Inc., "Form 10-K," 1999, 4.

38. Amazon.com Inc., "Form 10-K," 1998, 3, http://media.corporate-ir.net/media _files/irol/97/97664/reports/123197_10k.pdf.

39. IPO, "Top 300 Organizations Granted U.S. Patents in 2018," IPO, 2019, https:// ipo.org/wp-content/uploads/2019/07/2018-Top-300-Final.pdf.

40. Peri Hartman et al., Method and system for placing a purchase order via a communications network, US Patent 5,960,411, filed September 12, 1997, and issued September 28, 1999.

41. Tim O'Reilly, "An Open Letter to Jeff Bezos," O'Reilly and Associates, 2000, http://www.oreilly.com/amazon_patent/amazon_patent.comments.html; Richard Stallman, "(Formerly) Boycott Amazon!" GNU Operating System, accessed February 6, 2017, https://www.gnu.org/philosophy/amazon.html.

42. David M. Kristol and Lou Montulli, "RFC2109: HTTP State Management Mechanism," Network Working Group Request for Comments, 1997, https://tools.ietf .org/html/rfc2109; See Alexander R. Galloway, *Protocol: How Control Exists after Decentralization* (Cambridge, MA: MIT Press, 2004), 133–137, for further information on RFCs.

43. Paul Barton-Davis, "I Oppose Amazon.com's 1-Click Patent," Equal Area, 2000, http://www.equalarea.com/paul/amazon-1click.html.

44. Jeffrey P. Bezos, "An Open Letter from Jeff Bezos," Amazon.com, April 15, 2000, http://web.archive.org/web/20000415152112/http://www.amazon.com/exec/obidos/subst/misc/patents.html. The database never materialized.

45. Information on the patent's development was discovered through the USPTO's Public Patent Application Information Retrieval (PAIR) system, which offers digitized documentation via the "Image File Wrapper" tab: https://portal.uspto.gov/pair/PublicPair. The public PAIR database records over 1,300 pages of bureaucracy, correspondence, and a lengthy editorial account of changes to the claims.

46. Frank Nuovo, Portable communication device, US Patent Application Publication 2002/0050981, filed June 25, 2001, and issued May 2, 2002.

47. Gregg E. Zehr et al., Page turner for handheld electronic book reader device, US Patent 8,018,431, issued September 13, 2011.

48. Amazon.com Inc., "Form 10-K," 2019, 25, http://web.archive.org/web/20210105150403/http://d18rn0p25nwr6d.cloudfront.net/CIK-0001018724/bed19367-fa6b-41ff-a973-df1951obobba.pdf.

49. David Azari et al., Public-domain analyzer, US Patent 9,691,068, filed December 15, 2011, and issued June 27, 2017.

50. John William Eichelberg, Brock Robert Gardner, and Alan Donald Gillooly, Cooling system for data center, US Patent 9,690,337, filed December 9, 2013, and issued June 27, 2017.

51. James David Meyers and Kurt Wesley Piersol, Methods and devices for selectively ignoring captured audio data, US Patent 9,691,378, filed November 5, 2015, and issued June 27, 2017.

52. Scott Gerard Carmack, Narasimha Rao Lakkakula, and Nima Sharifi Mehr, Detecting of navigation data spoofing based on image data, US Patent 9,689,686, filed September 25, 2015, and issued June 27, 2017; Daniel Buchmueller et al., Stabilized airborne drop delivery, US Patent 9,688,404, issued June 27, 2017.

53. Hyo Yoon Kang, "Science inside Law: The Making of a New Patent Class in the International Patent Classification," *Science in Context* 25, no. 4 (2012): 551–594.

54. Sonjeev Jahagirdar et al., Recognizing text from frames of image data using contextual information, US Patent 9,355,336, filed April 23, 2014, and issued May 31, 2016.

55. Nick Wingfield, "Amazon Pushes Facial Recognition to Police. Critics See Surveillance Risk," *New York Times*, May 24, 2018, Technology, https://www.nytimes.com/2018/05/22/technology/amazon-facial-recognition.html.

56. Hans Radder, "Exploring Philosophical Issues in the Patenting of Scientific and Technological Inventions," *Philosophy and Technology* 26, no. 3 (2013): 283–300.

57. Jeffrey P. Bezos, Secure method for communicating credit card data when placing an order on a nonsecure network, US Patent 5,727,163, filed March 30, 1995, and issued March 10, 1998.

58. Nathaniel S. Borenstein, "Perils and Pitfalls of Practical Cybercommerce," *Communications of the ACM* 39, no. 6 (June 1996): 36–44.

59. Bezos, Secure method, 1.

60. Neil C. Roseman et al., User interfaces and methods for facilitating user-to-user sales, US Patent 7,472,077, filed May 9, 2002, and issued December 30, 2008.

61. Hilliard B. Siegel, Udi Manber, and Jonathan Leblang, Method and system for providing annotations of a digital work, US Patent 8,131,647, filed January 19, 2005, and issued March 6, 2012.

62. Andrew V. Harbick, Ryan J. Snodgrass, and Joel R. Spiegel, Playlist-based detection of similar digital works and work creators, US Patent 8,468,046, filed August 2, 2012, and issued June 18, 2013.

63. Shoshana Zuboff, *The Age of Surveillance Capitalism: The Fight for a Human Future at the New Frontier of Power* (London: Profile Books, 2019), 14.

64. Mark Davis, "Five Processes in the Platformisation of Cultural Production: Amazon and Its Publishing Ecosystem," *Australian Humanities Review* 66 (May 2020): 93.

65. Simon Peter Rowberry, "The Limits of Big Data for Analyzing Reading," *Participations* 16, no. 1 (May 2019): 237–257.

66. Pankaj C. Patel, Arash Azadegan, and Lisa M. Ellram, "The Effects of Strategic and Structural Supply Chain Orientation on Operational and Customer-Focused Performance," *Decision Sciences* 44, no. 4 (2013): 713–753.

67. Bezos chose Seattle not only to be close to the talent accumulated by Microsoft and the University of Washington but also because of the proximity to Ingram, one of the two biggest book distributors at the time. Stone, *Everything Store*, 31.

68. Amazon.com Inc., "Annual Report 2017," 2018, 16, http://phx.corporate-ir.net /External.File?item=UGFyZW50SUQ9NjkyMDIxfENoaWxkSUQ9NDAyOTkyfFR 5cGU9MQ==&t=1.

69. David Ingold and Spencer Soper, "Amazon Doesn't Consider the Race of Its Customers. Should It?" Bloomberg, 2016, http://www.bloomberg.com/graphics /2016-amazon-same-day/.

70. Daniel McGinn, "The Numbers in Jeff Bezos's Head," *Harvard Business Review* 92, no. 11 (November 2014): 58.

71. Bezos, "2015 Letter to Shareholders."

72. Jonathan Zittrain, *The Future of the Internet* (London: Penguin, 2009).

73. M. Warner, "Can Amazon Be Saved?" *Fortune* 144, no. 11 (November 26, 2001): 156.

74. Amazon.com Inc., "Amazon.com Launches Three Innovations to Advance E-Commerce for Shoppers, Sellers," Amazon Press Room, September 30, 1999, http://phx.corporate-ir.net/phoenix.zhtml?c=176060&p=irol-newsArticle&ID =502889.

75. Dan Nosowitz, "A Penny for Your Books," *New York Times*, October 26, 2015, http:// www.nytimes.com/2015/10/25/magazine/a-penny-for-your-books.html.

76. Amazon.com Inc., "About Amazon—Our Innovations—Fulfillment by Amazon," accessed June 29, 2017, https://www.amazon.com/p/feature/pxekbkm47y7c9fd.

77. Amazon.com Inc., "Annual Report 2017."

78. Ben Thompson, "Amazon's New Customer," Stratechery, June 19, 2017, https:// stratechery.com/2017/amazons-new-customer/.

79. Amazon.com Inc., "Securely Accept Payments Online," Amazon Pay, 2017, https:// pay.amazon.com/uk/.

80. Chris Anderson, *The Longer Long Tail* (London: Random House Business Books, 2009).

81. A total of Amazon's "used," "new," and "collectible" books available on the books home page from Amazon.com on June 2, 2017.

82. Miles J. Ward, Physical store online shopping control, US Patent 9,665,881, filed May 4, 2012, and issued May 30, 2017.
83. Amazon.com Inc., "Amazon Books," 2017, https://www.amazon.com/b?ie=UTF8 &node=13270229011.
84. Amazon.com Inc., "Amazon Go," 2016, https://www.amazon.com/b?ie=UTF8 &node=16008589011.
85. Nick Wingfield, "Inside Amazon Go, a Store of the Future," *New York Times*, January 21, 2018, Technology, https://www.nytimes.com/2018/01/21/technology /inside-amazon-go-a-store-of-the-future.html.

Chapter 3

1. For a summary of how Amazon's fulfillment centers operate, see Alessandro Delfanti, "Machinic Dispossession and Augmented Despotism: Digital Work in an Amazon Warehouse," *New Media and Society*, December 2, 2019, https://doi .org/10.1177/1461444819891613.
2. Ted Striphas, *The Late Age of Print: Everyday Book Culture from Consumerism to Control* (New York: Columbia University Press, 2011), 92–93.
3. John W. Warren, "Zen and the Art of Metadata Maintenance," *Journal of Electronic Publishing* 18, no. 3 (June 17, 2015), https://doi.org/10.3998/3336451.0018.305.
4. Striphas, *Late Age*, 94.
5. Striphas, *Late Age*, 94.
6. CNET, "Amazon, B&N Settle Lawsuit," CNET, October 21, 1997, https://www .cnet.com/news/amazon-b-n-settle-lawsuit/.
7. CamelCamelCamel, "Amazon Price Tracker, Amazon Price History Charts, Price Watches, and Price Drop Alerts," camelcamelcamel.com, accessed June 27, 2016, http://uk.camelcamelcamel.com/.
8. Michael Eisen, "Amazon's $23,698,655.93 Book about Flies," *It Is NOT Junk* (blog), April 22, 2011, http://www.michaeleisen.org/blog/?p=358.
9. Amazon.com Inc., "Amazon.com Invites Music Lovers to Help Build the Ultimate Music Store," Amazon Press Room, April 23, 1998, http://phx.corporate-ir.net /phoenix.zhtml?c=176060&p=irol-newsArticle&ID=502993.
10. It is unclear what Amazon will do once the industry moves solely to ISBN-13.
11. "U.P.C.s, Barcodes, & Prefixes—GS1 US," accessed July 3, 2017, https://www.gs1 us.org/upcs-barcodes-prefixes/overview.
12. Zoë Wykes, *ISBN-13 for Dummies, Special Edition* (Hoboken: Wiley, 2005).
13. Striphas, *Late Age*, 102.
14. AFNIL, "AFNIL," 2017, http://www.afnil.org/.
15. See, e.g., Amazon.com Inc., "Les jeunes dans la société Broché," Amazon.fr, 2011, https://www.amazon.fr/jeunes-dans-société-Hélène-Dubouis/dp/B0065 GAW9M/.
16. Christopher F. Weight et al., Identifying book title sets, US Patent 9,881,009, filed March 15, 2011, and issued January 30, 2018.
17. Karina Luke, "BIC Statement on Best Practice for Subtitle Field in Metadata Feeds," BIC, March 9, 2018, http://www.bic.org.uk/files/pdfs/BIC%20State ment%20on%20Best%20Practice%20for%20Sub-title%20field%20FINAL %209th%20March%202018.pdf.

18. ORCID, "ORCID: Connecting Research and Researchers," ORCID, 2018, https://orcid.org/.

19. See Jeremy Wade Morris, "Curation by Code: Infomediaries and the Data Mining of Taste," *European Journal of Cultural Studies* 18, nos. 4–5 (2015): 446–463.

20. Paul Ford, "Does Amazon Data Speak for Itself?" *New Republic*, February 18, 2016, https://newrepublic.com/article/129026/amazons-data-speak-itself.

21. Amazon.com Inc., "Ian Bogost Newsgames," Amazon.com, July 13, 2017, http://web.archive.org/web/20170713121105/https://www.amazon.com/s/ref=nb_sb_noss?url=search-alias%3Dstripbooks&field-keywords=ian+bogost+newsgames&rh=n%3A283155%2Ck%3Aian+bogost+newsgames.

22. Brian Krebs, "Money Laundering via Author Impersonation on Amazon?" *Krebs on Security* (blog), February 20, 2018, https://krebsonsecurity.com/2018/02/money-laundering-via-author-impersonation-on-amazon/.

23. Teresa Elsey, "Building Ebooks That Last," YouTube, May 2, 2019, https://www.youtube.com/watch?v=8OOHyBT-Lo.

24. Sonjeev Jahagirdar et al., Recognizing text from frames of image data using contextual information, US Patent 9,355,336, filed April 23, 2014, and issued May 31, 2016.

25. Robert Darnton, "What Is the History of Books?" in *The Book History Reader*, ed. David Finkelstein and Alistair McCleery, 2nd ed. (Oxford: Routledge, 2006), 9–26; Barbara Tillett, "What Is FRBR? A Conceptual Model for the Bibliographic Universe" (Washington, DC: Library of Congress, 2004), http://www.loc.gov/cds/downloads/FRBR.PDF.

26. Leslie Howsam, *Old Books and New Histories: An Orientation to Studies in Book and Print Culture* (Toronto: University of Toronto Press, 2006); Peter D. McDonald, "Implicit Structure and Explicit Interactions: Pierre Bourdieu and the History of the Book," *The Library*, 6th ser., 19, no. 2 (June 1997): 105–121; Thomas R. Adams and Nicolas Barker, "A New Model for the Study of the Book," in *A Potencie of Life: Books in Society*, ed. Nicolas Barker (London: British Library, 2001), 5–43; Padmini Ray Murray and Claire Squires, "The Digital Publishing Communications Circuit," *Book 2.0* 3, no. 1 (2013): 3–23.

27. Robert Darnton, "Booksellers / Literary Demand," A Literary Tour De France, 2016, www.robertdarnton.org/literarytour/booksellers.

28. Francisco J. Kane Jr., Tom Killalea, and Llewyn Mason, Recommendations based on progress data, US Patent 9,153,141, filed June 30, 2009, and issued October 6, 2015; Charles L. Ward et al., Selecting content-enhanced applications, US Patent 9,268,734, filed March 14, 2011, and issued February 23, 2016; Janna Hamaker et al., Aligning content items to identify differences, US Patent 9,069,767, filed March 17, 2011, and issued June 30, 2015.

29. Hamaker et al., Aligning content items to identify differences, figure 5.

30. Martin Paul Eve, "'You Have to Keep Track of Your Changes': The Version Variants and Publishing History of David Mitchell's *Cloud Atlas*," *Open Library of Humanities* 2, no. 2 (2016): 1, https://doi.org/10.16995/olh.82.

31. John B. Thompson, *Merchants of Culture: The Publishing Business in the Twenty-First Century*, 2nd ed. (London: Polity, 2012), 340.

32. Shoshana Zuboff, *The Age of Surveillance Capitalism: The Fight for a Human Future at the New Frontier of Power* (London: Profile Books, 2019), 75.

33. Josh Quittner, "Jeff Bezos: Bio: An Eye on the Future," *Time*, December 27, 1999, http://content.time.com/time/magazine/article/0,9171,992928,00.html.

34. It should come as no surprise that Amazon engineers have explored the possibilities of creating what they term "opaque recommendations"; see Rashmi Arun Patankar, Jeffrey Matthew Bilger, and Colin Ian Bodell, Providing opaque recommendations, US Patent 10,049,397, filed March 6, 2013, and issued August 14, 2018.

35. Ed Finn, "New Literary Cultures: Mapping the Digital Networks of Toni Morrison," in *From Codex to Hypertext: Reading at the Turn of the Twenty-First Century*, ed. Anouk Lang (Amherst and Boston: University of Massachusetts Press, 2012), 180.

36. Finn, "New Literary"; Ed Finn, "Becoming Yourself: The Afterlife of Reception," in *The Legacy of David Foster Wallace*, ed. Samuel Cohen and Lee Konstantinou (Iowa City: University of Iowa Press, 2012), 151–176; Ed Finn, "Revenge of the Nerd: Junot Díaz and the Networks of American Literary Imagination," *Digital Humanities Quarterly* 7, no. 1 (2013), http://www.digitalhumanities.org/dhq/vol/7/1/000148/000148.html.

37. Julian McAuley et al., "Image-Based Recommendations on Styles and Substitutes," in *Proceedings of the 38th International ACM SIGIR Conference on Research and Development in Information Retrieval*, 2015, 43–52; Ruining He and Julian McAuley, "Ups and Downs: Modeling the Visual Evolution of Fashion Trends with One-Class Collaborative Filtering," in *Proceedings of the 25th International Conference on World Wide Web* (ACM, 2016), 507–517. For further information about the data set and methodology, see appendix A.

38. Andrei Broder et al., "Graph Structure in the Web," *Computer Networks* 33, nos. 1–6 (June 2000): 309–320.

39. Clare Swanson, "The Bestselling Books of 2014," *Publishers Weekly*, January 2, 2015, https://www.publishersweekly.com/pw/by-topic/industry-news/bookselling/article/65171-the-fault-in-our-stars-tops-print-and-digital.html.

40. Timothy Graham, "Platforms and Hyper-choice on the World Wide Web," *Big Data and Society* 5, no. 1 (June 1, 2018), https://doi.org/10.1177/2053951718765878.

41. James Marcus, *Amazonia: Five Years at the Epicenter of the Dot.com Juggernaut* (New York: New Press, 2004), 4.

42. Aisha Gani, "Amazon Sues 1,000 'Fake Reviewers,'" *The Guardian*, October 18, 2015, Technology, http://www.theguardian.com/technology/2015/oct/18/amazon-sues-1000-fake-reviewers.

43. Thu-Huong Ha, "Amazon Just Deleted over 900 Reviews of Hillary Clinton's New Book," *Quartz* (blog), September 13, 2017, https://qz.com/1076357/hillary-clintons-what-happened-amazon-just-deleted-over-900-reviews-of-hillary-clintons-new-book/.

44. Daniel Allington, "'Power to the Reader' or 'Degradation of Literary Taste'? Professional Critics and Amazon Customers as Reviewers of *The Inheritance of Loss*," *Language and Literature* 25, no. 3 (2016): 254–278.

45. Ann Steiner, "Private Criticism in the Public Space: Personal Writing on Literature in Readers' Reviews on Amazon," *P@rticipations* 5, no. 2 (2008), https://www.participations.org/Volume%205/Issue%202/5_02_steiner.htm.

46. Jodie Archer and Matthew L. Jockers, *The Bestseller Code* (London: Allen Lane, 2016); Claire Squires, "Taste and/or Big Data? Post-digital Editorial Selection," *Critical Quarterly* 59, no. 3 (2017): 24–38.

47. Mark Davis, "E-books in the Global Information Economy," *European Journal of Cultural Studies* 18, nos. 4–5 (2015): 520.

Chapter 4

1. Jonathan Sterne, *MP3: The Meaning of a Format* (Durham, NC: Duke University Press, 2012), 7.

2. Jennifer Schuessler, "A Tribute to the Printer Aldus Manutius, and the Roots of the Paperback," *New York Times*, February 26, 2015, http://www.nytimes.com/2015/02/27/arts/design/a-grolier-club-tribute-to-the-printer-aldus-manutius.html.

3. Matthew Kirschenbaum, "Book.Files: Preservation of Digital Assets in the Contemporary Publishing Industry; A Report" (College Park, MD, and New York: University of Maryland and Book Industry Study Group, April 2020), 25, https://drum.lib.umd.edu/handle/1903/25605.

4. For a summary of the processes of text rendering, see Scott Weingart's discussion of the transmission of a text message in "The Route of a Text Message, a Love Story," *Vice* (blog), February 22, 2019, https://www.vice.com/en_us/article/kzdn8n/the-route-of-a-text-message-a-love-story.

5. Geoffrey C. Bowker, *Memory Practices in the Sciences* (Cambridge, MA: MIT Press, 2005).

6. Daniel Pargman and Jacob Palme, "ASCII Imperialism," in *Standards and Their Stories: How Quantifying, Classifying, and Formalizing Practices Shape Everyday Life*, ed. Martha Lampland and Susan Leigh Star (Ithaca, NY: Cornell University Press, 2009), 186.

7. Jay Greene, "E-books' Brass Band," *BusinessWeek*, April 3, 2000, https://web.archive.org/web/20060623065325/http:/www.businessweek.com/archives/2000/b3675033.arc.htm.

8. Open eBook Authoring Group, "Supporters," Open eBook, October 4, 1999, http://web.archive.org/web/19991004043319/http://openebook.org/who.htm.

9. Information on the formats can be found in Gary Hillerson, "Palm File Format Specification," 2001, original unavailable via Wayback Machine, available at http://lauriedavis9.tripod.com/copilot/download/Palm_File_Format_Specs.pdf.

10. "MemoWare—the PDA Document Repository," May 10, 2000, https://web.archive.org/web/20000510062641/http://www.memoware.com/.

11. Guido Henkel, "The Horrors of Kindle Format X," *Guido Henkel* (blog), October 27, 2015, http://guidohenkel.com/2015/10/the-horrors-of-kindle-format-x/.

12. Amazon.com Inc., "How to Make Books Available for the Kindle Platform. Version 2018.2," Amazon Kindle Publishing Guidelines, 2018, http://kindlegen.s3.amazonaws.com/AmazonKindlePublishingGuidelines.pdf.

13. Amazon.com Inc., "How to Make Books Available."

14. Amazon.com Inc., "How to Make Books Available," 19.

15. Jonathan Zittrain, *The Future of the Internet* (London: Penguin, 2009), 3.

16. Matthew G. Kirschenbaum, *Mechanisms: New Media and the Forensic Imagination* (Cambridge, MA: MIT Press, 2012), 133.

17. Doug Dorst and J. J. Abrams, *S.* [Kindle for Mac 1.20.2], AZW, B00G99SI06 (Canongate, 2014).

18. The source code reveals that the publisher treated *S.* as a comic book.

19. Igor Skochinsky, "Hacking the Kindle Part 3: Root Shell and Runtime System," *Reversing Everything* (blog), December 21, 2007, http://igorsk.blogspot.com/2007 /12/hacking-kindle-part-3-root-shell-and.html.

20. Aviram Zagorie et al., Device specific presentation control for electronic book reader devices, US Patent 8,423,889, filed December 11, 2008, and issued April 16, 2013; Steven K. Weiss et al., Dynamic display dependent markup language interface, US Patent 8,453,051, filed March 31, 2008, and issued May 28, 2013.

21. Weiss et al., Dynamic display.

22. Henkel, "The Horrors of Kindle Format X."

23. Henkel, "The Horrors of Kindle Format X."

24. See also Kirschenbaum's discussion of JPEG's materiality in *Mechanisms*, 142– 146.

25. Amazon.com Inc., "Kindle (8th Generation) Source Code," 2017, https://s3.ama zonaws.com/kindledownloads/Kindle_src_5.8.10_3202100019.tar.gz.

26. Amazon.com Inc., "How to Make Books Available for the Kindle Platform. Version 2018.2," 36–37.

27. Amazon.com Inc., "Amazon Ion," GitHub, 2017, https://amzn.github.io/ion-docs /index.html.

28. Jiminy Panoz, "Re: Thoughts on the Future of EPUB 3," epub3@w3.org, January 19, 2018, https://lists.w3.org/Archives/Public/public-epub3/2018Jan/0012.html.

29. Franklin Electronic Publishers Inc., "Mobipocket and Franklin Electronic Publishers Announce Opening of EBookBase, the First Wholesale Ebook Distribution Service Exclusively Targeted at Mobile Devices," 2003, http://www .prnewswire.com/news-releases/mobipocket-and-franklin-electronic-pub lishers-announce-opening-of-ebookbase-the-first-wholesale-ebook-distri bution-service-exclusively-targeted-at-mobile-devices-72419177.html.

30. Rowland Manthorpe, "Cory Doctorow Dreams of a DRM-Free Utopia—So He's Suing the US Government to Get It," *Wired UK*, April 25, 2017, http://www.wired .co.uk/article/cory-doctorow-walkaway-science-fiction-drm.

31. Kirschenbaum, "Book.Files," 19.

32. The DRM is generated through a private key unique to each customer along with the device's serial number. Ryan J. Snodgrass et al., Ebook encryption using variable keys, US Patent 8,826,036, filed June 28, 2010, and issued September 2, 2014.

33. Walter Isaacson, *Steve Jobs: The Exclusive Biography* [Kindle for iPad 4.10], AZW3, B005J3IEZQ (Little, Brown Book Group, 2011), loc. 185.

34. Brian Abel Ragen, "Reading Becomes Electric: The Amazon Kindle," *Papers on Language and Literature* 44, no. 3 (Summer 2008): 331–332.

35. Sravan Babu Bodapati and Venkatraman Kalyanapasupathy, Automated identification of start-of-reading location for ebooks, US Patent 10,042,880, filed January 6, 2016, and issued August 7, 2018.

36. Pargman and Palme, "ASCII Imperialism."

37. Mobipocket, "OPF X-Metadata Tags," Mobipocket Developer Center, 2007, http://web.archive.org/web/20090116182003/http://www.mobipocket.com /dev/article.asp?BaseFolder=prcgen&File=tagref_opfxmetadata.xml.

38. Anubhav Kushwaha, Digital work compression, US Patent 9,646,015, filed June 3, 2014, and issued May 9, 2017.

39. Robert A. Wisher and J. Peter Kincaid, "Personal Electronic Aid for Maintenance: Final Summary Report" (Alexandria, VA: US Army Research Institute for the Behavioral and Social Sciences, March 1989).

40. Eric A. Menninga, "Eric Menninga," LinkedIn, 2018, https://www.linkedin.com /in/eric-menninga-3716bb1.

41. Mark Davis and Michel Suignard, "UTR #36: Unicode Security Considerations," Unicode Technical Reports, 2014, http://www.unicode.org/reports/tr36/, documents some of core security issues with Unicode.

42. Lokesh Joshi and Eric A. Menninga, Generation of electronic books, US Patent 9,081,529, filed June 22, 2012, and issued July 14, 2015.

43. Joshi and Menninga, Generation of electronic books.

44. Jiminy Panoz, "Ebooks, Beta Testing, and the Apocalypse," GitHub, 2017, https:// jaypanoz.github.io/ebookcraft2017/#/.

Chapter 5

1. Brad Stone, *The Everything Store: Jeff Bezos and the Age of Amazon* (London: Bantam, 2013), 81.

2. Amazon.com Inc., "The Lab126 Vision," Lab126, 2014, 126, http://web.archive .org/web/20140701154134/http://lab126.com/our-vision.htm.

3. "Kindle: Amazon's Original Wireless Reading Device," Amazon.com, 2011, http://www.amazon.com/dp/B000FI73MA. The 112 titles are calculated from the combination of hardback and paperback fiction (mass market and trade) and "advice, how to and miscellaneous."

4. See, e.g., Mark Sweney, "'Screen Fatigue' Sees UK Ebook Sales Plunge 17% as Readers Return to Print," *The Guardian*, April 27, 2017, https://www.theguardian .com/books/2017/apr/27/screen-fatigue-sees-uk-ebook-sales-plunge-17-as -readers-return-to-print.

5. Catherine Neilan, "Digital Will Overtake Print in 2018, Says FBF Survey," *The Bookseller*, 2008, https://www.thebookseller.com/news/digital-will-overtake -print-2018-says-fbf-survey; Ana Arias Terry, "Electronic Ink Technologies: Showing the Way to a Brighter Future," *Library Hi Tech* 19, no. 4 (2001): 376–389.

6. It is notable that this page appears without much fanfare on the Kindle Direct Publishing (KDP) website rather than on a web page related to both traditional and self-published works. This signifies an aspirational element in the KDP marketing program, and because some authors can sell as well as traditionally published authors, new authors are more likely to buy into this system. Amazon. com Inc., "Kindle Million Club," accessed May 30, 2016, https://kdp.amazon .com/help?topicId=A3OG0G04TL5KMG.

7. New York Times Book Review, "About the Best Sellers," *New York Times Book Review*, 2017, https://www.nytimes.com/books/best-sellers/methodology/.

8. Rachel Deahl, "The YA Bestseller Brought Down by the YA Community," *Publishers Weekly*, August 24, 2017, https://www.publishersweekly.com/pw/by-topic /childrens/childrens-book-news/article/74592-the-ya-book-that-has-the -ya-community-crying-foul.html.

9. Calvin Reid, "Random House, Modern Library to Offer E-books," *Publishers Weekly* 247, no. 32 (August 7, 2000): 10.

10. Xuemei Tian and Bill Martin, "Impacting Forces on eBook Business Models Development," *Publishing Research Quarterly* 27, no. 3 (2011): 237.

11. Amazon.com Inc., "La Belle Sauvage: The Book of Dust Volume One (Book of Dust Series) Kindle Edition," Amazon.co.uk, 2017, https://www.amazon.co.uk/dp/B01N5URPMC/; Amazon.com Inc., "Good Night Stories for Rebel Girls Kindle Edition," Amazon.co.uk, 2017, https://www.amazon.co.uk/dp/B01MZ9ARCZ/.

12. "Budget 2020: VAT on E-books and Newspapers Scrapped," BBC News, March 11, 2020, http://web.archive.org/web/20200312133446/https://www.bbc.co.uk/news/technology-51832899.

13. John Maxwell, "XML Production Workflows? Start with the Web," *Journal of Electronic Publishing* 13, no. 1 (Winter 2010), http://hdl.handle.net/2027/spo.3336451.0013.106.

14. Aegitas, "Aegitas Digital Publishing," Aegitas Digital Publishing, 2017, https://www.aegitas.com; OverDrive, "Enhanced Media Publishing," OverDrive, 2017, https://www.overdrive.com/publishers/enhanced-media-publishing; "Bartleby.com: Great Books Online—Quotes, Poems, Novels, Classics and Hundreds More," Bartleby.com, 2018, http://www.bartleby.com/.

15. Jacob Flynn, Rebecca Giblin, and François Petitjean, "What Happens When Books Enter the Public Domain? Testing Copyright's Underuse Hypothesis across Australia, New Zealand, the United States and Canada," *University of New South Wales Law Journal* 42, no. 4 (November 2019), https://papers.ssrn.com/sol3/papers.cfm?abstract_id=3401684##.

16. Whitney Anne Trettien, "A Deep History of Electronic Textuality: The Case of *English Reprints Jhon Milton Areopagitica*," *Digital Humanities Quarterly* 7, no. 1 (2013), http://www.digitalhumanities.org/dhq/vol/7/1/000150/000150.html.

17. Stephen H. Branch, ed., *Stephen H. Branch's Alligator* 1, no. 18 (August 21, 1858), Project Gutenberg, 2017, http://www.gutenberg.org/ebooks/55004.

18. Amazon.com Inc., "Stephen H Branch's Alligator—Kindle Edition by Stephen H Branch," Amazon.com, 2017, https://www.amazon.com/dp/B075RCFPTX/.

19. Steven Levy, "The Future of Reading," *Newsweek*, November 26, 2007, 58.

20. Anna Sewell and Jose Emorca Flores, *Black Beauty (Kindle in Motion Edition)* [Kindle for iPhone 6.3.1], KFX, B01N6QRN08 (Two Lions, 2017).

21. Caryn J. Adams, "Random House v. Rosetta Books," *Berkeley Technology Law Journal* 17, no. 1 (2002): 29–46.

22. Adams, "Random House v. Rosetta Books," 35.

23. Kelvin Smith, *The Publishing Business: From P-books to E-books* (Lausanne: AVA Publishing, 2012), 36.

24. Amazon.com Inc., "Clancy on Kindle," Amazon Kindle's Blog, 2009, http://web.archive.org/web/20090217191756/http://www.amazon.com/gp/blog/A1F8Z0JAEIDVRY/.

25. Paul Feldstein, "Routes into the American Book Trade, 2008" (London: Publishers Association, 2008).

26. Rebecca Rosen, "The Missing 20th Century: How Copyright Protection Makes Book Vanish," *The Atlantic*, March 30, 2012, http://www.theatlantic.com/technology/archive/2012/03/the-missing-20th-century-how-copyright-makes-books-vanish/255282/.

27. "MIT Press Announces a New Collaboration," MIT Press, 2017, https://mitpress.mit.edu/blog/mit-press-announces-new-collaboration.

28. Teresa Elsey, "When Nothing Ever Goes Out of Print: Maintaining Backlist Ebooks," *Medium* (blog), April 6, 2016, https://medium.com/@teresaelsey/when-nothing-ever-goes-out-of-print-maintaining-backlist-ebooks-fcd63e680667.

29. Elsey, "When Nothing Ever Goes Out of Print."

30. Terje Colbjørnsen, "The Construction of a Bestseller: Theoretical and Empirical Approaches to the Case of the Fifty Shades Trilogy as an eBook Bestseller," *Media, Culture and Society* 36, no. 8 (2014): 1100–1117.

31. Colbjørnsen, 1111. Given Amazon's stranglehold on the ebook market in both the United Kingdom and United States, equivalent comparative data are difficult to acquire.

32. Timothy Laquintano, *Mass Authorship and the Rise of Self-Publishing* (Iowa City: University of Iowa Press, 2016), 34.

33. dtpadmin, "Why Should I Publish My Content on Digital Text Platform?" Digital Text Platform Forum, May 17, 2007, http://web.archive.org/web/2007112303262 4/http://forums.digitaltextplatform.com:80/dtpforums/thread.jspa?threadID=56&tstart=15.

34. Laquintano, *Mass Authorship*, 105.

35. Publishers Association, *PA Publishing Yearbook 2016* (London: Publishers Association, 2017), 1; Sweney, "Screen Fatigue."

36. Locke claimed that two of his books were *New York Times* Best Sellers, but this could not be independently verified. *Lethal People* appeared on the ebook fiction chart between May 8 and 22, 2011.

37. Publishers Weekly, "S&S to Distribute Kindle Bestseller John Locke," *Publishers Weekly*, August 22, 2011, https://www.publishersweekly.com/pw/by-topic/digital/content-and-e-books/article/48433-s-s-to-distribute-kindle-bestseller-john-locke.html.

38. David Streitfeld, "Book Reviewers for Hire Meet a Demand for Online Raves," *New York Times*, August 25, 2012, http://www.nytimes.com/2012/08/26/business/book-reviewers-for-hire-meet-a-demand-for-online-raves.html.

39. M. J. Franklin, "Amazon Just Revealed the Most Popular Kindle Books of All Time," *Mashable*, November 14, 2017, http://mashable.com/2017/11/14/amazon-kindle-most-popular-books-all-time/.

40. Amazon.com Inc., "Terms and Conditions," Kindle Direct Publishing, September 1, 2016, https://kdp.amazon.com/terms-and-conditions.

41. Thu-Huong Ha, "Amazon Has Laid Out Exactly How to Game Its Self-Publishing Platform," *Quartz* (blog), September 20, 2017, https://qz.com/1077996/self-publishing-on-amazon-amzn-how-an-author-can-hack-a-books-success-sales-and-royalties/.

42. Brian Krebs, "Money Laundering via Author Impersonation on Amazon?" *Krebs on Security* (blog), February 20, 2018, https://krebsonsecurity.com/2018/02/money-laundering-via-author-impersonation-on-amazon/.

43. David Gaughran, "Amazon Has a Fake Book Problem," *David Gaughran* (blog), June 3, 2017, https://davidgaughran.com/amazon-has-a-fake-book-problem/.

44. David Gaughran, "Scammers Break the Kindle Store," *David Gaughran* (blog), July 15, 2017, https://davidgaughran.com/scammers-break-the-kindle-store/.

45. David Gaughran, "Amazon's Hall of Spinning Knives," *David Gaughran* (blog), October 20, 2017, https://davidgaughran.com/amazons-hall-of-spinning-knives/.

46. Laquintano, *Mass Authorship*; Alison Baverstock, "Why Self-Publishing Needs to Be Taken Seriously," *Logos* 23, no. 4 (2012): 41–46; Laura Mandell, "The Original Author: How Digital Technology Reconceptualizes the Author (and the Self)," *International Journal of the Book* 1 (2003): 207–213; Trettien, "Deep History."

47. Strawberry Saroyan, "Amanda Hocking, Storyseller," *New York Times*, June 17, 2011, http://www.nytimes.com/2011/06/19/magazine/amanda-hocking-storyseller .html.

48. Canelo, "Vision," Canelo, 2017, https://www.canelo.co/vision/.

49. Abandoned Bookshop, "About," 2017, https://www.abandonedbookshop.com /about/.

50. Jennifer Alsever, "The Kindle Effect," *Fortune*, December 30, 2016, http://fortune .com/2016/12/30/amazon-kindle-digital-self-publishing/.

51. James Marcus, *Amazonia: Five Years at the Epicenter of the Dot.com Juggernaut* (New York: New Press, 2004), 217.

52. Amazon.com Inc., "Amazon Shorts," Amazon.com Message, December 7, 2006, http://web.archive.org/web/20061207162318/http://www.amazon.com:80/exec /obidos/tg/feature/-/570212/.

53. Dwight Garner, "Miniature E-Books Let Journalists Stretch Legs," *New York Times*, March 6, 2012, Books, https://www.nytimes.com/2012/03/07/books/kin dle-singles-genre-between-magazine-articles-and-books.html.

54. George Packer, "Cheap Words," *New Yorker*, February 10, 2014, https://www.new yorker.com/magazine/2014/02/17/cheap-words.

55. WashPostPR, "The Washington Post Launches Most Comprehensive Bestselling Books Lists," *Washington Post*, February 8, 2018, WashPost PR Blog, https:// www.washingtonpost.com/pr/wp/2018/02/08/the-washington-post-launches -most-comprehensive-bestselling-books-lists/.

56. Amazon.com Inc., "Fiction—Most Read—Week of May 14, 2017," Amazon Charts, 2017, https://www.amazon.com/charts/2017-05-14/mostread/fiction?ref=chrt _bk_rd_fc_sh_lp.

57. Amazon.com Inc., "Fiction—Most Read."

58. Ozgun Atasoy and Carey K. Morewedge, "Digital Goods Are Valued Less Than Physical Goods," *Journal of Consumer Research*, October 9, 2017, https://doi.org /10.1093/jcr/ucx102.

59. Alynda Wheat, "10 Years, 10 Books—a Look Back at Kindle Best Sellers," This Week in Books, 2017, https://www.amazon.com/article/twib/kindle-tenth-anni versary.html.

60. Amazon.com Inc., "The Pillars of the Earth," Kindle Store, 2007, http://web .archive.org/web/20071122135800/http://www.amazon.com:80/The-Pillars -of-the-Earth/dp/B000UZPI2U.

Chapter 6

1. D. F. McKenzie, "'What's Past Is Prologue': The Bibliographical Society and History of the Book," in *Making Meanings: "Printers of the Mind" and Other Essays*, ed. Peter D. McDonald and Michael Suarez (Amherst and Boston: University of Massachusetts Press, 2002), 259.

2. Katherine Cowdrey, "Touchpress Unveils New Strategic Direction and Rebrands as Amphio," *The Bookseller*, 2016, https://www.thebookseller.com/news/touch press-announces-new-strategic-direction-and-rebrand-amphio-407456.

3. Amazon has never publicly stated how many Kindle devices are in circulation. The number of users (around 45 million in June 2016) is easier to deduce from Amazon's metadata, but a user may have multiple devices or use the app on another platform.

4. Ted Nelson, "Dream Machines," in *Computer Lib / Dream Machines* (Redmond, WA: Tempus, 1987), 32.

5. Simone Murray, *The Digital Literary Sphere* (Baltimore, MD: Johns Hopkins University Press, 2018).

6. Paul Benzon, "Bootleg Paratextuality and Digital Temporality: Towards an Alternate Present of the DVD," *Narrative* 21, no. 1 (2013): 92.

7. Ellen McCracken, "Expanding Genette's Epitext/Peritext Model for Transitional Electronic Literature: Centrifugal and Centripetal Vectors on Kindles and iPads," *Narrative* 21, no. 1 (2013): 107.

8. Gilles Jean Roger Belin and Hannah Rebecca Lewbel, Cover display, US Patent 9,495,322, filed September 21, 2010, and issued November 15, 2016.

9. Elizabeth Caroline Cranfill, Mikio Inose, and Stephen O. Lemay, Display screen or portion thereof with animated graphical user interface, US Patent D 670,713, filed December 19, 2011, and issued November 13, 2012.

10. Johanna Drucker, *SpecLab: Digital Aesthetics and Projects in Speculative Computing* (Chicago: University of Chicago Press, 2009), 165.

11. Amazon.com Inc., "All-New Kindle Oasis," Amazon.com, October 12, 2017, http://web.archive.org/web/20171012113732/https://www.amazon.com/dp/B06 XD5YCKX.

12. Walter Manching Tseng et al., Generating a game related to a digital work, US Patent 9,449,526, filed March 19, 2012, and issued September 20, 2016.

13. Tully Barnett, "Platforms for Social Reading: The Material Book's Review," *Scholarly and Research Communication* 6, no. 4 (2015), https://doi.org/10.22230/src .2015v6n4a211.

14. Amazon.com Inc., "Read More Challenging Books," Amazon.com, March 17, 2015, http://web.archive.org/web/20150317030835/https://www.amazon.com/gp /feature.html?ie=UTF8&docId=1002989731.

15. Amazon.com Inc., "The Lab126 Vision," Lab126, 2014, http://web.archive.org /web/20140701154134/http://lab126.com/our-vision.htm.

16. Suzanne Collins, *The Hunger Games* [Kindle for Mac 1.20.2], AZW, B0083JCCX8 (Scholastic & Quadrum, 2012).

17. James C. Petts et al., Ebook citation enhancement, US Patent 9,639,877, filed July 6, 2012, and issued May 2, 2017.

18. Amazon.com Inc., "Kindle with Special Offers," Amazon Advertising, November 9, 2016, http://web.archive.org/web/20161109151930/https://advertising .amazon.com/ad-specs/en/kindle.

19. John Cook, "Shelfari: An Online Meeting Place for Bibliophiles," Seattle PI, October 10, 2006, http://web.archive.org/web/20160305202110/http://www .seattlepi.com/business/article/Shelfari-an-online-meeting-place-for-bib liophiles-1216875.php.

20. Michael Arrington, "Amazon Invests in Shelfari," *TechCrunch* (blog), February 25, 2007, http://social.techcrunch.com/2007/02/25/amazon-invests-in-shelfari/.

21. Shelfari, "Questions and Feedback," November 13, 2009, http://web.archive .org/web/20091113093818/http://www.shelfari.com:80/faq/29.

22. Shelfari, "*Harry Potter and the Deathly Hallows* (Harry Potter 7) by J. K. Rowling," October 23, 2011, http://web.archive.org/web/20111023055435/http://www.shel fari.com:80/books/1064883/Harry-Potter-and-the-Deathly-Hallows.

23. Shelfari, "About the Shelfari Librarians & Editors Group," February 25, 2011, http://web.archive.org/web/20110225161532/http://www.shelfari.com/groups /10713/about.

24. Goodreads, "Got a Kindle E-Reader? Now Your Goodreads Want to Read List Is on the Kindle Home Page!" Goodreads Blog, January 27, 2017, http://web.archive .org/web/20170127192507/https://www.goodreads.com/blog/show/611-got-a -kindle-e-reader-now-your-goodreads-want-to-read-list-is-on-the-ki.

25. Amazon has filed several patents related to natural language processing (NLP), including Stan Weidner Salvador and Vlad Magdin, Predictive natural language processing models, US Patent 9,336,772, filed March 6, 2014, and issued May 10, 2016; Imre Attila Kiss, Lambert Mathias, and Jeffrey Penrod Adams, Named entity recognition with personalized models, US Patent 9,190,055, issued November 17, 2015; Simon Overell and William Tunstall-Pedoe, Extracting structured knowledge from unstructured text, US Patent 9,110,882, filed May 12, 2011, and issued August 18, 2015.

26. Walter Isaacson, *Steve Jobs: The Exclusive Biography* [Kindle for iPad 4.10], AZW3, B005J3IEZQ (Little, Brown Book Group, 2011), loc. 199.

27. Oxford Dictionaries, *New Oxford American Dictionary* [Kindle for Android 7.11.0.115], AZW3, B003ODIZL6 (Oxford University Press, 2008), loc. 180914.

28. Theo J. D. Bothma and D. J. Prinsloo, "Automated Dictionary Consultation for Text Reception: A Critical Evaluation of Lexicographic Guidance in Linked Kindle e-Dictionaries," *Lexicographica* 29, no. 1 (2013): 165–198.

29. Bothma and Prinsloo, "Automated Dictionary Consultation."

30. See, e.g., Joseph Michael Reagle Jr., *Good Faith Collaboration: The Culture of Wikipedia* (Cambridge, MA: MIT Press, 2010), chap. 2; Jaron Lanier, *You Are Not a Gadget* (London: Penguin, 2011), 142.

31. Bram Stoker, *Dracula* [Kindle for iPhone 6.3.1], AZK, B00084B5TK8 (Amazon Media EU S.à r.l., 2012), loc. 45.

32. Incidentally, the introduction of Shelfari in 2011 marked a time when Amazon was more interested in creating annotations for the book itself, although these data would often be scraped from Wikipedia.

33. Teresa Elsey, "When Nothing Ever Goes Out of Print: Maintaining Backlist Ebooks," *Medium* (blog), April 6, 2016, https://medium.com/@teresaelsey/when -nothing-ever-goes-out-of-print-maintaining-backlist-ebooks-fcd63e680667.

34. Oxford Dictionaries, *New Oxford*, loc. 533264.

35. As evidenced in Tom Killalea and Janna S. Hamaker, Disambiguation of term meaning, US Patent 8,250,071, filed June 30, 2010, and issued August 21, 2012.

36. Daniel B. Rausch, Determining reading levels of electronic books, US Patent 8,744,855, filed August 9, 2010, and issued June 3, 2014.

37. Amazon.com Inc., "Reading Enhancements," Amazon.co.uk Help, 2012, https:// www.amazon.co.uk/gp/help/customer/display.html?nodeId=200729910.

38. Joshua M. Goodspeed et al., Identifying topics in a digital work, US Patent 9,613,003, filed March 28, 2012, and issued April 4, 2017.

39. Jan Wright, "The Devil Is in the Details: Indexes versus Amazon's X-Ray," *The Indexer* 30, no. 1 (2012): 15.

40. Elsey, "When Nothing Ever Goes Out of Print."

41. Wright, "The Devil Is in the Details," 16.

42. Richard Wrangham, *Catching Fire: How Cooking Made Us Human* (London: Profile Books, 2010), 296–297.

43. This feature is not unique to the Kindle, as it is a regular feature of digital indexing software packages such as Cindex and is part of the development of the EPUB Indexes specification.

44. A 2015 patent attempted to mitigate the effect of spoilers by providing context information relative to the reader's current location in the text. Mehal Shah, Dynamic character biographies, US Patent 9,690,451, filed April 9, 2015, and issued June 27, 2017.

45. Donna Tartt, *The Goldfinch* [Kindle for Android 7.11.0.115], AZW3, B00C74SHRK (Little, Brown, 2013), loc. 2942.

46. Tartt, *The Goldfinch* [Kindle for Android], loc. 12690.

47. As with most elements of the Kindle's technical infrastructure, this in itself varies according to hardware-software setup. I conducted this analysis with Kindle for Mac 1.12.24, as these inconsistencies arose on the platform when I was conducting data collection for chapter 6.

48. John Milton, *Paradise Lost* [Kindle for Mac 1.12.24], AZW, B004UJSYO6 (Amazon Media EU S.à r.l., 2011).

49. Scott Dixon, Edge navigation user interface, US Patent 9,026,932, filed April 16, 2010, and issued May 5, 2015.

50. Dixon, Edge navigation user interface, col. 1.

51. Intel-GE Care Innovations, "Intel Reader," Intel-GE Care Innovations, 2009, http://web.archive.org/web/20110225013439/http://www.careinnovations.com/Products/Reader/Default.aspx.

52. Amazon.com Inc., "Word Runner," Kindle Store, October 6, 2017, http://web.archive.org/web/20171006083018/https://www.amazon.com/Word-Runner-Kindle-Store/b?ie=UTF8&node=11953645011.

53. Bob Brown and Craig Saper, *The Readies* (Roving Eye Press, 2014).

54. David A. Balota, "Speed Reading: You Can't Always Get What You Want, but Can You Sometimes Get What You Need?" *Psychological Science in the Public Interest* 17, no. 1 (2016): 1–3.

55. Geoffrey A. Fowler and Jeffrey A. Trachtenberg, "New Kindle Audio Feature Causes a Stir," *Wall Street Journal*, February 10, 2009, Tech, http://www.wsj.com/articles/SB123419309890963869.

56. Amazon.com Inc., "Statement from Amazon.com regarding Kindle 2's Experimental Text-to-Speech Feature," February 27, 2009, https://press.aboutamazon.com/news-releases/news-release-details/statement-amazoncom-regarding-kindle-2s-experimental-text-speech.

57. Amazon.com Inc., "Statement from Amazon.com."

58. The separation is strong enough that critics who are vocally against Amazon are enchanted by Audible's offerings.

59. Amazon.com Inc., "Whispersync for Voice," Amazon.com, April 15, 2016, http://web.archive.org/web/20160415082009/http://www.amazon.co.uk/gp/feature.html?ie=UTF8&docId=1000812303.

60. Amazon.com Inc., "Amazon Kindle Lite—2MB. Read Millions of EBooks," Android Apps on Google Play, November 8, 2017, http://web.archive.org/web/20171108124044/https://play.google.com/store/apps/details?id=com.amazon.klite.

Chapter 7

1. James Marcus, *Amazonia: Five Years at the Epicenter of the Dot.com Juggernaut* (New York: New Press, 2004).

2. Amazon.com Inc., "Kindle User Guide (2nd Edition)," 2007, http://s3.amazonaws.com/kindle/Kindle_User_Guide.pdf.

3. Michael G. Curtis, Facilitating discussion group formation and interaction, US Patent 8,892,630, filed September 29, 2008, and issued November 18, 2014.

4. Amazon.com Inc., "Reading Group Guides and More," Book Clubs, January 15, 2012, http://web.archive.org/web/20120115102914/http://www.amazon.com:80/gp/feature.html?ie=UTF8&docId=1000487921.

5. Deanna Glaze, "Amazon Kindle," I am monkeyshine, 2010, http://web.archive.org/web/20141018134751/http://deanna-glaze.squarespace.com/test ms-page-1.

6. No official reason was given for restricting access to the database, but it was likely due to the value of the data in an age when publishers are beginning to become more interested in the reading habits of their customers. Kobo, "Publishing in the Era of Big Data," 2014, http://cafe.kobo.com/_ir/159/20149/Publishing%20in%20the%20Era%20of%20Big%20Data%20-%20Kobo%20Whitepaper%20Fall%202014.pdf.

7. Hanning Zhou, Jian Liang, and Sherif M. Yacoub, On-demand generating e-book content with advertising, US Patent 9,892,427, filed September 2, 2014, and issued February 13, 2018.

8. Shoshana Zuboff, *The Age of Surveillance Capitalism: The Fight for a Human Future at the New Frontier of Power* (London: Profile Books, 2019), 513.

9. Lauren Cameron, "Marginalia and Community in the Age of the Kindle: Popular Highlights in *The Adventures of Sherlock Holmes*," *Victorian Review* 38, no. 2 (2012): 81–99; Simon Peter Rowberry, "Commonplacing the Public Domain," *Language and Literature* 25, no. 2 (2016); Tully Barnett, "Social Reading: The Kindle's Social Highlighting Function and Emerging Reading Practices," *Australian Humanities Review* 56 (May 2014): 141–162.

10. Amazon.com Inc., "Annual Report 2017," 2018, [vii], http://phx.corporate-ir.net/External.File?item=UGFyZW50SUQ9NjkyMDIxfENoaWxkSUQ9NDAyOTky fFR5cGU9MQ==&t=1.

11. Amazon.com Inc., "@author," Amazon.com, September 25, 2011, http://web.archive.org/web/20110925001802/http://www.amazon.com:80/gp/feature.html?ie=UTF8&docId=1000714331.

12. Emily Margaret Anderson et al., Author interactions using online social networks, US Patent 9,183,172, filed June 22, 2011, and issued November 10, 2015.

13. See, e.g., Naomi S. Baron, *Words Onscreen: The Fate of Reading in a Digital World* (Oxford: Oxford University Press, 2015).

14. Anne Mangen, Bente R. Walgermo, and Kolbjørn Brønnick, "Reading Linear Texts on Paper versus Computer Screen: Effects on Reading Comprehension," *International Journal of Educational Research* 58 (2013): 61–68; Baron, *Words Onscreen*; Matt Hayler, *Challenging the Phenomena of Technology: Embodiment, Expertise, and Evolved Knowledge* (Basingstoke: Palgrave Macmillan, 2015).

15. Bram Stoker, *Dracula* [Kindle for iPhone 6.3.1], AZK, B0084B5TK8 (Amazon Media EU S.à r.l., 2012).

16. Joseph Michael Reagle Jr., *Good Faith Collaboration: The Culture of Wikipedia* (Cambridge, MA: MIT Press, 2010), 50.

17. Emily Margaret Anderson and Tom Killalea, Personal user highlight from popular highlights, US Patent 9,965,150, filed October 27, 2014, and issued May 8, 2018.

18. This can have the strange effect of needing to resynchronize Kindle files after downloading them initially.

19. Robin Sloan, *Mr. Penumbra's 24-Hour Bookstore, a Novel* [Kindle Cloud Reader 011201999], B00A25NLOU (Farrar, Straus and Giroux, 2012), loc. 377.

20. Sloan, *Mr. Penumbra's 24-Hour Bookstore*.

21. Cameron, "Marginalia and Community," 91–95.

22. Donna Tartt, *The Goldfinch* (London: Abacus, 2014), 864.

23. Killalea et al., Aggregation of highlights.

24. Walter Isaacson, *Steve Jobs: The Exclusive Biography* [Kindle Touch 5.3.7.3], AZW3, B005J3IEZQ (Little, Brown Book Group, 2011), loc. 375.

25. Andrew Sims, "The Most Moving Parts of 'Cursed Child,' According to Kindle," *Hypable* (blog), August 12, 2016, http://www.hypable.com/cursed-child-kindle -popular-highlights/; Virginia Heffernan, "E-Readers Collective," *New York Times*, October 15, 2010, http://www.nytimes.com/2010/10/17/magazine/17FOB-medium -t.html.

26. Jordan Ellenberg, "The Summer's Most Unread Book Is . . . ," *Wall Street Journal*, July 3, 2014, Life and Style, http://www.wsj.com/articles/the-summers-most -unread-book-is-1404417569.

27. Kobo, "Publishing in the Era of Big Data," 4.

28. Kobo, "Publishing in the Era of Big Data"; Pavel Braslavski et al., "Large-Scale Log Analysis of Digital Reading," ASIST 2016, https://dl.acm.org/doi/ abs/10.5555/3017447.3017491.

29. The aggregated average highlight location was calculated by multiplying the indexed locations and volumes and then adding the resulting numbers together.

30. J. K. Rowling, *Harry Potter and the Philosopher's Stone* [Kindle for Mac 1.20.2], AZW, B019PIOJYU (Pottermore, 2015), loc. 3267.

31. Rowling, *Harry Potter and the Philosopher's Stone*, loc. 3631.

32. Kobo, "Publishing in the Era of Big Data"; Amazon undertakes similar analysis, as identified in Francisco J. Kane Jr., Tom Killalea, and Llewyn Mason, Recommendations based on progress data, US Patent 9,153,141, filed June 30, 2009, and issued October 6, 2015.

33. Timothy Laquintano, *Mass Authorship and the Rise of Self-Publishing* (Iowa City: University of Iowa Press, 2016), 107.

34. Jane Austen, *Pride and Prejudice* [Kindle for Mac 1.20.2], AZW, B000JMLFLW (Public Domain Books, 2010), loc. 2205.

35. Austen, *Pride and Prejudice*, loc. 1.

36. In total, a quarter of highlights relating to *Pride and Prejudice and Zombies* ignore the zombies in favor of the classic aphorisms from Austen's original, demonstrating how readers converge on these statements. Seth Grahame-Smith and Jane Austen, *Pride and Prejudice and Zombies* [Kindle for Mac 1.20.2], AZW, B004HW7E6U (Quirk Books, 2009), version v3.1r1.

37. Barnett, "Social Reading."

Chapter 8

1. Brad Stone, "Amazon Erases Orwell Books from Kindle Devices," *New York Times*, July 17, 2009, http://www.nytimes.com/2009/07/18/technology/companies/18 amazon.html.

2. Jeffrey P. Bezos, "An Apology from Amazon," Customer Discussions, 2009, https://www.amazon.com/tag/kindle/forum/cdForum=Fx1D7SY3BVSESG&cdThread =Tx1FXQPSF67X1IU.

3. Jared Newman, "Amazon Settles Kindle '1984' Lawsuit," *PC World*, October 1, 2009, https://www.pcworld.com/article/172953/amazon_kindle_1984_lawsuit.html.

4. Silvio Lorusso and Sebastian Schmeig, *56 Broken Kindle Screens* (Lulu, 2012).

5. iFixit, "Kindle 1st Generation Repair," iFixit, 2017, https://www.ifixit.com/Device /Kindle_1st_Generation.

6. Garnet Hertz and Jussi Parikka, "Zombie Media: Circuit Bending Media Archaeology into an Art Method," *Leonardo* 45, no. 5 (2012): 424–430.

7. Hertz and Parikka, "Zombie Media," 426.

8. Marcus Blosch and Jackie Fenn, "Understanding Gartner's Hype Cycles," Gartner Research, August 20, 2018, https://www.gartner.com/en/documents/3887767 /understanding-gartner-s-hype-cycles; Hertz and Parikka, "Zombie Media," 428.

9. Matt Peckham, "Play *Doom* on a Printer—Thanks to a Serious Security Flaw," *Wired*, September 23, 2014, http://www.wired.com/2014/09/doom-printer/.

10. David Given, "Hacking the Kindle," *Cowlark.com* (blog), December 10, 2015, http:// web.archive.org/web/20121022145738/http://cowlark.com/kindle/combined .html.

11. Geoffroy Tremblay, "KindleBerry Pi," *Ponnuki—Electronic Media Art and Yoga* (blog), 2012, http://www.ponnuki.net/2012/09/kindleberry-pi/.

12. N. K. Sheridon and M. A. Berkovitz, "The Gyricon—a Twisting Ball Display," *Proceedings of the Society for Information Display* 18, no. 34 (1977): 289–293.

13. MobileRead, "Kindlet Index," MobileRead Wiki, 2016, http://wiki.mobileread .com/wiki/Kindlet_Index.

14. "Acorn," "DIY Kindle Voice Control (Simulating Key Presses)—MobileRead Forums," MobileRead Forums, 2011, https://www.mobileread.com/forums/show thread.php?t=118480.

15. fbdev, "Kinamp (v2) Audio Player for Kindle," MobileRead Forums, 2011, https:// www.mobileread.com/forums/showthread.php?t=147854.

16. Nick Montfort, "Continuous Paper: The Early Materiality and Workings of Electronic Literature," 2005, http://nickm.com/writing/essays/continuous_paper

_mla.html; Andrew de Quincey, "KIF: An Infocom Text Adventure Interpreter for the Kindle," *Andrew de Quincey's Livejournal* (blog), October 9, 2010, http://adq .livejournal.com/108011.html.

17. Montfort, "Continuous Paper."

18. Amazon.com Inc., "Amazon Announces Kindle Development Kit—Software Developers Can Now Build Active Content for Kindle," Amazon Press Room, 2010, http://phx.corporate-ir.net/phoenix.zhtml?c=176060&p=irol-newsArticle &ID=1377349.

19. Amazon.com Inc., "Catan: USM," Kindle Store, 2012, http://web.archive.org/web /20171013122311/https://www.amazon.com/Catan/dp/B007JV4WGQ/?tag =terrania-20.

20. Nate Hoffelder, "Amazon Drops Support for Kindle Active Content from the Kindle Voyage," Digital Reader, October 27, 2014, https://the-digital-reader.com /2014/10/27/amazon-drops-support-kindle-active-content-kindle-voyage/.

21. Nick Montfort and Ian Bogost, *Racing the Beam: The Atari Video Computer System* (Cambridge, MA: MIT Press, 2009).

22. Peter Purgathofer, *DIY Kindle Scanner*, Vimeo, 2013, http://vimeo.com/73675285.

23. Amazon.com Inc., "Annual Report 2017," 2018, [7], http://phx.corporate-ir.net /External.File?item=UGFyZW50SUQ9NjkyMDIxfENoaWxkSUQ9NDAyOTkyfFR 5cGU9MQ==&t=1.

24. The Legal Deposit Libraries (Non-print Works) Regulations 2013, no. 777 § (2013); for a scholarly analysis of this shift, see Paul Gooding and Melissa Terras, *Electronic Legal Deposit: Shaping the Libraries of the Future* (London: Facet Publishing, 2020).

25. The Legal Deposit Libraries (Non-print Works) Regulations 2013, 5.

26. The Legal Deposit Libraries (Non-print Works) Regulations 2013.

27. National Library of Scotland, "The Silent Corner / Dean Koontz," National Library of Scotland, 2017, http://main-cat.nls.uk/vwebv/holdingsInfo?bibId=9420635.

28. Library of Congress, "Textual Works and Musical Compositions," Recommended Formats Statement, 2017, http://web.archive.org/web/20190708145942/https:// www.loc.gov/preservation/resources/rfs/textmus.html.

29. Kunsthal Aarhus, "Ubermorgen—the Project Formerly Known as Kindle Forkbomb," Kunsthal Aarhus, 2013.

30. Finn Brunton, *Spam: A Shadow History of the Internet* (Cambridge, MA: MIT Press, 2013), 167.

31. Shoshana Zuboff, *The Age of Surveillance Capitalism: The Fight for a Human Future at the New Frontier of Power* (London: Profile Books, 2019), 96.

32. Clifford Lynch, "Stewardship in the 'Age of Algorithms,'" *First Monday* 22, no. 12 (December 2017), https://doi.org/10.5210/fm.v22i12.8097.

33. Amazon.com Inc., "Announcement: This Amazon Forum Is Retiring October 13, 2017," Kindle Forum, 2017, http://web.archive.org/web/20171004091808 /https://www.amazon.com/forum/kindle/ref=cdForum=Fx1D7SY3BVSESG&cd Thread=Tx13YCUTDID1DJD.

34. Amazon.com Inc., "Kindle Popular Highlights," 2014, https://kindle.amazon.com /most_popular.

Chapter 9

1. J. Yellowlees Douglas, *The End of Books—or Books without End? Reading Interactive Narratives* (Ann Arbor: University of Michigan Press, 2000).
2. W3C, "W3C Publishing Working Group," W3C, 2017, https://www.w3.org/publishing/groups/publ-wg/.
3. Jessica Pressman, "The Aesthetics of Bookishness in Twenty-First-Century Literature," *Michigan Quarterly Review* 48, no. 4 (Fall 2009).
4. Sudeep Sharma, "Netflix and the Documentary Boom," in *The Netflix Effect: Technology and Entertainment in the 21st Century*, ed. Kevin McDonald and Daniel Smith-Rowse (London: Bloomsbury, 2016), 143–154.
5. Angus Phillips, "Have We Passed Peak Book? The Uncoupling of Book Sales from Economic Growth," *Publishing Research Quarterly* 33, no. 3 (2017): 310–327.
6. Start-up data from Thad McIlroy's survey of publishing start-ups between 2007 and 2017. Further start-ups have shut down since the report. Thad McIlroy, "Startups within the U.S. Book Publishing Industry," *Publishing Research Quarterly* 33, no. 1 (2017): 1–9; Lisa Campbell, "Dropbox Buys Readmill," *The Bookseller*, 2014, https://www.thebookseller.com/news/dropbox-buys-readmill.

Appendix A

1. Charlie Rose, "Interview with Jeff Bezos," February 26, 2009, https://charlierose.com/videos/22164.
2. Peri Hartman et al., Method and system for placing a purchase order via a communications network, US Patent 5,960,411, filed September 12, 1997, and issued September 28, 1999.
3. Brigham Young University, "NOW Corpus (News on the Web)," BYU Corpora, 2017, corpus.byu.edu/now/.
4. Tony McEnery and Andrew Hardie, *Corpus Linguistics* (Cambridge: Cambridge University Press, 2011), 122–123.
5. Christopher F. Weight et al., Book version mapping, US Patent 9,846,688, filed December 28, 2010, and issued December 19, 2017.
6. Julian McAuley et al., "Image-Based Recommendations on Styles and Substitutes," in *Proceedings of the 38th International ACM SIGIR Conference on Research and Development in Information Retrieval* (New York: ACM, 2015), 43–52; Ruining He and Julian McAuley, "Ups and Downs: Modeling the Visual Evolution of Fashion Trends with One-Class Collaborative Filtering," in *Proceedings of the 25th International Conference on World Wide Web* (ACM, 2016), 507–517.
7. Matthew G. Kirschenbaum, *Mechanisms: New Media and the Forensic Imagination* (Cambridge, MA: MIT Press, 2012), 133.
8. Kirschenbaum, *Mechanisms*, 10.

Appendix B

1. Modern Language Association of America, *MLA Handbook*, 8th ed. (New York: Modern Language Association of America, 2016), sec. 3.3.3.
2. *The Chicago Manual of Style* (Chicago: University of Chicago Press, 2017), sec. 14.159–160, http://chicagomanualofstyle.org/home.html.

3. Nathan Altice, *I AM ERROR: The Nintendo Family Computer / Entertainment System Platform* (Cambridge, MA: MIT Press, 2015), 333.

4. Altice, *I AM ERROR*, 336.

5. Altice, *I AM ERROR*; Jerome McDonough et al., "Twisty Little Passages Almost All Alike: Applying the FRBR Model to a Classic Computer Game," *Digital Humanities Quarterly* 4, no. 2 (2010), http://www.digitalhumanities.org/dhq/vol/4/2/0000 89/000089.html.

6. Matthew G. Kirschenbaum, *Mechanisms: New Media and the Forensic Imagination* (Cambridge, MA: MIT Press, 2012).

7. Rollin Milroy, *About Agrippa* (Vancouver: Heavenly Monkey, 2015); Alan Liu et al., "The *Agrippa* Files," 2005, http://agrippa.english.ucsb.edu/.

8. Kirschenbaum, *Mechanisms*.

9. Amazon.com Inc., "Bone Music," Kindle Store, 2018, https://www.amazon.co.uk /gp/product/B07354S1K7/.

10. Fredson Bowers, *Principles of Bibliographical Description* (New York: Russell & Russell, 1962), 197.

11. Ben Goldacre, *Bad Science* [Kindle for Android 8.0.0.68], AZW3, B002RI9ORI (HarperCollins, 2013), version 2013-09-03, loc. 5317.

12. Eoghan Casey, *Digital Evidence and Computer Crime: Forensic Science, Computers and the Internet*, 3rd ed. (Amsterdam: Elsevier, 2011), 22–23.

13. Peter Sorotokin et al., "EPUB Canonical Fragment Identifiers 1.1," 2017, http:// www.idpf.org/epub/linking/cfi/.

Bibliography

Kindle Ebooks

Albanese, Andrew Richard (2013). *The Battle of $9.99: How Apple, Amazon, and the Big Six Publishers Changed the E-book Business Overnight* [Kindle for PC 1.21.0]. KFX. B00DH8JCOC. PWxyz. Loc. 981.

Austen, Jane (2010). *Pride and Prejudice* [Kindle for Mac 1.20.2]. AZW. B000JMLFLW. Public Domain Books. Loc. 4584.

Collins, Suzanne (2012). *The Hunger Games* [Kindle for Mac 1.20.2]. AZW. B0083JCCX8. Scholastic & Quadrum. Loc. 4501.

Dorst, Doug, and J. J. Abrams (2014). *S.* [Kindle for Mac 1.20.2]. AZW. B00G99SIO6. Canongate. Loc. 518.

Goldacre, Ben (2013) *Bad Science* [Kindle for Android 8.0.0.68]. AZW3. B002RI9ORI. HarperCollins. Version 2013-09-03. Loc. 5474.

Franzen, Jonathan (2011). *The Corrections* [Kindle for Mac 1.20.2]. AZW. B0043VDEE6. Fourth Estate. Version 2016-02-17. Loc. 10612.

Grahame-Smith, Seth, and Jane Austen (2009). *Pride and Prejudice and Zombies* [Kindle for Mac 1.20.2]. AZW. B004HW7E6U. Quirk Books. Version v3.1r1. Loc. 3681.

Isaacson, Walter (2011). *Steve Jobs: The Exclusive Biography* [Kindle for iPad 4.10]. AZW3. B005J3IEZQ. Little, Brown Book Group. Loc. 12321.

Isaacson, Walter. (2011). *Steve Jobs: The Exclusive Biography* [Kindle Touch 5.3.7.3]. AZW3. B005J3IEZQ. Little, Brown Book Group. Loc. 12321.

Lenart, K. (2010). *Simple Word Find—Sports Edition* [Kindle for Mac 1.20.2]. AZW. B004EEPOYK. K. Lenart and Advanced Design Professions. Loc. 214.

Milton, John (2011). *Paradise Lost* [Kindle for Mac 1.12.24]. AZW. B004UJSYO6. Amazon Media EU S.à r.l. 4609.

Oxford Dictionaries (2008). *New Oxford American Dictionary* [Kindle for Android 7.11.0.115]. AZW3. B003ODIZL6. Oxford University Press. Loc. 683493.

Rowling, J. K. (2015). *Harry Potter and the Philosopher's Stone* [Kindle for Mac 1.20.2]. AZW. B019PIOJYU. Pottermore. Loc. 3912.

Sewell, Anna, and Jose Emorca Flores (2017). *Black Beauty (Kindle in Motion Edition)* [Kindle for iPhone 6.3.1]. KFX. B01N6QRN08. Two Lions. Loc. 2595.

Sloan, Robin (2012). *Mr. Penumbra's 24-Hour Bookstore, a Novel* [Kindle Cloud Reader 011201999]. B00A25NLOU. Farrar, Straus and Giroux. Loc. 4158.

Stephenson, Neal (1998). *The Diamond Age* [Kindle Cloud Reader 011201999]. B002RI9DQ0. Penguin Random House. Loc. 8301.

Stoker, Bram (2012). *Dracula* [Kindle for iPhone 6.3.1]. AZK. B00B84B5TK8. Amazon Media EU S.à r.l. Loc. 5741.

Tartt, Donna (2013). *The Goldfinch* [Kindle for Android 7.11.0.115]. AZW3. B00C74SHRK. Little, Brown. Loc. 13582.

Достоевский, Федор Михайлович (2014). *Преступление и наказание (Russian Edition)* [Kindle Touch 5.3.7.3]. AZW3. B00KHRXSMI. Общественное достояние. Loc. 13971.

Secondary Sources

Abandoned Bookshop. "About," 2017. https://www.abandonedbookshop.com/about/.

Abbate, Janet. *Inventing the Internet*. Cambridge, MA: MIT Press, 2000.

"Acorn." "DIY Kindle Voice Control (Simulating Key Presses)—MobileRead Forums." MobileRead Forums, 2011. https://www.mobileread.com/forums/showthread .php?t=118480.

Adams, Caryn J. "Random House v. Rosetta Books." *Berkeley Technology Law Journal* 17, no. 1 (2002): 29–46.

Adams, Thomas R., and Nicolas Barker. "A New Model for the Study of the Book." In *A Potencie of Life: Books in Society*, edited by Nicolas Barker, 5–43. London: British Library, 2001.

Aegitas. "Aegitas Digital Publishing." Aegitas Digital Publishing, 2017. https://www .aegitas.com.

AFNIL. "AFNIL," 2017. http://www.afnil.org/.

Allen School. "Carlos Guestrin and Emily Fox Join the University of Washington." *Allen School News* (blog), April 27, 2012. https://news.cs.washington.edu/2012/04/27 /carlos-guestrin-and-emily-fox-join-the-university-of-washington/.

Allington, Daniel. "'Power to the Reader' or 'Degradation of Literary Taste'? Professional Critics and Amazon Customers as Reviewers of *The Inheritance of Loss*." *Language and Literature* 25, no. 3 (2016): 254–278.

Alsever, Jennifer. "The Kindle Effect." *Fortune*, December 30, 2016. http://fortune .com/2016/12/30/amazon-kindle-digital-self-publishing/.

Altice, Nathan. *I AM ERROR: The Nintendo Family Computer / Entertainment System Platform*. Cambridge, MA: MIT Press, 2015.

Amazon Web Services. "AWS Programs for Research and Education," 2017. http://aws .amazon.com/grants/.

Amazon.com Inc. "2006 Annual Report." Seattle: Amazon.com, 2007. http://media .corporate-ir.net/media_files/irol/97/97664/2006AnnualReport.pdf.

Amazon.com Inc. "2019 Annual Report." Seattle: Amazon.com, 2020. https://s2 .q4cdn.com/299287126/files/doc_financials/2020/ar/2019-Annual-Report.pdf.

Amazon.com Inc. "About Amazon—Our Innovations—Fulfillment by Amazon." Accessed June 29, 2017. https://www.amazon.com/p/feature/pxekbkm47y7c9fd.

Amazon.com Inc. "About Your Kindle [2006 Version for FCC]," 2006. https://apps.fcc
.gov/eas/GetApplicationAttachment.html?id=862803.

Amazon.com Inc. "All-New Kindle Oasis." Amazon.com, October 12, 2017. http://web
.archive.org/web/20171012113732/https://www.amazon.com/dp/B06XD5YCKX.

Amazon.com Inc. "Amazon Announces Kindle Development Kit—Software Developers Can Now Build Active Content for Kindle." Amazon Press Room, 2010.
https://press.aboutamazon.com/news-releases/news-release-details/amazon
-announces-kindle-development-kit-software-developers-can.

Amazon.com Inc. "Amazon Books," 2017. https://www.amazon.com/b?ie=UTF8&
node=13270229011.

Amazon.com Inc. "Amazon Catalyst," 2017. https://catalyst.amazon.com/.

Amazon.com Inc. "Amazon Fiona Reading Light [X7198.2014]." Computer History
Museum, 2006. http://www.computerhistory.org/collections/catalog/102747856.

Amazon.com Inc. "Amazon Fiona Rear Cover [102747848]." Computer History Museum,
2006. http://www.computerhistory.org/collections/catalog/102747848.

Amazon.com Inc. "Amazon Fiona Rear Cover [102747850]." Computer History Museum,
2006. http://www.computerhistory.org/collections/catalog/102747850.

Amazon.com Inc. "Amazon Go," 2016. https://www.amazon.com/b?ie=UTF8&node
=16008589011.

Amazon.com Inc. "Amazon Ion." GitHub, 2017. https://amzn.github.io/ion-docs/index
.html.

Amazon.com Inc. "Amazon Kindle 3G Coverage," 2017. http://web.archive.org/web
/20190326131601/http://cliento.cellmaps.com/viewer.html?view=intl&cov=3.

Amazon.com Inc. "Amazon Kindle Lite—2MB. Read Millions of EBooks." Android Apps
on Google Play, November 8, 2017. http://web.archive.org/web/20171108124044
/https://play.google.com/store/apps/details?id=com.amazon.klite.

Amazon.com Inc. "Amazon Kindle Project Fiona Prototype Unit [X7198.2014]." Computer History Museum, 2005. http://www.computerhistory.org/collections/catalog
/102747839.

Amazon.com Inc. "Amazon Prime Air." Amazon.com, 2013. http://www.amazon.com
/b?node=8037720011.

Amazon.com Inc. "Amazon Shorts." Amazon.com Message, December 7, 2006.
http://web.archive.org/web/20061207162318/http://www.amazon.com:80/exec
/obidos/tg/feature/-/570212/.

Amazon.com Inc. "Amazon Upgrade." Amazon Device Support, 2016. https://www
.amazon.com/gp/help/customer/display.html?ie=UTF8&nodeId=110744011.

Amazon.com Inc. "Amazon.com Invites Music Lovers to Help Build the Ultimate
Music Store." Amazon Press Room, April 23, 1998. https://press.aboutamazon
.com/news-releases/news-release-details/amazoncom-invites-music-lovers
-help-build-ultimate-music-store.

Amazon.com Inc. "Amazon.com Launches Three Innovations to Advance E-Commerce
for Shoppers, Sellers." Amazon Press Room, September 30, 1999. https://press
.aboutamazon.com/news-releases/news-release-details/amazoncom-launches
-three-innovations-advance-e-commerce-shoppers.

Amazon.com Inc. "Announcement: This Amazon Forum Is Retiring October 13, 2017."
Kindle Forum, 2017. http://web.archive.org/web/20171004091808/https://
www.amazon.com/forum/kindle/ref=cdForum=Fx1D7SY3BVSESG&cdThread
=Tx13YCUTDID1DJD.

Amazon.com Inc. "Annual Report 2017," 2018. http://web.archive.org/web/20210
623092704/https://s2.q4cdn.com/299287126/files/doc_financials/annual
/Amazon_AR.PDF.

Amazon.com Inc. "@author." Amazon.com, September 25, 2011. http://web.archive
.org/web/20110925001802/http://www.amazon.com:80/gp/feature.html?ie
=UTF8&docId=1000714331.

Amazon.com Inc. "Bone Music." Kindle Store, 2018. http://web.archive.org/web
/20180206133911/https://www.amazon.co.uk/gp/product/B07354S1K7/.

Amazon.com Inc. "Catan: USM." Kindle Store, 2012. http://web.archive.org/web
/20171013122311/https://www.amazon.com/Catan/dp/B007JV4WGQ/?tag=ter
rania-20.

Amazon.com Inc. "Clancy on Kindle." Amazon Kindle's Blog, 2009. http://web
.archive.org/web/20090217191756/http://www.amazon.com/gp/blog/A1F8Z
oJAEIDVRY/.

Amazon.com Inc. "Critical Software Update for Kindle E-Readers." Amazon.com
Help, 2016. http://www.amazon.com/gp/help/customer/display.html?nodeId
=201994710&tag=mro60-20.

Amazon.com Inc. "Fiction—Most Read—Week of May 14, 2017." Amazon Charts, 2017.
https://www.amazon.com/charts/2017-05-14/mostread/fiction?ref=chrt_bk_rd
_fc_sh_lp.

Amazon.com Inc. "Form 10-K," 1998. http://media.corporate-ir.net/media_files/irol
/97/97664/reports/123197_10k.pdf.

Amazon.com Inc. "Form 10-K," 1999. http://web.archive.org/web/20210623093958
/https://d18rnop25nwr6d.cloudfront.net/CIK-0001018724/07ab23e8-be7f
-44ba-9765-44979c4516a1.pdf.

Amazon.com Inc. "Form 10-K," 2019. http://web.archive.org/web/20210105150403
/http://d18rnop25nwr6d.cloudfront.net/CIK-0001018724/bed19367-fa6b-41ff
-a973-df19510bobba.pdf.

Amazon.com Inc. "Form 10-Q: Q2 2020," June 2020. http://d18rnop25nwr6d.cloud
front.net/CIK-0001018724/a77b5839-99b8-4851-8f37-0b012f9292b9.pdf.

Amazon.com Inc. "Good Night Stories for Rebel Girls Kindle Edition." Amazon.co.uk,
2017. https://www.amazon.co.uk/dp/B01MZ9ARCZ/.

Amazon.com Inc. "How to Make Books Available for the Kindle Platform. Version
2018.2." Amazon Kindle Publishing Guidelines, 2018. http://kindlegen.s3.ama
zonaws.com/AmazonKindlePublishingGuidelines.pdf.

Amazon.com Inc. "Ian Bogost Newsgames." Amazon.com, July 13, 2017. http://web
.archive.org/web/20170713121105/https://www.amazon.com/s/ref=nb_sb_noss
?url=search-alias%3Dstripbooks&field-keywords=ian+bogost+newsgames&rh
=n%3A283155%2Ck%3Aian+bogost+newsgames.

Amazon.com Inc. "Kindle (8th Generation) Source Code," 2017. https://s3.ama
zonaws.com/kindledownloads/Kindle_src_5.8.10_3202100019.tar.gz.

Amazon.com Inc. "Kindle: Amazon's Original Wireless Reading Device." Amazon.
com, 2011. http://www.amazon.com/dp/B000FI73MA.

Amazon.com Inc. "Kindle DX Wireless Reading Device." Amazon.com, 2010. http://
web.archive.org/web/20100131052954/http://www.amazon.com:80/Kindle
-Wireless-Reading-Device-Display/dp/B0015TCML0.

Amazon.com Inc. "Kindle Keyboard 3G, Free 3G + Wi-Fi, 6" E Ink Display." Amazon.com, 2010. https://www.amazon.com/Kindle-Wireless-Reading-Display-Globally/dp/B002LVUX1W/.

Amazon.com Inc. "Kindle Million Club." Accessed May 30, 2016. https://kdp.amazon.com/help?topicId=A3OGoGo4TL5KMG.

Amazon.com Inc. "Kindle Popular Highlights," 2014. https://kindle.amazon.com/most_popular.

Amazon.com Inc. "Kindle Source Code 1.0.0.292." Kindle Amazon Web Services, 2007. https://s3.amazonaws.com/kindle/Kindle_src.1.0.0.292.tar.

Amazon.com Inc. "Kindle Source Code 2.2." Kindle Amazon Web Services, 2009. https://kindle.s3.amazonaws.com/Kindle_src_2.0_291330095.tar.gz.

Amazon.com Inc. "Kindle User Guide (2nd Edition)," 2007. http://s3.amazonaws.com/kindle/Kindle_User_Guide.pdf.

Amazon.com Inc. "Kindle Wireless Reading Device (6" Display, Global Wireless, Latest Generation)." Kindle Store, November 27, 2009. http://web.archive.org/web/20091127191626/http://www.amazon.com:80/Kindle-Wireless-Reading-Display-Generation/dp/B0015T963C.

Amazon.com Inc. "Kindle with Special Offers." Amazon Advertising, November 9, 2016. http://web.archive.org/web/20161109151930/https://advertising.amazon.com/ad-specs/en/kindle.

Amazon.com Inc. "La Belle Sauvage: The Book of Dust Volume One (Book of Dust Series) Kindle Edition." Amazon.co.uk, 2017. https://www.amazon.co.uk/dp/B01N5URPMC/.

Amazon.com Inc. "Lab126." Lab126, 2005. http://web.archive.org/web/20051124085428/http://www.lab126.com:80/.

Amazon.com Inc. "The Lab126 Vision." Lab126, 2014. http://web.archive.org/web/20140701154134/http://lab126.com/our-vision.htm.

Amazon.com Inc. "Les jeunes dans la société Broché." Amazon.fr, 2011. https://www.amazon.fr/jeunes-dans-société-Hélène-Dubouis/dp/B0065GAW9M/.

Amazon.com Inc. "Page Flip." Amazon.com, 2016. https://www.amazon.com/b?ie=UTF8&node=13632018011.

Amazon.com Inc. "The Pillars of the Earth." Kindle Store, 2007. http://web.archive.org/web/20071122135800/http://www.amazon.com:80/The-Pillars-of-the-Earth/dp/B000UZPI2U.

Amazon.com Inc. "Read More Challenging Books." Amazon.com, March 17, 2015. http://web.archive.org/web/20150317030835/https://www.amazon.com/gp/feature.html?ie=UTF8&docId=1002989731.

Amazon.com Inc. "Read Your Books Online," September 27, 2014. http://web.archive.org/web/20140927045348/https://www.amazon.com/gp/digital/sitb/help/learn.html/ref=si3_learn_dtls?ie=UTF8&details=1&navbar=0.

Amazon.com Inc. "Reading Enhancements." Amazon.co.uk Help, 2012. https://www.amazon.co.uk/gp/help/customer/display.html?nodeId=200729910.

Amazon.com Inc. "Reading Group Guides and More." Book Clubs, January 15, 2012. http://web.archive.org/web/20120115102914/http://www.amazon.com:80/gp/feature.html?ie=UTF8&docId=1000487921.

Amazon.com Inc. "Search Inside!" Amazon.co.uk Help, 2017. https://www.amazon.co.uk/gp/help/customer/display.html/?nodeId=200182580.

Amazon.com Inc. "Securely Accept Payments Online." Amazon Pay, 2017. https://pay
.amazon.com/uk/.

Amazon.com Inc. "Statement from Amazon.com Regarding Kindle 2's Experimental Text-to-Speech Feature," February 27, 2009. https://press.aboutamazon.com
/news-releases/news-release-details/statement-amazoncom-regarding
-kindle-2s-experimental-text-speech.

Amazon.com Inc. "Stephen H Branch's Alligator—Kindle Edition by Stephen H
Branch." Amazon.com, 2017. https://www.amazon.com/dp/B075RCFPTX/.

Amazon.com Inc. "Terms and Conditions." Kindle Direct Publishing, September 1,
2016. https://kdp.amazon.com/terms-and-conditions.

Amazon.com Inc. "Whispersync for Voice." Amazon.com, April 15, 2016. http://web
.archive.org/web/20160415082009/http://www.amazon.co.uk/gp/feature.html
?ie=UTF8&docId=1000812303.

Amazon.com Inc. "Word Runner." Kindle Store, October 6, 2017. http://web.archive
.org/web/20171006083018/https://www.amazon.com/Word-Runner-Kindle
-Store/b?ie=UTF8&node=11953645011.

Andersen Consulting. "Reading in the New Millennium, a Bright Future for Ebook
Publishing: Facilitating Open Standards." Washington, DC: AAP Annual Meeting,
March 22, 2000. http://web.archive.org/web/20021227113121/http://www.pub
lishers.org/digital/dec2000anderson.ppt.

Anderson, Chris. *The Longer Long Tail*. London: Random House Business Books, 2009.

Anderson, Emily Margaret, and Tom Killalea. Personal user highlight from popular
highlights. US Patent 9,965,150, filed October 27, 2014, and issued May 8, 2018.

Anderson, Emily Margaret, Tom Killalea, Daniel Leng, and Peter A. Larsen. Author
interactions using online social networks. US Patent 9,183,172, filed June 22,
2011, and issued November 10, 2015.

Antley, Jeremy. "From Data Self to Data Serf." *Peasant Muse* (blog), 2012. http://www
.peasantmuse.com/2012/06/from-data-self-to-data-serf.html.

Apperley, Thomas, and Jussi Parikka. "Platform Studies' Epistemic Threshold." *Games
and Culture* 13, no. 4 (2018): 327–348.

Archer, Jodie, and Matthew L. Jockers. *The Bestseller Code*. London: Allen Lane, 2016.

Arrington, Michael. "Amazon Invests in Shelfari." *TechCrunch* (blog), February 25,
2007. http://social.techcrunch.com/2007/02/25/amazon-invests-in-shelfari/.

Atasoy, Ozgun, and Carey K. Morewedge. "Digital Goods Are Valued Less Than Physical Goods." *Journal of Consumer Research*, October 9, 2017. https://doi.org/10
.1093/jcr/ucx102.

Azari, David, Lee M. Miller, Maksym Kovalenko, Jonathan D. Sanford, Anthony C.
Martinelli, Alan Kipust, and Kelly Watson. Public-domain analyzer. US Patent
9,691,068, filed December 15, 2011, and issued June 27, 2017.

Bai, Peng Fei, Robert Andrew Hayes, Mingliang Jin, Lingling Shui, Zi Chuan Yi, Li
Wang, Xiao Zhang, and Guofu Zhou. "Review of Paper-Like Display Technologies." *Progress in Electromagnetics Research* 147 (2014): 95–116.

Balota, David A. "Speed Reading: You Can't Always Get What You Want, but Can You
Sometimes Get What You Need?" *Psychological Science in the Public Interest* 17, no.
1 (2016): 1–3.

Barnett, Tully. "Platforms for Social Reading: The Material Book's Review." *Scholarly and Research Communication* 6, no. 4 (2015). https://doi.org/10.22230/src
.2015v6n4a211.

Barnett, Tully. "Social Reading: The Kindle's Social Highlighting Function and Emerging Reading Practices." *Australian Humanities Review* 56 (May 2014): 141–162.

Baron, Naomi S. *Words Onscreen: The Fate of Reading in a Digital World*. Oxford: Oxford University Press, 2015.

"Bartleby.com: Great Books Online—Quotes, Poems, Novels, Classics and Hundreds More." Bartleby.com, 2018. http://www.bartleby.com/.

Barton-Davis, Paul. "I Oppose Amazon.com's 1-Click Patent." Equal Area, 2000. http://www.equalarea.com/paul/amazon-1click.html.

Baverstock, Alison. "Why Self-Publishing Needs to Be Taken Seriously." *Logos* 23, no. 4 (2012): 41–46.

BBC News. "Budget 2020: VAT on E-books and Newspapers Scrapped." BBC News, March 11, 2020. http://web.archive.org/web/20200312133446/https://www.bbc.co.uk/news/technology-51832899.

Belin, Gilles Jean Roger, and Hannah Rebecca Lewbel. Cover display. US Patent 9,495,322, filed September 21, 2010, and issued November 15, 2016.

Benzon, Paul. "Bootleg Paratextuality and Digital Temporality: Towards an Alternate Present of the DVD." *Narrative* 21, no. 1 (2013): 88–104.

Bezos, Jeffrey P. "An Apology from Amazon." Customer Discussions, 2009. https://www.amazon.com/tag/kindle/forum/cdForum=Fx1D7SY3BVSESG&cdThread=Tx1FXQPSF67X1IU.

Bezos, Jeffrey P. "An Open Letter from Jeff Bezos." Amazon.com, April 15, 2000. http://web.archive.org/web/20000415152112/http://www.amazon.com/exec/obidos/subst/misc/patents.html.

Bezos, Jeffrey P. "2015 Letter to Shareholders." Investor Relations, 2016. https://amazonir.gcs-web.com/annual-reports.

Bezos, Jeffrey P. *Opening Keynote—MIT World*. MIT, 2006.

Bezos, Jeffrey P. Secure method for communicating credit card data when placing an order on a non-secure network. US Patent 5,727,163, filed March 30, 1995, and issued March 10, 1998.

Birkerts, Sven. *The Gutenberg Elegies: The Fate of Reading in an Electronic Age*. New York: Fawcett Columbine, 1994.

Block, Ryan. "Amazon Kindle: Meet Amazon's E-book Reader." *Engadget*, September 11, 2006. https://www.engadget.com/2006/09/11/amazon-kindle-meet-amazons-e-book-reader/.

Blosch, Marcus, and Jackie Fenn, "Understanding Gartner's Hype Cycles," Gartner Research, August 20, 2018, https://www.gartner.com/en/documents/3887767/understanding-gartner-s-hype-cycles.

Blum, Andrew. *Tubes: Behind the Scenes at the Internet*. London: Viking, 2012.

Bodapati, Sravan Babu, and Venkatraman Kalyanapasupathy. Automated identification of start-of-reading location for ebooks. US Patent 10,042,880, filed January 6, 2016, and issued August 7, 2018.

Boellstorff, Tom, and Braxton Soderman. "Transplatform: Culture, Context, and the Intellivision/Atari VCS Rivalry." *Games and Culture* 14, no. 6 (2019): 680–703.

Bookeen. "Bookeen Cybook." Bookeen, 2007. http://web.archive.org/web/20071002212414/http://www.bookeen.com:80/specs/ebook-specs.aspx.

Borenstein, Nathaniel S. "Perils and Pitfalls of Practical Cybercommerce." *Communications of the ACM* 39, no. 6 (June 1996): 36–44.

Borsuk, Amaranth, and Brad Bouse. *Between Page and Screen*. Los Angeles: Siglio, 2012.

Bothma, Theo J. D., and D. J. Prinsloo. "Automated Dictionary Consultation for Text Reception: A Critical Evaluation of Lexicographic Guidance in Linked Kindle e-Dictionaries." *Lexicographica* 29, no. 1 (2013): 165–198.

Bowers, Fredson. *Principles of Bibliographical Description*. New York: Russell & Russell, 1962.

Bowker, Geoffrey C. *Memory Practices in the Sciences*. Cambridge, MA: MIT Press, 2005.

Branch, Stephen H., ed. *Stephen H. Branch's Alligator* 1, no. 18 (August 21, 1858). Project Gutenberg, 2017. http://www.gutenberg.org/ebooks/55004.

Brandt, Richard. *One Click: Jeff Bezos and the Rise of Amazon.com*. London: Portfolio Penguin, 2011.

Braslavski, Pavel, Vivien Petras, Valery Likhosherstov, and Maria Gäde. "Large-Scale Log Analysis of Digital Reading." ASIST 2016. https://dl.acm.org/doi/abs/10.5555/3017447.3017491.

Brigham Young University. "NOW Corpus (News on the Web)." BYU Corpora, 2017. corpus.byu.edu/now/.

Broadcom Corp. v. Qualcomm Inc., 501 F. 3d 297 (Court of Appeals, 3rd Circuit 2007).

Broder, Andrei, Ravi Kumar, Farzin Maghoul, Prabhakar Raghavan, Sridhar Rajagopalan, Raymie Stata, Andrew Tomkins, and Janet Wiener. "Graph Structure in the Web." *Computer Networks* 33, nos. 1–6 (June 2000): 309–320.

Brown, Bob, and Craig Saper. *The Readies*. Roving Eye Press, 2014.

Brunton, Finn. *Spam: A Shadow History of the Internet*. Cambridge, MA: MIT Press, 2013.

Buchmueller, Daniel, Louis Leroi LeGrand III, Jack Erdozain Jr., Scarlett Elizabeth Koller, Eric Alexander Riehl, and Trevor Barr Walker. Stabilized airborne drop delivery. US Patent 9,688,404, issued June 27, 2017.

Burns, Stephanie. "FCC ID No. UUU-L7E20070323 Short Term Confidentiality Request." Federal Communications Commission, October 19, 2007. http://web.archive.org/web/20210623100724/https://fccid.io/UUU-L7E20070323/Letter/Short-Term-Confidentiality-Request-862773.pdf.

Burrington, Ingrid. "Why Amazon's Data Centers Are Hidden in Spy Country." *The Atlantic*, January 8, 2016. http://www.theatlantic.com/technology/archive/2016/01/amazon-web-services-data-center/423147/.

Bush, Vannevar. "As We May Think." *The Atlantic* 176 (July 1945): 101–108.

Business Wire. "Prime View International Reaches Agreement to Acquire E Ink." Business Wire, June 1, 2009. http://web.archive.org/web/20100920185513/https://www.businesswire.com/news/home/20090601005656/en/Prime-View-International-Reaches-Agreement-Acquire-Ink.

Cadwalladr, Carole. "My Week as an Amazon Insider." *The Guardian*, December 1, 2013, Technology. http://www.theguardian.com/technology/2013/dec/01/week-amazon-insider-feature-treatment-employees-work.

CamelCamelCamel. "Amazon Price Tracker, Amazon Price History Charts, Price Watches, and Price Drop Alerts." camelcamelcamel.com. Accessed June 27, 2016. http://uk.camelcamelcamel.com/.

Cameron, Lauren. "Marginalia and Community in the Age of the Kindle: Popular Highlights in *The Adventures of Sherlock Holmes*." *Victorian Review* 38, no. 2 (2012): 81–99.

Campbell, Lisa. "Dropbox Buys Readmill." *The Bookseller*, 2014. https://www.thebook seller.com/news/dropbox-buys-readmill.

Canelo. "Vision." Canelo, 2017. https://www.canelo.co/vision/.

Carmack, Scott Gerard, Narasimha Rao Lakkakula, and Nima Sharifi Mehr. Detecting of navigation data spoofing based on image data. US Patent 9,689,686, filed September 25, 2015, and issued June 27, 2017.

Casey, Eoghan. *Digital Evidence and Computer Crime: Forensic Science, Computers and the Internet*. 3rd ed. Amsterdam: Elsevier, 2011.

Chamberlain, Gethin. "Underpaid and Exhausted: The Human Cost of Your Kindle." *The Guardian*, June 9, 2018, Technology. http://www.theguardian.com/technol ogy/2018/jun/09/human-cost-kindle-amazon-china-foxconn-jeff-bezos.

Chen, Brian X. "iPhone 4's 'Retina' Display Claims Are False Marketing." *Wired*, June 9, 2010. https://www.wired.com/2010/06/iphone-4-retina/.

The Chicago Manual of Style. Chicago: University of Chicago Press, 2017. http://chicago manualofstyle.org/home.html.

CNET. "Amazon, B&N Settle Lawsuit." CNET, October 21, 1997. https://www.cnet.com /news/amazon-b-n-settle-lawsuit/.

Colbjørnsen, Terje. "The Construction of a Bestseller: Theoretical and Empirical Approaches to the Case of the Fifty Shades Trilogy as an eBook Bestseller." *Media, Culture and Society* 36, no. 8 (2014): 1100–1117.

Coldewey, Devin. "How the Kindle Was Designed through 10 Years and 15 Generations." *TechCrunch* (blog), 2017. http://social.techcrunch.com/2017/11/20/how -the-kindle-was-designed-through-10-years-and-15-generations/.

Coleman, Gabriella. *Coding Freedom: The Ethics and Aesthetics of Hacking*. Princeton, NJ: Princeton University Press, 2013.

Cook, John. "Shelfari: An Online Meeting Place for Bibliophiles." Seattle PI, October 10, 2006. http://web.archive.org/web/20160305202110/http://www.seattlepi .com/business/article/Shelfari-an-online-meeting-place-for-bibliophiles -1216875.php.

Corns, Thomas N. "The Early Modern Search Engine: Indices, Title Pages, Marginalia and Contents." In *The Renaissance Computer: Knowledge Technology in the First Age of Print*, edited by Neil Rhodes and Jonathan Sawday, 95–105. London: Routledge, 2000.

Costello, Megan. "'Radio Paper' from E Ink." *Publishers Weekly* 248, no. 12 (March 19, 2001).

Cowdrey, Katherine. "Touchpress Unveils New Strategic Direction and Rebrands as Amphio." *The Bookseller*, 2016. https://www.thebookseller.com/news/touchpress -announces-new-strategic-direction-and-rebrand-amphio-407456.

Cranfill, Elizabeth Caroline, Mikio Inose, and Stephen O. Lemay. Display screen or portion thereof with animated graphical user interface. US Patent D 670,713, filed December 19, 2011, and issued November 13, 2012.

Cuneo, Joshua. "'Hello, Computer': The Interplay of *Star Trek* and Modern Computing." In *Science Fiction and Computing: Essays on Interlinked Domains*, edited by David L. Ferro and Eric G. Swedin, 131–147. Jefferson, NC: McFarland, 2011.

Curtis, Michael G. Facilitating discussion group formation and interaction. US Patent 8,892,630, filed September 29, 2008, and issued November 18, 2014.

Darnton, Robert. "Booksellers / Literary Demand." A Literary Tour de France, 2016. www.robertdarnton.org/literarytour/booksellers.

Darnton, Robert. "What Is the History of Books?" In *The Book History Reader*, edited by David Finkelstein and Alistair McCleery, 2nd ed., 9–26. Oxford: Routledge, 2006.

Davis, Mark. "E-books in the Global Information Economy." *European Journal of Cultural Studies* 18, nos. 4–5 (2015): 514–529.

Davis, Mark. "Five Processes in the Platformisation of Cultural Production: Amazon and Its Publishing Ecosystem." *Australian Humanities Review* 66 (May 2020): 83–103.

Davis, Mark, and Michel Suignard. "UTR #36: Unicode Security Considerations." Unicode Technical Reports, 2014. http://www.unicode.org/reports/tr36/.

Deahl, Rachel. "The YA Bestseller Brought Down by the YA Community." *Publishers Weekly*, August 24, 2017. https://www.publishersweekly.com/pw/by-topic/child rens/childrens-book-news/article/74592-the-ya-book-that-has-the-ya-com munity-crying-foul.html.

Delfanti, Alessandro. "Machinic Dispossession and Augmented Despotism: Digital Work in an Amazon Warehouse." *New Media and Society*, December 2, 2019. https://doi.org/10.1177/1461444819891613.

Delfanti, Alessandro, and Bronwyn Frey. "Humanly Extended Automation or the Future of Work Seen through Amazon Patents." *Science, Technology, and Human Values*, July 29, 2020. https://doi.org/10.1177/0162243920943665.

Denny, Neill. "The Kindle Has Landed." *The Bookseller*, October 9, 2009. https://www.thebookseller.com/blogs/kindle-has-landed.

Dixon, Scott. Edge navigation user interface. US Patent 9,026,932, filed April 16, 2010, and issued May 5, 2015.

Douglas, J. Yellowlees. *The End of Books—or Books without End? Reading Interactive Narratives*. Ann Arbor: University of Michigan Press, 2000.

Driscoll, Beth, and Claire Squires. "'Oh Look, a Ferry'; or The Smell of Paper Books." *Lifted Brow*, October 24, 2018. https://www.theliftedbrow.com/liftedbrow/2018/10/24/oh-look-a-ferry-or-the-smell-of-paper-books-by-beth-driscoll-and-claire-squires.

Drucker, Johanna. *SpecLab: Digital Aesthetics and Projects in Speculative Computing*. Chicago: University of Chicago Press, 2009.

dtpadmin. "Why Should I Publish My Content on Digital Text Platform?" Digital Text Platform Forum, May 17, 2007. http://web.archive.org/web/20071123032624/http://forums.digitaltextplatform.com:80/dtpforums/thread.jspa?threadID=56&tstart=15.

E Ink. "E Ink Pearl Imaging Film," 2017. http://www.eink.com/sell_sheets/pearl_spec_sheet.pdf.

eBay. "Search: Kindle DX." eBay, 2018. http://web.archive.org/web/20180122115624/https://www.ebay.com/sch/i.html?_from=R40&_sacat=0&LH_Complete=1&LH_Sold=1&_nkw=kindle+dx&_sop=16.

Edwards, Paul N., Steven J. Jackson, Geoffrey C. Bowker, and Cory P. Knobel. "Understanding Infrastructure: Dynamics, Tensions, and Design," 2007. http://hdl.handle.net/2027.42/49353.

Eichelberg, John William, Brock Robert Gardner, and Alan Donald Gillooly. Cooling system for data center. US Patent 9,690,337, filed December 9, 2013, and issued June 27, 2017.

Eisen, Michael. "Amazon's $23,698,655.93 Book about Flies." *It Is NOT Junk* (blog), April 22, 2011. http://www.michaeleisen.org/blog/?p=358.

Eisenstein, Elizabeth L. *The Printing Press as an Agent of Change*. Cambridge: Cambridge University Press, 1980.

Ellenberg, Jordan. "The Summer's Most Unread Book Is . . ." *Wall Street Journal*, July 3, 2014, Life and Style. http://www.wsj.com/articles/the-summers-most-unread-book-is-1404417569.

Elsey, Teresa. "Building Ebooks That Last." YouTube, May 2, 2019. https://www.youtube.com/watch?v=8OOHyBT-Lo.

Elsey, Teresa. "When Nothing Ever Goes Out of Print: Maintaining Backlist Ebooks." *Medium* (blog), April 6, 2016. https://medium.com/@teresaelsey/when-nothing-ever-goes-out-of-print-maintaining-backlist-ebooks-fcd63e680667.

Eve, Martin Paul. "'You Have to Keep Track of Your Changes': The Version Variants and Publishing History of David Mitchell's *Cloud Atlas*." *Open Library of Humanities* 2, no. 2 (2016): 1. https://doi.org/10.16995/olh.82.

fbdev. "Kinamp (v2) Audio Player for Kindle." MobileRead Forums, 2011. https://www.mobileread.com/forums/showthread.php?t=147854.

Febvre, Lucien, and Henri-Jean Martin. *The Coming of the Book: The Impact of Printing, 1450–1800*. Edited by Geoffrey Nowell-Smith and David Wootton. Translated by David Gerard. London: Verso, 2010.

Feldstein, Paul. "Routes into the American Book Trade, 2008." London: Publishers Association, 2008.

Fernandez, Emilio A. Microprocessor based simulated book. US Patent 4,855,725, filed December 28, 1988, and issued August 8, 1989.

Finn, Ed. "Becoming Yourself: The Afterlife of Reception." In *The Legacy of David Foster Wallace*, edited by Samuel Cohen and Lee Konstantinou, 151–176. Iowa City: University of Iowa Press, 2012.

Finn, Ed. "New Literary Cultures: Mapping the Digital Networks of Toni Morrison." In *From Codex to Hypertext: Reading at the Turn of the Twenty-First Century*, edited by Anouk Lang, 177–202. Amherst and Boston: University of Massachusetts Press, 2012.

Finn, Ed. "Revenge of the Nerd: Junot Díaz and the Networks of American Literary Imagination." *Digital Humanities Quarterly* 7, no. 1 (2013). http://www.digitalhumanities.org/dhq/vol/7/1/000148/000148.html.

Flynn, Jacob, Rebecca Giblin, and François Petitjean. "What Happens When Books Enter the Public Domain? Testing Copyright's Underuse Hypothesis across Australia, New Zealand, the United States and Canada." *University of New South Wales Law Journal* 42, no. 4 (November 2019). https://papers.ssrn.com/sol3/papers.cfm?abstract_id=3401684##.

Ford, Paul. "Does Amazon Data Speak for Itself?" *New Republic*, February 18, 2016. https://newrepublic.com/article/129026/amazons-data-speak-itself.

Forston, Danny, and Simon Duke. "Alexa, What Shall We Do Next? Take Over the World, Jeff." *Sunday Times*, June 18, 2017.

Fowler, Geoffrey A. "E-Readers: They're Hot Now, but the Story Isn't Over." *Wall Street Journal*, December 1, 2009, Tech. http://www.wsj.com/articles/SB10001424052748704328104574519851557848662.

Fowler, Geoffrey A., and Jeffrey A. Trachtenberg. "New Kindle Audio Feature Causes a Stir." *Wall Street Journal*, February 10, 2009, Tech. http://www.wsj.com/articles/SB123419309890963869.

Fowler, Gerald C., and Terence D. Hughey. Reading machine. US Patent 4,160,242, filed June 28, 1977, and issued July 3, 1979.

Franklin Electronic Publishers Inc. "Mobipocket and Franklin Electronic Publishers Announce Opening of EBookBase, the First Wholesale Ebook Distribution Service Exclusively Targeted at Mobile Devices," 2003. http://web.archive.org/web/20031011064358/http://biz.yahoo.com/prnews/031008/phwo11_1.html.

Franklin, M. J. "Amazon Just Revealed the Most Popular Kindle Books of All Time." *Mashable*, November 14, 2017. http://mashable.com/2017/11/14/amazon-kindle-most-popular-books-all-time/.

Galloway, Alexander R. *Protocol: How Control Exists after Decentralization*. Cambridge, MA: MIT Press, 2004.

Gani, Aisha. "Amazon Sues 1,000 'Fake Reviewers.'" *The Guardian*, October 18, 2015, Technology. http://www.theguardian.com/technology/2015/oct/18/amazon-sues-1000-fake-reviewers.

Garner, Dwight. "Miniature E-Books Let Journalists Stretch Legs." *New York Times*, March 6, 2012, Books. https://www.nytimes.com/2012/03/07/books/kindle-singles-genre-between-magazine-articles-and-books.html.

Gaughran, David. "Amazon Has a Fake Book Problem." *David Gaughran* (blog), June 3, 2017. https://davidgaughran.com/amazon-has-a-fake-book-problem/.

Gaughran, David. "Amazon's Hall of Spinning Knives." *David Gaughran* (blog), October 20, 2017. https://davidgaughran.com/amazons-hall-of-spinning-knives/.

Gaughran, David. "Scammers Break the Kindle Store." *David Gaughran* (blog), July 15, 2017. https://davidgaughran.com/scammers-break-the-kindle-store/.

Gemstar TV Guide International. "Another Important EBook Announcement." Gemstar eBook, February 9, 2006. http://web.archive.org/web/20060209023520/http://www.gemstar-ebook.com:80/cgi-bin/WebObjects/eBookstore.woa/wa/.

Genette, Gérard, and Marie Maclean. "Introduction to the Paratext." *New Literary History* 22, no. 2 (Spring 1991): 261–272.

Gill, Harsimran. "'The Ebook Is a Stupid Product: No Creativity, No Enhancement,' Says the Hachette Group CEO." Scroll.in, 2018. https://scroll.in/article/868871/the-ebook-is-a-stupid-product-no-creativity-no-enhancement-says-the-hachette-group-ceo.

Gillespie, Tarleton. "The Politics of 'Platforms.'" *New Media and Society* 12, no. 3 (2010): 347–364.

Given, David. "Hacking the Kindle." *Cowlark.com* (blog), December 10, 2015. http://web.archive.org/web/20121022145738/http://cowlark.com/kindle/combined.html.

Glaze, Deanna. "Amazon Kindle." I am monkeyshine, 2010. http://web.archive.org/web/20141018134751/http://deanna-glaze.squarespace.com/test-ms-page-1.

Gooding, Paul, and Melissa Terras. *Electronic Legal Deposit: Shaping the Libraries of the Future*. London: Facet Publishing, 2020.

Goodreads. "Got a Kindle E-Reader? Now Your Goodreads Want to Read List Is on the Kindle Home Page!" Goodreads Blog, January 27, 2017. http://web.archive.org/web/20170127192507/https://www.goodreads.com/blog/show/611-got-a-kindle-e-reader-now-your-goodreads-want-to-read-list-is-on-the-ki.

Goodspeed, Joshua M., Janna S. Hamaker, Adam J. Iser, Tom Killalea, Abhishek Patnia, and Alla Taborisskaya. Identifying topics in a digital work. US Patent 9,613,003, filed March 28, 2012, and issued April 4, 2017.

Graham, Timothy. "Platforms and Hyper-choice on the World Wide Web." *Big Data and Society* 5, no. 1 (June 1, 2018). https://doi.org/10.1177/2053951718765878.

Greene, Jay. "E-books' Brass Band." *BusinessWeek*, April 3, 2000. https://web.archive .org/web/20060623065325/http:/www.businessweek.com/archives/2000 /b3675033.arc.htm.

Greenfield, Rebecca. "Amazon's Kindle MatchBook: Good Idea, Not Such a Great Deal." *The Atlantic*, September 3, 2013. https://www.theatlantic.com/technology /archive/2013/09/amazons-kindle-matchbook-program-isnt-good-deal-most -time/311521/.

Ha, Thu-Huong. "Amazon Has Laid Out Exactly How to Game Its Self-Publishing Platform." *Quartz* (blog), September 20, 2017. https://qz.com/1077996/self-pub lishing-on-amazon-amzn-how-an-author-can-hack-a-books-success-sales -and-royalties/.

Ha, Thu-Huong. "Amazon Just Deleted over 900 Reviews of Hillary Clinton's New Book." *Quartz* (blog), September 13, 2017. https://qz.com/1076357/hillary-clin tons-what-happened-amazon-just-deleted-over-900-reviews-of-hillary -clintons-new-book/.

Hamaker, Janna, Tom Killalea, Christopher F. Weight, Bruno A. Posokhow, and Daniel B. Rausch. Aligning content items to identify differences. US Patent 9,069,767, filed March 17, 2011, and issued June 30, 2015.

Harbick, Andrew V., Ryan J. Snodgrass, and Joel R. Spiegel. Playlist-based detection of similar digital works and work creators. US Patent 8,468,046, filed August 2, 2012, and issued June 18, 2013.

Hart, Michael. "Re: 3.301 e-Texts (65)." *Humanist*, July 29, 1989. https://humanist.kdl .kcl.ac.uk/Archives/Virginia/v03/0305.html.

Hartman, Peri, Jeffrey P. Bezos, Shel Kaphan, and Joel Spiegel. Method and system for placing a purchase order via a communications network. US Patent 5,960,411, filed September 12, 1997, and issued September 28, 1999.

Hayes, Robert A., and B. J. Feenstra. "Video-Speed Electronic Paper Based on Elec-trowetting." *Nature* 425, no. 6956 (September 2003): 383–385.

Hayler, Matt. *Challenging the Phenomena of Technology: Embodiment, Expertise, and Evolved Knowledge*. Basingstoke: Palgrave Macmillan, 2015.

He, Ruining, and Julian McAuley. "Ups and Downs: Modeling the Visual Evolution of Fashion Trends with One-Class Collaborative Filtering." In *Proceedings of the 25th International Conference on World Wide Web*, 507–517. New York: ACM, 2016.

Heffernan, Virginia. "E-Readers Collective." *New York Times*, October 15, 2010. http:// www.nytimes.com/2010/10/17/magazine/17FOB-medium-t.html.

Heller, Steven. "Who Named the Kindle (and Why)?" *Print Magazine* (blog). Accessed July 27, 2015. http://www.printmag.com/article/who-named-the-kindle-and -why/.

Henkel, Guido. "The Horrors of Kindle Format X." *Guido Henkel* (blog), October 27, 2015. http://guidohenkel.com/2015/10/the-horrors-of-kindle-format-x/.

Hennen, Thomas J. "OCLC Invitational Conference: Public Librarians Take Cool View of Future." *American Libraries* 19, no. 5 (1988): 390–392.

Hertz, Garnet, and Jussi Parikka. "Zombie Media: Circuit Bending Media Archaeology into an Art Method." *Leonardo* 45, no. 5 (2012): 424–430.

Hillerson, Gary. "Palm File Format Specification," 2001. Original unavailable via Wayback Machine. http://lauriedavis9.tripod.com/copilot/download/Palm_File _Format_Specs.pdf.

Hilts, Paul. "Book Tech Looks at E-Publishing." *Publishers Weekly* 248, no. 10 (March 5, 2001): 46.

Hoffelder, Nate. "Amazon Drops Support for Kindle Active Content from the Kindle Voyage." Digital Reader, October 27, 2014. https://the-digital-reader.com/2014 /10/27/amazon-drops-support-kindle-active-content-kindle-voyage/.

Howsam, Leslie. *Old Books and New Histories: An Orientation to Studies in Book and Print Culture.* Toronto: University of Toronto Press, 2006.

IBM. "Virtualization in Education," 2007. http://www-07.ibm.com/solutions/in /education/download/Virtualization%20in%20Education.pdf.

IDPF. "EPUB 3 Open Container Format (OCF) 3.0.1." EPUB 3, 2014. http://www.idpf .org/epub/301/spec/epub-ocf.html.

IDPF. "EPUB 3 Overview." EPUB 3, 2014. http://www.idpf.org/epub/301/spec/epub -overview.html.

IDPF. "EPUB 3 Publications 3.0.1." EPUB 3, 2014. http://www.idpf.org/epub/301 /spec/epub-publications.html.

iFixit. "Kindle 1st Generation Repair." iFixit, 2017. https://www.ifixit.com/Device /Kindle_1st_Generation.

IKEA Singapore. "Experience the Power of a Bookbook™." YouTube, September 3, 2014. https://www.youtube.com/watch?v=MOXQo7nURso.

Ingold, David, and Spencer Soper. "Amazon Doesn't Consider the Race of Its Customers. Should It?" Bloomberg, April 21, 2016. http://www.bloomberg.com/graph ics/2016-amazon-same-day/.

Intel. "Marvell to Purchase Intel's Communications and Application Processor Business for $600 Million." Intel Press Room, 2006. https://www.intel.com/press room/archive/releases/2006/20060627corp.htm.

Intel-GE Care Innovations. "Intel Reader." Intel-GE Care Innovations, 2009. http:// web.archive.org/web/20110225013439/http://www.careinnovations.com/Prod ucts/Reader/Default.aspx.

IPO. "Top 300 Organizations Granted U.S. Patents in 2018." IPO, 2019. https://ipo.org /wp-content/uploads/2019/07/2018-Top-300-Final.pdf.

Irani, Lilly. "Difference and Dependence among Digital Workers: The Case of Amazon Mechanical Turk." *South Atlantic Quarterly* 114, no. 1 (2015): 225–234.

Jackson, H. J. *Marginalia: Readers Writing in Books.* New Haven, CT: Yale University Press, 2002.

Jahagirdar, Sonjeev, Matthew Joseph Cole, David Paul Ramos, Utkarsh Prateek, Emilie Noelle McConville, Ankur Datta, Laura Varnum Finney, et al. Recognizing text from frames of image data using contextual information. US Patent 9,355,336, filed April 23, 2014, and issued May 31, 2016.

Johns, Adrian. *The Nature of the Book: Print and Knowledge in the Making.* Chicago: University of Chicago Press, 1998.

Johnston, John E., and Gregg E. Zehr. Configurable keypad for an electronic device. US Patent 8,692,736, filed June 14, 2007, and issued April 8, 2014.

Johnstone, Bob. "Electronic Paperbacks." *Wired*, March 1, 1994. https://www.wired
.com/1994/03/electronic-paperbacks/.

Jones, Derek T., and Oleksandr Berezhnyy. Electronic book pagination. US Patent
9,892,094, filed June 19, 2014, and issued February 13, 2018.

Joshi, Lokesh, and Eric A. Menninga. Generation of electronic books. US Patent
9,081,529, filed June 22, 2012, and issued July 14, 2015.

Kane, Francisco J., Jr., Tom Killalea, and Llewyn Mason. Recommendations based
on progress data. US Patent 9,153,141, filed June 30, 2009, and issued October
6, 2015.

Kang, Hyo Yoon. "Science inside Law: The Making of a New Patent Class in the International Patent Classification." *Science in Context* 25, no. 4 (2012): 551–594.

Kantor, Jodi, and David Streitfeld. "Inside Amazon: Wrestling Big Ideas in a Bruising Workplace." *New York Times*, August 15, 2015. http://www.nytimes.com/2015
/08/16/technology/inside-amazon-wrestling-big-ideas-in-a-bruising-work
place.html.

Karlinsky, Neal. "The Inside Story of How the Kindle Was Born." US Day One Blog,
November 15, 2017. https://blog.aboutamazon.com/devices/the-inside-story-of
-how-the-kindle-was-born.

Kay, A., and A. Goldberg. "Personal Dynamic Media." *Computer* 10, no. 3 (March
1977): 31–41.

Kilgour, Frederick. *The Evolution of the Book*. New York: Oxford University Press, 1998.

Killalea, Tom, Thomas Dimson, Janna Hamaker, and Eugene Kalenkovich. Aggregation of highlights. US Patent 9,087,032, filed January 26, 2009, and issued July
21, 2015.

Killalea, Tom, and Janna S. Hamaker. Disambiguation of term meaning. US Patent
8,250,071, filed June 30, 2010, and issued August 21, 2012.

"Kindle DX Marks Gear Shift for Amazon." *The Bookseller*, May 22, 2009, 8.

"Kindle Ready on UK Launchpad." *The Bookseller*, October 2, 2009, 3.

King, Stephen. "Messages from Stephen." StephenKing.com, 2000. http://web
.archive.org/web/20081007114133/http://stephenking.com/stephens_messages
.html.

Kirschenbaum, Matthew G. "Book.Files: Preservation of Digital Assets in the Contemporary Publishing Industry; A Report." College Park, MD, and New York: University of Maryland and Book Industry Study Group, April 2020. https://drum.lib
.umd.edu/handle/1903/25605.

Kirschenbaum, Matthew G. *Mechanisms: New Media and the Forensic Imagination*.
Cambridge, MA: MIT Press, 2012.

Kirschenbaum, Matthew, and Sarah Werner. "Digital Scholarship and Digital Studies:
The State of the Discipline." *Book History* 17 (2014): 406–458.

Kiss, Imre Attila, Lambert Mathias, and Jeffrey Penrod Adams. Named entity recognition with personalized models. US Patent 9,190,055, issued November 17, 2015.

knc1. "K5 Notice from Amazon." MobileRead Forums, March 4, 2016. https://www
.mobileread.com/forums/showpost.php?p=3274121&postcount=8.

Knecht, G. Bruce. "Wall Street Whiz Finds Niche Selling Books on the Internet." *Wall Street
Journal*, May 16, 1996. http://www.wsj.com/articles/SB832204437381952500.

Knight, Jeffrey Todd. *Bound to Read: Compilations, Collections, and the Making of Renaissance Literature*. Philadelphia: University of Pennsylvania Press, 2013.

Kobo. "Publishing in the Era of Big Data," 2014. http://cafe.kobo.com/_ir/159/20149
/Publishing%20in%20the%20Era%20of%20Big%20Data%20-%20Kobo
%20Whitepaper%20Fall%202014.pdf (link no longer exists).

Krebs, Brian. "Money Laundering via Author Impersonation on Amazon?" *Krebs on Security* (blog), February 20, 2018. https://krebsonsecurity.com/2018/02/money
-laundering-via-author-impersonation-on-amazon/.

Kristol, David M., and Lou Montulli. "RFC2109: HTTP State Management Mechanism." Network Working Group Request for Comments, 1997. https://tools.ietf
.org/html/rfc2109.

Kunsthal Aarhus. "Ubermorgen—the Project Formerly Known as Kindle Forkbomb." Kunsthal Aarhus, 2013.

Kushwaha, Anubhav. Digital work compression. US Patent 9,646,015, filed June 3, 2014, and issued May 9, 2017.

Lanier, Jaron. *You Are Not a Gadget*. London: Penguin, 2011.

Laquintano, Timothy. *Mass Authorship and the Rise of Self-Publishing*. Iowa City: University of Iowa Press, 2016.

The Legal Deposit Libraries (Non-print Works) Regulations 2013, no. 777 (2013).

Levy, Steven. "The Future of Reading." *Newsweek*, November 26, 2007, 57–64.

Library of Congress. "Textual Works and Musical Compositions." Recommended Formats Statement, 2017. http://web.archive.org/web/20190708145942/https://
www.loc.gov/preservation/resources/rfs/textmus.html.

Liu, Alan, Paxton Hehmeyer, James Hodge, Kimberly Knight, David Roh, and Elizabeth Swanstrom. "The *Agrippa* Files," 2005. http://agrippa.english.ucsb.edu/.

Liu, Wendy. "Coronavirus Has Made Amazon a Public Utility—So We Should Treat It like One." *The Guardian*, April 17, 2020, Opinion. https://www.theguardian.com
/commentisfree/2020/apr/17/amazon-coronavirus-public-utility-workers.

Livingstone, David. "Homefront." *Star Trek: Deep Space Nine*. CBS, January 1, 1996.

Lorusso, Silvio, and Sebastian Schmeig. *56 Broken Kindle Screens*. Lulu, 2012.

Luke, Karina. "BIC Statement on Best Practice for Subtitle Field in Metadata Feeds." BIC, March 9, 2018. http://www.bic.org.uk/files/pdfs/BIC%20Statement
%20on%20Best%20Practice%20for%20Sub-title%20field%20FINAL%209th
%20March%202018.pdf.

Lynch, Clifford. "Stewardship in the 'Age of Algorithms.'" *First Monday* 22, no. 12 (December 2017). https://doi.org/10.5210/fm.v22i12.8097.

Mandell, Laura. "The Original Author: How Digital Technology Reconceptualizes the Author (and the Self)." *International Journal of the Book* 1 (2003): 207–213.

Mangen, Anne, Bente R. Walgermo, and Kolbjørn Brønnick. "Reading Linear Texts on Paper versus Computer Screen: Effects on Reading Comprehension." *International Journal of Educational Research* 58 (2013): 61–68.

Manjoo, Farhad. "Which Tech Giant Would You Drop?" *New York Times*, May 10, 2017. https://www.nytimes.com/interactive/2017/05/10/technology/Ranking-Apple
-Amazon-Facebook-Microsoft-Google.html.

Manthorpe, Rowland. "Cory Doctorow Dreams of a DRM-Free Utopia—So He's Suing the US Government to Get It." *Wired UK*, April 25, 2017. http://www.wired.co.uk
/article/cory-doctorow-walkaway-science-fiction-drm.

Marcus, James. *Amazonia: Five Years at the Epicenter of the Dot.com Juggernaut*. New York: New Press, 2004.

Marmarelli, Trina, and Martin Ringle. "The Reed College Kindle Study." Reed College, 2010.

Maxwell, John. "E-Book Logic: We Can Do Better." *Papers of the Bibliographical Society of Canada* 51, no. 1 (2013). http://jps.library.utoronto.ca/index.php/bsc/article /view/20761/16996.

Maxwell, John. "XML Production Workflows? Start with the Web." *Journal of Electronic Publishing* 13, no. 1 (Winter 2010). http://hdl.handle.net/2027/spo.3336451.0013 .106.

McAuley, Julian, Christopher Targett, Qinfeng Shi, and Anton van den Hengel. "Image-Based Recommendations on Styles and Substitutes." In *Proceedings of the 38th International ACM SIGIR Conference on Research and Development in Information Retrieval*, 43–52. ACM, 2015.

McCracken, Ellen. "Expanding Genette's Epitext/Peritext Model for Transitional Electronic Literature: Centrifugal and Centripetal Vectors on Kindles and iPads." *Narrative* 21, no. 1 (2013): 105–124.

McDonald, Peter D. "Implicit Structure and Explicit Interactions: Pierre Bourdieu and the History of the Book." *The Library*, 6th ser., 19, no. 2 (June 1997): 105–121.

McDonough, Jerome, Matthew Kirschenbaum, Doug Reside, Neil Fraistat, and Dennis Jerz. "Twisty Little Passages Almost All Alike: Applying the FRBR Model to a Classic Computer Game." *Digital Humanities Quarterly* 4, no. 2 (2010). http:// www.digitalhumanities.org/dhq/vol/4/2/000089/000089.html.

McEnery, Tony, and Andrew Hardie. *Corpus Linguistics*. Cambridge: Cambridge University Press, 2011.

McGinn, Daniel. "The Numbers in Jeff Bezos's Head." *Harvard Business Review* 92, no. 11 (November 2014): 58–61.

McIlroy, Thad. "Startups within the U.S. Book Publishing Industry." *Publishing Research Quarterly* 33, no. 1 (2017): 1–9.

McKenzie, D. F. "'What's Past Is Prologue': The Bibliographical Society and History of the Book." In *Making Meanings: "Printers of the Mind" and Other Essays*, edited by Peter D. McDonald and Michael Suarez, 259–275. Amherst and Boston: University of Massachusetts Press, 2002.

McKitterick, David. *Print, Manuscript and the Search for Order, 1450–1830*. Cambridge: Cambridge University Press, 2003.

"MemoWare—the PDA Document Repository," May 10, 2000. https://web.archive.org /web/20000510062641/http://www.memoware.com/.

Menninga, Eric A. "Eric Menninga." LinkedIn, 2018. https://www.linkedin.com/in /eric-menninga-3716bb1.

Merchant, Brian. "How Google, Microsoft, and Big Tech Are Automating the Climate Crisis." Gizmodo, February 21, 2019. https://gizmodo.com/how-google-micro soft-and-big-tech-are-automating-the-1832790799.

Meyers, James David, and Kurt Wesley Piersol. Methods and devices for selectively ignoring captured audio data. US Patent 9,691,378, filed November 5, 2015, and issued June 27, 2017.

Mickle, Tripp. "Among the iPhone's Biggest Transformations: Apple Itself." *Wall Street Journal*, June 20, 2017, Tech. https://www.wsj.com/articles/among-the-iphones -biggest-transformations-apple-itself-1497951003.

Milliot, Jim. "Amazon Upgrade Tops 100,000 Titles." *Publishers Weekly*, December 24, 2007, 5.

Milliot, Jim. "The Nook Arrives." *Publishers Weekly*, October 26, 2009, 6.

Milroy, Rollin. *About Agrippa*. Vancouver: Heavenly Monkey, 2015.

"MIT Press Announces a New Collaboration." MIT Press, 2017. https://mitpress.mit
.edu/blog/mit-press-announces-new-collaboration.

MobileRead. "Kindlet Index." MobileRead Wiki, 2016. http://wiki.mobileread.com
/wiki/Kindlet_Index.

Mobipocket. "OPF X-Metadata Tags." Mobipocket Developer Center, 2007. http://web
.archive.org/web/20090116182003/http://www.mobipocket.com/dev/article
.asp?BaseFolder=prcgen&File=tagref_opfxmetadata.xml.

Modern Language Association of America. *MLA Handbook*. 8th ed. New York: Modern
Language Association of America, 2016.

Montfort, Nick. "Continuous Paper: The Early Materiality and Workings of Electronic Literature," 2005. http://nickm.com/writing/essays/continuous_paper
_mla.html.

Montfort, Nick, and Ian Bogost. *Racing the Beam: The Atari Video Computer System*.
Cambridge, MA: MIT Press, 2009.

Morris, Jeremy Wade. "Curation by Code: Infomediaries and the Data Mining of
Taste." *European Journal of Cultural Studies* 18, nos. 4–5 (2015): 446–463.

Murray, Simone. *The Digital Literary Sphere*. Baltimore, MD: Johns Hopkins University Press, 2018.

Nakamura, Lisa. "'Words with Friends': Socially Networked Reading on Goodreads."
PMLA 128, no. 1 (2013): 238–243.

National Library of Scotland. "The Silent Corner / Dean Koontz." National Library
of Scotland, 2017. http://main-cat.nls.uk/vwebv/holdingsInfo?bibId=9420635.

Neate, Rupert. "Amazon's Jeff Bezos Pays Out $38bn in Divorce Settlement." *The
Guardian*, June 30, 2019, Technology. https://www.theguardian.com/technol-
ogy/2019/jun/30/amazon-jeff-bezos-ex-wife-mackenzie-handed-38bn-in
-divorce-settlement.

Neilan, Catherine. "Amazon Urges Indies to Digitise." *The Bookseller*, March 13, 2009,
10.

Neilan, Catherine. "Digital Will Overtake Print in 2018, Says FBF Survey." *The Bookseller*, 2008. https://www.thebookseller.com/news/digital-will-overtake-print
-2018-says-fbf-survey.

Neill, Graeme, and Catherine Neilan. "Amazon Launches Kindle Worldwide." *The
Bookseller*, October 12, 2009, 3.

Nelson, Theodor Holm. *Computer Lib / Dream Machines*. Redmond, WA: Tempus, 1987.

New York Times Book Review. "About the Best Sellers." *New York Times Book Review*,
2017. https://www.nytimes.com/books/best-sellers/methodology/.

New York Times Editorial Desk. "King Closure." *New York Times*, December 1, 2000,
A36.

Newman, Jared. "Amazon Settles Kindle '1984' Lawsuit." *PC World*, October 1, 2009.
https://www.pcworld.com/article/172953/amazon_kindle_1984_lawsuit.html.

Noorda, Rachel, and Stevie Marsden. "Twenty-First Century Book Studies: The State
of the Discipline." *Book History* 22, no. 1 (2019): 370–397.

Nosowitz, Dan. "A Penny for Your Books." *New York Times*, October 26, 2015. http://
www.nytimes.com/2015/10/25/magazine/a-penny-for-your-books.html.

Nuovo, Frank. Portable communication device. US Patent Application Publication no.
2002/0050981, filed June 25, 2001, and issued May 2, 2002.

O'Donovan, Caroline, and Ken Bensinger. "The Cost of Next-Day Delivery: How Amazon Escapes the Blame for Its Deadly Last Mile." BuzzFeed News, September 6, 2019. https://www.buzzfeednews.com/article/carolineodonovan/amazon -next-day-delivery-deaths.

Ooba, Seiichi, Shingo Ooue, Hiroyuki Ueda, Hirotoshi Endo, Makoto Murakoshi, and Masashi Yanagida. Dictionary reading device. US Patent 3,612,676, filed November 22, 1968, and issued October 12, 1971.

Open eBook Authoring Group. "Supporters." Open eBook, October 4, 1999. http:// web.archive.org/web/19991004043319/http://openebook.org/who.htm.

ORCID. "ORCID: Connecting Research and Researchers." ORCID, 2018. https://orcid .org/.

O'Reilly, Tim. "An Open Letter to Jeff Bezos." O'Reilly and Associates, 2000. http:// www.oreilly.com/amazon_patent/amazon_patent.comments.html.

Ota, Isao. Electrophoretic display device. US Patent 3,668,106, filed April 9, 1970, and issued June 6, 1972.

Ota, I., J. Ohnishi, and M. Yoshiyama. "Electrophoretic Image Display (EPID) Panel." *Proceedings of the IEEE* 61, no. 7 (July 1973): 832–836.

OverDrive. "Enhanced Media Publishing." OverDrive, 2017. https://www.overdrive .com/publishers/enhanced-media-publishing.

Overell, Simon, and William Tunstall-Pedoe. Extracting structured knowledge from unstructured text. US Patent 9,110,882, filed May 12, 2011, and issued August 18, 2015.

Packer, George. "Cheap Words." *New Yorker*, February 10, 2014. https://www.new yorker.com/magazine/2014/02/17/cheap-words.

Panoz, Jiminy. "Ebooks, Beta Testing, and the Apocalypse." GitHub, 2017. https://jay-panoz.github.io/ebookcraft2017/#/.

Panoz, Jiminy. "Re: Thoughts on the Future of EPUB 3." epub3@w3.org, January 19, 2018. https://lists.w3.org/Archives/Public/public-epub3/2018Jan/0012.html.

Pargman, Daniel, and Jacob Palme. "ASCII Imperialism." In *Standards and Their Stories: How Quantifying, Classifying, and Formalizing Practices Shape Everyday Life*, edited by Martha Lampland and Susan Leigh Star, 177–199. Ithaca, NY: Cornell University Press, 2009.

Parkes, M. B. *Pause and Effect: An Introduction to the History of Punctuation in the West*. Aldershot: Scolar Press, 1992.

Patankar, Rashmi Arun, Jeffrey Matthew Bilger, and Colin Ian Bodell. Providing opaque recommendations. US Patent 10,049,397, filed March 6, 2013, and issued August 14, 2018.

Patel, Pankaj C., Arash Azadegan, and Lisa M. Ellram. "The Effects of Strategic and Structural Supply Chain Orientation on Operational and Customer-Focused Performance." *Decision Sciences* 44, no. 4 (2013): 713–753.

Pearson. "Penguin Signs Up to 'Search Inside!' Programme with Amazon.co.uk." Pearson, 2006. https://www.pearson.com/corporate/news/media/news -announcements/2006/10/penguin-signs-up-to-search-inside!-programme -with-amazoncouk.html.

Peckham, Matt. "Play *Doom* on a Printer—Thanks to a Serious Security Flaw." *Wired*, September 23, 2014. http://www.wired.com/2014/09/doom-printer/.

Perez, Thomas E., Samuel R. Bagenstos, John L. Wodatch, Allison Nichol, and Kate Nicholson. "Letter of Resolution between the United States and Reed College."

Information and Technical Assistance on the Americans with Disabilities Act, 2009. http://www.ada.gov/reed_college.htm.

Petts, James C., Aaron James Dykstra, Laura Ellen Grit, Lindsey Christina Fowler, Dennis H. Harding, George M. Ionkov, and Samuel A. Minter. Ebook citation enhancement. US Patent 9,639,877, filed July 6, 2012, and issued May 2, 2017.

Phillips, Angus. "Have We Passed Peak Book? The Uncoupling of Book Sales from Economic Growth." *Publishing Research Quarterly* 33, no. 3 (2017): 310–327.

Plantin, Jean-Christophe, Carl Lagoze, Paul N. Edwards, and Christian Sandvig. "Infrastructure Studies Meet Platform Studies in the Age of Google and Facebook." *New Media and Society* 20, no. 1 (2018): 293–310.

Platt, Charles. "Digital Ink." *Wired*, May 1, 1997. https://www.wired.com/1997/05/ff-digitalink/.

Preda, Alex. "Socio-technical Agency in Financial Markets: The Case of the Stock Ticker." *Social Studies of Science* 36, no. 5 (2006): 753–782.

Pressman, Jessica. "The Aesthetics of Bookishness in Twenty-First-Century Literature." *Michigan Quarterly Review* 48, no. 4 (Fall 2009).

Publishers Association. *PA Publishing Yearbook 2016*. London: Publishers Association, 2017.

Publishers Weekly. "S&S to Distribute Kindle Bestseller John Locke." *Publishers Weekly*, August 22, 2011. https://www.publishersweekly.com/pw/by-topic/digital/content-and-e-books/article/48433-s-s-to-distribute-kindle-bestseller-john-locke.html.

Purgathofer, Peter. *DIY Kindle Scanner*. Vimeo, 2013. http://vimeo.com/73675285.

Quincey, Andrew de. "KIF: An Infocom Text Adventure Interpreter for the Kindle." *Andrew de Quincey's Livejournal* (blog), October 9, 2010. http://adq.livejournal.com/108011.html.

Quittner, Josh. "Jeff Bezos: Bio: An Eye on the Future." *Time*, December 27, 1999. http://content.time.com/time/magazine/article/0,9171,992928,00.html.

Radder, Hans. "Exploring Philosophical Issues in the Patenting of Scientific and Technological Inventions." *Philosophy and Technology* 26, no. 3 (2013): 283–300.

Ragen, Brian Abel. "Reading Becomes Electric: The Amazon Kindle." *Papers on Language and Literature* 44, no. 3 (Summer 2008): 328–332.

Rausch, Daniel B. Determining reading levels of electronic books. US Patent 8,744,855, filed August 9, 2010, and issued June 3, 2014.

Ray Murray, Padmini, and Claire Squires. "The Digital Publishing Communications Circuit." *Book 2.0* 3, no. 1 (2013): 3–23.

Reagle, Joseph Michael, Jr. *Good Faith Collaboration: The Culture of Wikipedia*. Cambridge, MA: MIT Press, 2010.

Reid, Calvin. "Random House, Modern Library to Offer E-books." *Publishers Weekly* 247, no. 32 (August 7, 2000): 10.

Reid, Calvin, and Karen Holt. "Barnes & Noble.com Exits E-book Market." *Publishers Weekly* 250, no. 37 (September 15, 2003): 9.

Reid, Calvin, and Steven Zeitchik. "Gemstar E-books Shutdown." *Publishers Weekly* 250, no. 25 (June 23, 2003): 10.

rodrigoccurvo. "Correct Mobi Location Formula (Maybe)." MobileRead Forums, 2011. https://www.mobileread.com/forums/showthread.php?t=159357.

Rose, Charlie. "Interview with Jeff Bezos," November 19, 2007. https://charlierose.com/videos/11791.

Rose, Charlie. "Interview with Jeff Bezos," February 26, 2009. https://charlierose.com/videos/22164.

Roseman, Neil C., Paul Kotas, Jeffrey P. Bezos, Bruce C. Moore, Richard L. Dalzell, and Jeffrey M. Blackburn. User interfaces and methods for facilitating user-to-user sales. US Patent 7,472,077, filed May 9, 2002, and issued December 30, 2008.

Rosen, Rebecca, "The Missing 20th Century: How Copyright Protection Makes Book Vanish." *The Atlantic*, March 30, 2012. http://www.theatlantic.com/technology/archive/2012/03/the-missing-20th-century-how-copyright-makes-books-vanish/255282/.

Rosenblatt, Bill. "Amazon.com Acquires Mobipocket." *Ebooklyn* (blog), 2005. http://web.archive.org/web/20160324100829/http://www.ebooklyn.net/p/amazon-com-acquires-mobipocket.html.

Rowberry, Simon Peter. "Commonplacing the Public Domain." *Language and Literature* 25, no. 2 (2016).

Rowberry, Simon Peter. "The Limits of Big Data for Analyzing Reading." *Participations* 16, no. 1 (May 2019): 237–257.

Rubincam, David P. Electronic book. US Patent 4,159,417, filed October 28, 1977, and issued June 26, 1979.

Run! "File:E-ink.svg." Wikipedia, 2006. https://en.wikipedia.org/wiki/File:E-ink.svg.

Salvador, Stan Weidner, and Vlad Magdin. Predictive natural language processing models. US Patent 9,336,772, filed March 6, 2014, and issued May 10, 2016.

Saroyan, Strawberry. "Amanda Hocking, Storyseller." *New York Times*, June 17, 2011. http://www.nytimes.com/2011/06/19/magazine/amanda-hocking-storyseller.html.

Satariano, Adam, Karl Russell, Troy Griggs, Blacki Migliozzi, and Chang W. Lee. "How the Internet Travels across Oceans." *New York Times*, March 10, 2019, Technology. https://www.nytimes.com/interactive/2019/03/10/technology/internet-cables-oceans.html.

Schaffert, R. M., and C. D. Oughton. "Xerography: A New Principle of Photography and Graphic Reproduction." *Journal of the Optical Society of America* 38, no. 12 (December 1948): 991–998.

Schlesinger, Jacob M. "Walkman of Words: Sony's Data Discman Can Squeeze an Encyclopedia into a Portable Electronic Book." *Wall Street Journal*, October 21, 1991, r12.

Schuessler, Jennifer. "A Tribute to the Printer Aldus Manutius, and the Roots of the Paperback." *New York Times*, February 26, 2015. http://www.nytimes.com/2015/02/27/arts/design/a-grolier-club-tribute-to-the-printer-aldus-manutius.html.

Seely Brown, John. "1997 Objectives," 1997. Mark Weiser papers, ca. 1975–1999. Series 5, box 41, folder 10.

Shah, Mehal. Dynamic character biographies. US Patent 9,690,451, filed April 9, 2015, and issued June 27, 2017.

Sharma, Sudeep. "Netflix and the Documentary Boom." In *The Netflix Effect: Technology and Entertainment in the 21st Century*, edited by Kevin McDonald and Daniel Smith-Rowse, 143–154. London: Bloomsbury, 2016.

Shelfari. "About the Shelfari Librarians & Editors Group," February 25, 2011. http://web.archive.org/web/20110225161532/http://www.shelfari.com/groups/10713/about.

Shelfari. "*Harry Potter and the Deathly Hallows* (Harry Potter 7) by J. K. Rowling," October 23, 2011. http://web.archive.org/web/20111023055435/http://www .shelfari.com:80/books/1064883/Harry-Potter-and-the-Deathly-Hallows.

Shelfari. "Questions and Feedback," November 13, 2009. http://web.archive.org/web /20091113093818/http://www.shelfari.com:80/faq/29.

Sheridon, N. K., and M. A. Berkovitz. "The Gyricon—a Twisting Ball Display." *Proceedings of the Society for Information Display* 18, no. 34 (1977): 289–293.

Sherman, William H. *Used Books: Marking Readers in Renaissance England*. Philadelphia: University of Pennsylvania Press, 2008.

Siegel, Hilliard B., Udi Manber, and Jonathan Leblang. Method and system for providing annotations of a digital work. US Patent 8,131,647, filed January 19, 2005, and issued March 6, 2012.

Sims, Andrew. "The Most Moving Parts of 'Cursed Child,' According to Kindle." *Hypable* (blog), August 12, 2016. http://www.hypable.com/cursed-child-kindle -popular-highlights/.

Skochinsky, Igor. "Hacking the Kindle Part 3: Root Shell and Runtime System." *Reversing Everything* (blog), December 21, 2007. http://igorsk.blogspot.com/2007/12 /hacking-kindle-part-3-root-shell-and.html.

Sloan, Robin. "The Kindle Wink." *The Message* (blog), April 23, 2014. https://medium .com/message/the-kindle-wink-4f61cd5c84c5.

Smith, Kelvin. *The Publishing Business: From P-books to E-books*. Lausanne: AVA Publishing, 2012.

Snodgrass, Ryan J., James C. Slezak, Matthew E. Goldberg, Jeremie Leproust, Guillaume Jeulin, and Felix F. Antony. Ebook encryption using variable keys. US Patent 8,826,036, filed June 28, 2010, and issued September 2, 2014.

Somers, James. "Torching the Modern-Day Library of Alexandria." *The Atlantic*, April 20, 2017. https://www.theatlantic.com/technology/archive/2017/04/the-tragedy -of-google-books/523320/.

Sorotokin, Peter, Garth Conboy, Brady Duga, John Rivlin, Don Beaver, Kevin Ballard, Alastair Fettes, and Daniel Weck. "EPUB Canonical Fragment Identifiers 1.1," 2017. http://www.idpf.org/epub/linking/cfi/.

Squires, Claire. "Taste and/or Big Data? Post-digital Editorial Selection." *Critical Quarterly* 59, no. 3 (2017): 24–38.

Stallman, Richard. "(Formerly) Boycott Amazon!" GNU Operating System. Accessed February 6, 2017. https://www.gnu.org/philosophy/amazon.html.

Standage, Tom. *The Turk: The Life and Times of the Famous Eighteenth-Century Chess-Playing Machine*. New York: Berkley Trade, 2003.

Star, Susan Leigh, and Martha Lampland. "Reckoning with Standards." In *Standards and Their Stories: How Quantifying, Classifying, and Formalizing Practices Shape Everyday Life*, edited by Martha Lampland and Susan Leigh Star, 3–24. Ithaca, NY: Cornell University Press, 2009.

Starosielski, Nicole. *The Undersea Network*. Durham, NC: Duke University Press, 2015.

Stefik, Mark. "The Digital Document Company." Palo Alto, CA: Xerox PARC, July 29, 1995. Mark Weiser papers, ca. 1975–1999. Series 2, box 8, folder 12.

Steiner, Ann. "Private Criticism in the Public Space: Personal Writing on Literature in Readers' Reviews on Amazon." *P@rticipations* 5, no. 2 (2008). https://lup.lub .lu.se/record/1288297.

Sterne, Jonathan. *MP3: The Meaning of a Format*. Durham, NC: Duke University Press, 2012.

Stone, Brad. "Amazon Erases Orwell Books from Kindle Devices." *New York Times*, July 17, 2009. http://www.nytimes.com/2009/07/18/technology/companies /18amazon.html.

Stone, Brad. *The Everything Store: Jeff Bezos and the Age of Amazon*. London: Bantam, 2013.

Streitfeld, David. "Book Reviewers for Hire Meet a Demand for Online Raves." *New York Times*, August 25, 2012. http://www.nytimes.com/2012/08/26/business /book-reviewers-for-hire-meet-a-demand-for-online-raves.html.

Striphas, Ted. *The Late Age of Print: Everyday Book Culture from Consumerism to Control*. New York: Columbia University Press, 2011.

Swanson, Clare. "The Bestselling Books of 2014." *Publishers Weekly*, January 2, 2015. https://www.publishersweekly.com/pw/by-topic/industry-news/bookselling /article/65171-the-fault-in-our-stars-tops-print-and-digital.html.

Sweney, Mark. "Amazon Breaks Premier League Hold of Sky and BT with Prime Streaming Deal." *The Guardian*, June 7, 2018, Media. http://www.theguardian .com/media/2018/jun/07/amazon-breaks-premier-league-hold-of-sky-and -bt-with-streaming-deal.

Sweney, Mark. "'Screen Fatigue' Sees UK Ebook Sales Plunge 17% as Readers Return to Print." *The Guardian*, April 27, 2017. https://www.theguardian.com/books/2017 /apr/27/screen-fatigue-sees-uk-ebook-sales-plunge-17-as-readers-return-to -print.

Tartt, Donna. *The Goldfinch*. London: Abacus, 2014.

Telfer, Stephen J., and Michael D. McCreary. "A Full-Color Electrophoretic Display." *SID Symposium Digest of Technical Papers* 47, no. 1 (2016): 574–577.

Terry, Ana Arias. "Electronic Ink Technologies: Showing the Way to a Brighter Future." *Library Hi Tech* 19, no. 4 (2001): 376–389.

Thompson, Ben. "Amazon's New Customer." Stratechery, June 19, 2017. https://strat echery.com/2017/amazons-new-customer/.

Thompson, John B. *Merchants of Culture: The Publishing Business in the Twenty-First Century*. 2nd ed. London: Polity, 2012.

Thylstrup, Nanna Bonde. *The Politics of Mass Digitization*. Cambridge, MA: MIT Press, 2019.

Tian, Xuemei, and Bill Martin. "Impacting Forces on eBook Business Models Development." *Publishing Research Quarterly* 27, no. 3 (2011): 230–246.

Tillett, Barbara. "What Is FRBR? A Conceptual Model for the Bibliographic Universe." Washington, DC: Library of Congress, 2004. http://www.loc.gov/cds/downloads /FRBR.PDF.

Tremblay, Geoffroy. "KindleBerry Pi." *Ponnuki—Electronic Media Art and Yoga* (blog), 2012. http://www.ponnuki.net/2012/09/kindleberry-pi/.

Trettien, Whitney Anne. "A Deep History of Electronic Textuality: The Case of *English Reprints Jhon Milton Areopagitica*." *Digital Humanities Quarterly* 7, no. 1 (2013). http://www.digitalhumanities.org/dhq/vol/7/1/000150/000150.html.

Tseng, Walter Manching, Adam J. Iser, Michel L. Goldstein, Ravi Shankar Thangavel, Janna S. Hamaker, and Ankur Jain. Generating a game related to a digital work. US Patent 9,449,526, filed March 19, 2012, and issued September 20, 2016.

Tsukayama, Hayley. "Why Amazon Is Paying Nearly $1 Billion to Acquire Twitch." *Washington Post*, August 25, 2014, The Switch. https://www.washingtonpost.com/news/the-switch/wp/2014/08/25/amazon-said-to-be-close-to-acquiring-twitch/.

"U.P.C.s, Barcodes, & Prefixes." GS1 US. Accessed July 3, 2017. https://www.gs1us.org/upcs-barcodes-prefixes/overview.

Usbourne, David. "Amazon's Electronic Book Turns a New Page in the History of the Written Word." *The Independent*, November 20, 2007.

Van der Weel, Adriaan. *Changing Our Textual Minds: Towards a Digital Order of Knowledge*. Manchester: Manchester University Press, 2011.

Vogels, Werner. "Amazon and the Lean Cloud." HackFwd Build 0.7, posted to Vimeo, September 2011. https://vimeo.com/29719577.

Vogels, Werner. "How and Why Did Amazon Get into the Cloud Computing Business?" Quora, January 14, 2011. https://www.quora.com/How-and-why-did-Amazon-get-into-the-cloud-computing-business.

W3C. "W3C Publishing Working Group." W3C, 2017. https://www.w3.org/publishing/groups/publ-wg/.

Ward, Charles L., Donald Ryan Willhoit, Lars C. Ulness, Robert C. Borja Jr., James D. Mackraz, and Edward J. Gayles. Selecting content-enhanced applications. US Patent 9,268,734, filed March 14, 2011, and issued February 23, 2016.

Ward, Miles J. Physical store online shopping control. US Patent 9,665,881, filed May 4, 2012, and issued May 30, 2017.

Warner, M. "Can Amazon Be Saved?" *Fortune* 144, no. 11 (November 26, 2001): 156.

Warren, John W. "Zen and the Art of Metadata Maintenance." *Journal of Electronic Publishing* 18, no. 3 (2015). https://doi.org/10.3998/3336451.0018.305.

WashPostPR. "The Washington Post Launches Most Comprehensive Bestselling Books Lists." *Washington Post*, February 8, 2018, WashPost PR Blog. https://www.washingtonpost.com/pr/wp/2018/02/08/the-washington-post-launches-most-comprehensive-bestselling-books-lists/.

Weight, Christopher F., Andrew D. Birkett, Janna Hamaker, Tom Killalea, and Alexander William Robb Nelson. Identifying book title sets. US Patent 9,881,009, filed March 15, 2011, and issued January 30, 2018.

Weight, Christopher F., Janna Hamaker, Tom Killalea, Bruno A. Posokhow, and Daniel B. Rausch. Book version mapping. US Patent 9,846,688, filed December 28, 2010, and issued December 19, 2017.

Weingart, Scott B. "The Route of a Text Message, a Love Story." *Vice* (blog), February 22, 2019. https://www.vice.com/en_us/article/kzdn8n/the-route-of-a-text-message-a-love-story.

Weiss, Steven K., Craig S. Griffin, John Lattyak, Lawrence Arnold Lynch-Freshner, and Thomas A. Ryan. Dynamic display dependent markup language interface. US Patent 8,453,051, filed March 31, 2008, and issued May 28, 2013.

Weltevrede, Esther, and Erik Borra. "Platform Affordances and Data Practices: The Value of Dispute on Wikipedia." *Big Data and Society* 3, no. 1 (June 1, 2016). https://doi.org/10.1177/2053951716653418.

Wheat, Alynda. "10 Years, 10 Books—a Look Back at Kindle Best Sellers." This Week in Books, November 15, 2017. https://www.amazon.com/article/twib/kindle-tenth-anniversary.html.

Wingfield, Nick. "Amazon Pushes Facial Recognition to Police. Critics See Surveillance Risk." *New York Times*, May 24, 2018, Technology. https://www.nytimes.com/2018/05/22/technology/amazon-facial-recognition.html.

Wingfield, Nick. "Inside Amazon Go, a Store of the Future." *New York Times*, January 21, 2018, Technology. https://www.nytimes.com/2018/01/21/technology/inside-amazon-go-a-store-of-the-future.html.

Wisher, Robert A., and J. Peter Kincaid. "Personal Electronic Aid for Maintenance: Final Summary Report." Alexandria, VA: US Army Research Institute for the Behavioral and Social Sciences, March 1989.

Wolf, Gary. "The Great Library of Amazonia." *Wired*, December 1, 2003. http://www.wired.com/wired/archive/11.12/amazon.html.

Wrangham, Richard. *Catching Fire: How Cooking Made Us Human*. London: Profile Books, 2010.

Wright, Jan. "The Devil Is in the Details: Indexes versus Amazon's X-Ray." *The Indexer* 30, no. 1 (2012): 11–16.

Wykes, Zoë. *ISBN-13 for Dummies, Special Edition*. Hoboken, NJ: Wiley, 2005.

Yamazaki, Shunpei, and Toshiji Hamatani. Paperless portable book. US Patent 5,339,091, filed October 14, 1992, and issued August 16, 1994.

Zagorie, Aviram, Michael V. Rykov, Craig S. Griffin, and John Lattyak. Device specific presentation control for electronic book reader devices. US Patent 8,423,889, filed December 11, 2008, and issued April 16, 2013.

Zehr, Gregg E., John E. Johnston, Jateen P. Parekh, Symon J. Whitehorn, and Thomas J. Hobbs. Page turner for handheld electronic book reader device. US Patent 8,018,431, issued September 13, 2011.

Zehr, Gregg, and John Hollar. "Zehr, Gregg, Oral History," May 14, 2014. http://www.computerhistory.org/collections/catalog/102739920.

Zehr, Gregg, and Symon J. Whitehorn. Handheld electronic book reader device having dual displays. US Patent 8,950,682 , filed March 29, 2006, and issued July 6, 2010.

Zhou, Hanning, Jian Liang, and Sherif M. Yacoub. On-demand generating e-book content with advertising. US Patent 9,892,427, filed September 2, 2014, and issued February 13, 2018.

Zittrain, Jonathan. *The Future of the Internet*. London: Penguin, 2009.

Zuboff, Shoshana. *The Age of Surveillance Capitalism: The Fight for a Human Future at the New Frontier of Power*. London: Profile Books, 2019.

Index